Saint Augustine's *Confessions* have for fifteen centuries inspired and encouraged devoted readers. In his epic journey—at once exceptional and profoundly human—every man finds a mirror for perfection and the consolation of real hope.

In this modern translation of the immortal classic, scholar, poet, and novelist Rex Warner renders faithfully Augustine's vision and with consummate skill transposes into modern, readable English all the beauty, power, and drive that have made the *Confessions* a classic of Western culture.

Rex Warner was born in 1905 in Birmingham, England. He was a teacher in England and Egypt and the director of the British Institute in Athens, Greece, before coming to the United States in 1961, where he became the Tallman Professor of Classics at Bowdoin College and professor of English at the University of Connecticut. A noted translator of Greek and Latin, he was also the author of numerous novels and essays. He died in 1986.

Elizabeth Block is the author of the novel *A Gesture Through Time* and the recipient of a fiction fellowship from the Christopher Isherwood Foundation. Her writing has been featured on National Public Radio affiliates KQED and KSFR, and her short films have screened extensively throughout the United States.

Martin E. Marty is a Lutheran pastor and the Fairfax M. Cone Distinguished Service Professor Emeritus at the University of Chicago, where he taught chiefly at the Divinity School for some thirty-five years. Among his more than fifty books are *Righteous Empire: The Protestant Experience in America* and *Pilgrims in Their Own Land: 500 Years of Religion in America*.

THE
CONFESSIONS
OF
SAINT AUGUSTINE

TRANSLATED BY REX WARNER

WITH A NEW FOREWORD BY
ELIZABETH BLOCK
AND WITH AN INTRODUCTION
AND AFTERWORD BY
MARTIN E. MARTY

SIGNET CLASSICS

SIGNET CLASSICS
Published by New American Library, a division of
Penguin Group (USA) Inc., 375 Hudson Street,
New York, New York 10014, USA
Penguin Group (Canada), 90 Eglinton Avenue East, Suite 700, Toronto,
Ontario M4P 2Y3, Canada (a division of Pearson Penguin Canada Inc.)
Penguin Books Ltd., 80 Strand, London WC2R 0RL, England
Penguin Ireland, 25 St. Stephen's Green, Dublin 2,
Ireland (a division of Penguin Books Ltd.)
Penguin Group (Australia), 250 Camberwell Road, Camberwell, Victoria 3124,
Australia (a division of Pearson Australia Group Pty. Ltd.)
Penguin Books India Pvt. Ltd., 11 Community Centre, Panchsheel Park,
New Delhi - 110 017, India
Penguin Group (NZ), 67 Apollo Drive, Rosedale, North Shore 0632,
New Zealand (a division of Pearson New Zealand Ltd.)
Penguin Books (South Africa) (Pty.) Ltd., 24 Sturdee Avenue,
Rosebank, Johannesburg 2196, South Africa

Penguin Books Ltd., Registered Offices:
80 Strand, London WC2R 0RL, England

Published by Signet Classics, an imprint of New American Library, a division
of Penguin Group (USA) Inc. Previously published in a Mentor edition.

First Signet Classics Printing, February 2001
First Signet Classics Printing (Block Foreword), March 2009
20   19   18   17   16   15   14   13

Copyright © Rex Warner, 1963
Introduction and Afterword copyright © Martin E. Marty, 2001
Foreword copyright © Elizabeth Block, 2009
All rights reserved

Ⓒ REGISTERED TRADEMARK—MARCA REGISTRADA

Printed in the United States of America

Contents

Foreword

As an anthropology honors student at the University of Michigan, I came of age amidst the eloquent rhetoric of anti-confession. Contrary to the romantic and poetic admissions of Saint Augustine, a mass hysteria known as Michel Foucault's *The History of Sexuality* dominated the intellectual landscape. Serious about my academic pursuits, I read, observed, and discussed everything through Foucault's oblique prism. Like my contemporaries, I even tried (though repeatedly failed) to live up to his grand un-God-like-ness. Foucault's deity was discourse itself. Saint Augustine's confessions were evidence of Foucault's indisputable observations about knowledge and power. God was not truth and light but a man-made juggernaut. The point of life was not to move away from "sin" (something I was raised to believe didn't even exist), but to explode in it. Saint Augustine's mortal "region of unlikeness"—the imperfect human place where man is without God—was Foucault's raison d'être, and not just reason for being, but for producing and analyzing more discussion.

For Saint Augustine, biological sin and a career in the field of rhetoric were forbidden and dishonest sex partners who needed healing and truth. For Foucault and for my youthful devotion to his writings, biological sin (let alone biological truth) wasn't anything but a necessary rhetorical proposition in the first place.

And so, cloaked in predictable irony, I embraced—through much of my early and late youth—what Saint

Augustine might call immoral fiction outside of God's light. Sin was but a thrilling literary challenge.

Immersed in prolific and explicit interrogations of confession and representation, unconverted and cast in darkness's shadow, I spent years spinning fictional tales of taboo and forbidden loves. I questioned Saint Augustine's bathed-in-light savior, Almighty God. Redeeming the mortal body meant little to me—I was obsessed with the tall, dark, and handsome tale, the twists and turns of discourse and with proving that nothing can be proven; the world doesn't gush truthful human blood and guts, only floods of linguistic equivalents and parts of wholes. I was overcome with the immortality of art.

So enraptured was I with an unrepressive hypothesis of unlikeness, sometimes I even forgot, as I began to get older and dumber, I was a woman with a real ticking time bomb of (another version of immortality) a biological clock. The sandy, sooty time and its memory slipped through Saint Augustine's rhetorical hourglass of conversion, chaste love, and salvation. My eggs were tired of swaying the metronome hand at a reliable pace. The years unfurled and discourse overshadowed the truths of my body, sand passing through my life's hourglass.

Suddenly, as my body's last gasp for reproductive possibility began so loudly to beat, I couldn't hear anything else but the sin of loneliness tick-tock away and tear at my heart, a heart steeped in layers and layers of disembodied fictions, stories prancing through the speed of light so bright they were lying to me.

When I read Saint Augustine, I think of confession not so much as a straightforward exposé of one's wrongdoings. I think about how I would construct my own confession, and how that might compare or contrast to contemporary ideas of the popular or commercial memoir. I also ponder the Internet as a real reckless confessional—unlike Saint Augustine's—but nonetheless one that has truly replaced thoughtful and necessary reflection slowed down from the perspective of actually having lived long enough to extract from memory the deliberate ebbs and flows of living and its unwitting epiphanies. Perhaps the Internet has deprived us sensually of what the patient and almighty Story would never leave us wanting. Because Saint Augustine values the pressure of time bearing down upon the weight of redemption, his narrative remains worthy of repeated inspection against the backdrop of our own frenetically addictive contemporary high-def visual electronica.

Ultimately, biology is the basis for every human foible. Through the looking glass of memory, amidst all progressive human biological decay, we move forward. We move closer to God in his timelessness. As Augustine reminds us, "Your today is eternity, and so it was that you begot one who is coeternal with you to whom you said: This day have I begotten Thee." Somehow, Saint Augustine's escape from bodily sin into narrative confessional salvation reminds me of my own eager conversion from narrative "sin" into biological redemption. It also asserts that begetting is not just spiritual begetting.

Reaching toward some path above my depraved region of unlikeness—my fun house of language—I clamored for something more than myself, more than my writing, more than the man I had loved for so many years. I looked for anything, not really sure what I would find and how I would get there. At first, it seemed so easy. I turned to my husband and said, "It's time. What the hell have we been waiting for?"

It wasn't as if we hadn't already had lots of time to get pregnant. I was in my late thirties and he was in his early forties. But, like so many of our peers, we of the first postfeminist generation postponed and postponed (with great deliberation and debate) our biological destinies (not to mention we spent most of our twenties and thirties broke and without health insurance). Our redemption lay not in being saddled with a drooling, pooping, sobbing little one, but in liberation and freedom. For me (and for my husband), elbow room meant a religious devotion to crafting literary and artistic works. The thought of cramming our tiny urban apartment with tacky plastic toys and baby gear (let alone a precious, breathing little being) was about as suspect as a hedge fund CEO. We weren't exactly chasing Jack Kerouac, but we definitely thought meaningful existence resided well outside the cogs and wheels of a well-oiled mainstream. But then I realized (contrary to popular opinion), "What a fantastic context in which to raise a child." Besides, I have such a romantic lust for the city in which I live, how could I not introduce an impressionable new life into the glorious place in which I was lucky enough to become an adult. What an opportunity to give another life. And maybe I wasn't as selfish as those around me might like to believe.

My search for truth would be a total inversion of Saint Augustine's quest. And yet Saint Augustine's rhetoric offers a ripe textual rubric for me to unravel, at least perfunctorily—in reflective memory—my path to (narrative) redemption. I could get down and dirty with Saint A., precisely by using his journey to entertain my own hot button item of conversion. Saint Augustine offers a generous structural arc for anyone aching to explore, represent, and overcome a personal crisis (let alone a larger cultural-political-economic one) . . . though mine is hardly a conversion of religion—unless of course you consider looking into the eyes of your newborn child the holiest of all holiness—but rather a lifelong struggle, the understanding of which is cobbled together by memory's recollection of one's youthful exploits and evolution.

I was an awkwardly heady youth, obsessed with narrative constructions; the opposite pursuit became my noblesse oblige as a preface writer and as an aging woman. In the book you're holding, my personal tale of salvation precedes Saint Augustine's, on which my story is based. Yet his text enables me to enter into conversation in the first place. In other words, I would not be encouraged to write this preface in such a personal confessional manner had I not followed Saint Augustine's strategy. Yet my preface is supposed to shed light on the actual book.

Instead, I mirror and offer as a window *The Confessions*, so that one not so eager to engage or not so identified with Saint A. might take the text to her own corner of the world and interpret it as suits her own history and place. Such necessary intervention is what makes the journey readable and worthwhile, making us delight in Saint A.'s refracted memoirish reflections.

Yet confession as truth according to Saint Augustine and biological truth as I have come to encounter it stand in opposite corners. Biological truth, to Saint Augustine, lies in stark contrast to God. Biology, or rather the physical being bound by immediate gratification in time and space, rubs especially against the grain of God's eternity if you are referring to a woman's biological truth—be it her breast milk or her sexuality. A newborn baby suckling at her mother's breast need not endure as the work of motherhood. Rather, as Augustine proffers, breastfeeding a baby is not testimony of the mother-child bond, but the link between God and baby—as God's earliest nutritional supplement of redemption, whereby mother is mere vessel (her cup runneth over). And yet that is exactly what I sought—not Saint Augustine's description of his infancy—but my own flesh and blood suckling at my breast, simply because nothing (not even finding God) could possibly compare—and because as a female, I had the biological privilege (if not obligation). I looked eternity in the face; I considered the stoppage of all time, and of my womanly kind of interval. *Depraved*, Saint A. might say (as he would think in general about women), but yes, that bodily truth was my ambition, as spiritual salvation was Saint Augustine's.

So rather than apprehend and genuflect to what Saint Augustine implies as to the eternity and timelessness of God, I realized I was rapidly running out of my own duration; I had to go right to the most fleshy of sinful deeds and to the center of my body. Motherhood seemed to be the most truthful and comfortable saintliness I would be willing to muster.

At the moment we decided it was time to try to get

pregnant, my husband and I entered a reverse time warp. We became crazed and impatient adolescents. The sex act was our sole mission in life—as often as possible and in as many positions as necessary to create our perfect little zygote. As in our nonprocreative sex life, we did not buy the "missionary position is best" prescription for successful pregnancy that so many how-to-maximize-sperm-potency treatises reiterated.

Ironically, the heterosexual conceptual journey is one of those rare moments when our society makes it okay to talk about sex in quasi-frank terms (rather than in the power relation repressive terms to which Michel Foucault refers and Saint Augustine enacts in the presence of God). We're welcome to produce both scientific and anecdotal-casual reams about it and even to celebrate copulation and confess our exploits (in passing gossip at the kitchen table, the café, the watercooler, the bar, on the bus, in the locker room, etc.). The heterosexual reproductive onus may be the only situation in which as an American culture we encourage and praise unbridled sexual intimacy—or at least fertility, gloating as the ultimate human expression of traditional masculinity. And while I have never believed in compulsory motherhood as an example of my ability to love, I still wanted my baby—from conception to pregnancy to delivery and beyond.

Contrary to popular notions of memoir, Augustine's confession is actually a hybrid genre consisting of a second-person direct address to the moral authority in the position of redeeming the writer of her wrongdoings (in this case, you, the reader, are ultimately the judge). Also a philosophical genre, it locates and questions one's personal actions within a particular culture of knowledge and investigations of being and truth. In Augustine's case, time and memory are equal protagonists or, rather, inextricable links between confession and conversion. For me, Augustine's text serves as the occasion to confess my own redemption story. One cannot be saved without the passage of time and the reflection of one's journey through its transition. Finally, confession in

Saint A.'s purview exists as a highly idiosyncratic exegesis, as the personal becomes a way of eliciting critical and extended commentary on biblical text. While Augustine relies diligently on biblical citation and context to situate his salvation story, I supply *The Confessions* itself as a biblical reference point and as the reminder of "knowledge" as evidence, in the Old Testament sense of woman knowing man and the possibility of conception resulting from that (wink-wink) *knowledge*.

So from abstract (though not necessarily chaste) intellect to the race for carnal procreative *knowledge*, I fled for my own version of eternity. And as my late-thirties copulative exploits raged without the vengeance of a pregnancy, I began utterly to panic. All this unprotected sex and no baby? Is it too late, I mean, really, I'm almost—gulp—*forty*? I swear to you, I said to my husband, I will become a spiritual person if I get pregnant. I really have no need for God, but if this actually happens at my most desperate moment of womanhood, I will find something other than poetry and art to believe in. But, still. Nothing.

In the course of my thirty-ninth year, two car accidents bookended too much sex and too many visits to doctors and acupuncturists and any kind of healer I could either afford or fathom. Surely, God, you must be punishing me for repeatedly thumbing my nose at you; it's my fault for waiting this long, for thinking I could manage my biological fate the way I govern my career (but didn't I mention I was broke and without health insurance most of those prime procreative years?). Why won't you just give me a break? Or as Saint Augustine persists: "Do not forsake me now that I call upon you. . . ."

Thirty-nine years old, whiplash and painkillers in tow, my husband and I still managed never to give up—we just got less creative in our procreative acrobatics. Wham bam, thank you, ma'am, two days before my fortieth birthday, I was pregnant. Within a week, I miscarried. And then I resigned myself; I was not fated for the act of reproduction. I was ready to entertain my international adoption adventure.

Two months later, I sipped from a glass of water. It might as well have been a glass of metal, it tasted so vile. I knew exactly what it meant. I ran out of the house to the drugstore, purchased my pregnancy test. There you were, my little most magical God, talking to me from within, a plus sign on my stick of pee. And right then, salvation, you transported me from the depths of sin into a Godlike presence, my newfound *region of likeness*. And in the emergence and verisimilitude of my fetus, I have (harkening back to Michel Foucault) contributed (in the tradition of confessional repetition) to the widening archive of the pleasures of sex—sex that, contrary to Saint Augustine, was not the sin from which to arch away, but to move eagerly towards.

My conversion story encompasses a quest for cell division—ultimately in the form of my infant daughter—ascending as my greatest spiritual savior. Her birth brings about the biological and physical antidote to all narrative wrongdoing—all godless quests for God. Or so I would like to believe and facilitate in the small space of this preface. My daughter is exactly seven months old at the final inflection of this paragraph. Now, hushed seeker, after you read the timeless Saint Augustine text at the taciturn flick of this page, how will you tell your story?

—Elizabeth Block

Before *The Confessions*

"My parents were not well-off, small-town North Africans. . . ."

or

"I was Roman-born, in Tagaste, North Africa, in 354. . . ."

Those are the inoffensive regular ways to begin autobiographies. Augustine begins his *Confessions* irregularly, almost offensively:

"Great art thou, O Lord, and greatly to be praised, . . . And man wants to praise you. . . ."

Not until the ninth line does he use a personal pronoun, and then it is, for autobiographies, uncharacteristically in the plural. Yet it seizes the imagination of all but the most suspicious or cynical readers, with the book's most memorable line:

". . . you have made us for yourself, and our hearts are restless until they can find peace in you."

Not until eleven lines after this does the first person singular, the great subject of autobiographies, make an appearance:

"Let me seek you. . . ."

Such a first page can seem offensive, or can be so when commended to modern readers, because it presumes that they will identify with the author. That means that they, too, have restless hearts and are seeking. Read on and you will find that Augustine spends much time on the place where the restless discover peace, and seekers begin to find. This place is personified, to the point that one could credibly borrow a modern book title and call it *A Biography of God*, prismed through the life of a human. By what right shall a commender assume that readers, however restless and searching, have as their goal Augustine's God, or any transcendent being or person or force?

Answer: by no right. But that will not deter many who have been swept by the power, sometimes the frenzy, of these pages, from urging them upon others who care for autobiography.

Autobiography? One can get into intense debates as to whether *The Confessions* is an autobiography at all. A modern interpreter, Garry Wills, prefers to call it *The Testimony,* which goes beyond the idea of the confession of sin or the profession of faith. Others want us to think of the book as a long prayer, given the opening lines we have quoted, the prayerful momentum of all the pages, and the final word, which ends as prayers do, *Amen.* What all the revisers recognize is that, if this is an autobiography, it broke the mold for such books.

Break the mold it might. Still, historians of autobiography give it a prime place, even as they move on to see how later Western writers glued the pieces of the broken mold together and came up with books *something* like *Confessions.* Most of those that contemporaries read come from lesser distances than does this one from Augustine. Jean-Jacques Rousseau and Johann Wolfgang von Goethe offer bibliographical stops along the way. But more likely the subjects will be writers or generals, presidents or celebrities and scandal makers.

Augustine is different. How can readers identify with a North African from 1500 years ago? A Catholic, though most readers may not be such. A bishop, though few readers will be one. A bishop of Hippo, a back-country outpost, though Great Book Clubs, reading circles, and college classes whose members converge around this text are more likely to be urban, possibly urbane. The author of *The Confessions* (writing between 397–401) was evidently enjoying a midlife crisis, yet readers may be dealing with young-adult or old-age crises. Augustine, uninterpreted and seen out of the context of his times, would certainly be no hero of modern feminists, yet women, including feminists, find reasons to probe his book.

The ancient bishop and saint is distant from moderns in many ways. Even believers find much of his world remote. They do not postpone baptism, as he and his did, hoping to employ baptism as near the deathbed as possible, to wash away the accumulation of the sins that Augustine is forever writing about. Nonbelievers have to reckon with someone who today instead of writing *The Confessions* might head for the couch or seek prescriptions that might have addressed his childhood restlessness—the signs he tells us about sound suspiciously like those of Attention Deficit Disorder. Unlike many readers, he has no problem with the existence or identity of God. He is only concerned about finding peace in this God.

Any interpreter, teacher, or apologist who tries to remove the distance between Augustine and today's readers, does a disservice to both. He speaks despite, or because of, or through, the strangeness that this distance creates.

With that disclaimer in mind, it is time to make some claims about ways in which this strange, compelling voice from the long past can speak to all sorts of readers today.

First of all, *The Confessions* is indisputably a classic. It appears on most lists of "Top 10" or "Top 100" books in the West from the two millennia just past. Call it a classic, however, and one can dull or even doom its potential; can think of it as a dusty work that inspires awe but goes unread, except where demanding professors inflict it on students. Instead, one might think of a classic as a work of genius that, once having made its point and having had its effect in an extensive culture, reset the terms of life in that setting so that, though one may agree with it or not, admire it or not, one cannot "go behind" or "get back to the world" before it made its statement.

Thus the bearded god killers of a century and more ago, Darwin, Nietzsche, Marx, and Freud, wrote classics with which not all will agree and that meet scorn as much as admiration—but "behind" which one cannot go. They have to be reckoned with. So it is with Augustine and his classic *The Confessions*.

Next, the restless seekers in an age that prizes "soul" and "spirituality" and "the search," if they show a bit of patience with Augustine, are likely to find reasons to see elements of his world that match some in their own. He writes in a milieu marked by words historians use, such as "barbarian threat," "pagan lure," "secular practicality," "alternative philosophies"—in his case, Manicheeism and Neo-Platonism—all of which are present in contemporary culture, if under different names.

A third way in which *The Confessions* closes some of the gap between the author and our contemporaries has to do with an effect that has become apparent to readers through the ages. William Sloan, a modern publisher, reminded authors of autobiographies that readers do not open their books thinking and begging, "Tell me about you." By instinct (and these are my words and not exactly Sloan's) they are signaling, "Tell me about me, as I use you as a mirror to my soul or a window to my world." This does not mean that readers are necessarily narcissistic. It does mean that they cannot remove themselves from the transaction implied by our words "autobiographer" and "reader."

Fourth, having paid this book the ambiguous compliment of calling it a classic, we can pay the author the unambiguous one of calling him a genius. Like Augustine or not; be offended by him or charmed; share his version of the restless heart and the search to find peace or undertake a different journey, it makes no difference. It becomes clear that he is more than a virtuoso in the world of self-examination, a talent at relating to his God, a psychologically complex leader. He has a way of reaching into the abyss of human complexity and of grasping for the heights of human aspiration that dazzle.

As does the work of a Mozart or a Bach, geniuses in music who awe clarinet tootlers, weak basses, and makers of jazz. As does the work of Shakespeare, who may bore sophomores when incompetent teachers drone on about him, but stuns and enchants moviegoers who see modern adaptations or well-done classic versions of *Romeo and Juliet.* As do the works of Da Vinci, Michelangelo, and Rembrandt, in the eyes of casual gallerygoers, Sunday painters, and the aged in the craft studios of senior citizen settings. They provide academic deconstructionists and postmodern relativists with the best icons for their theoretical work, even as they speak to the restless heart in the classroom.

The Confessions, an ancient classic that addresses modern situations, a mirror held up to readers and a work of genius that induces awe, is in many ways a demanding, indeed a difficult, book. While common readers, common people, through the ages have seized it, he wrote it for elites, *spiritales,* "people of the spirit," whom the proud author wanted to impress.

It is not the difficulty that leads to the demanding. Often the clear content will be most disturbing. At times the reader may have to pause to demur, or growl, as when Augustine gets engrossed in concepts that, however appropriate, are at least on first hearing uncongenial. For example: original sin. Readers may be put off or become envious or keep their guard up as Augustine deals readily with his God, whom others find remote, "other," or nonexistent. Women, and not only women, may wince about the way he "used" his unnamed concubine of fifteen years, or was not fully responsible in respect to their child, Adeodatus. They will find his relation to his praying mother Monica at times cloying, at times off-putting. He shows no sign of having written *The Confessions* in order to produce a book that all will find congenial. He was a rhetorician who loved argument, and offers a text that induces argument and, one hopes, vehement disagreements. The enemies of a good reading of *The Confessions* would be apathy, cynicism, or too easy agreement with the author in what he sets out to do.

There are plenty of entertainments and tantalizers along the way to make the meeting of Augustinian demands easier. We note him making much of things: babies at the breast (I, 7), couples in love (VIII, 3), his own schoolboy boredom (I, 11), the fact that his mother was on the verge of alcoholism as a girl (IX, 8), his sexual fantasies and dreams (X, 30), the pleasures of music (X, 33). Some of his anecdotes amuse because they seem to make too much of trivial incidents in his past, though they turn out to be among the most revealing elements in his life plot.

Thus most commentators, and I would be among them, find revealing his account of a boyhood escapade concerning stolen pears. The incident would probably not have been disturbing enough to keep Patricius and Monica awake, and certainly would not have been recorded on Thagastean police blotters. Augustine and some "other wretched youths" late at night, "in our depraved way," stole all the fruit they could carry. "And this was not to feed ourselves; we may have tasted a few, but then we threw the rest to the pigs. Our real pleasure was simply in doing something that was not allowed." And then, from trivial heights to soulful depths: "Such was my heart, God, such was my heart which You had pity on when it was at the very bottom of the abyss."

Abyss? A pear tree and a pigsty? "And now let my heart tell you what it was looking for there, that I became evil for nothing, with no reason for wrongdoing

except the wrongdoing itself." He spent much of a life-
time, beginning with seven sections of *The Confessions*
Book II, picking away at the psychic scars this boring
incident left on his conscience. That pear tree seemed
to bother him more than did the flaws in his relation to
his parents, concubine, or son. Something is going on
here that demands probing. But rather than enter the
vast company of tutoring probers, I would like to turn
over those seven sections and the Books that surround
them to readers who may use them as a mirror or a
window. It is likely that most of them, most of us, are
restless because of incidents that trouble only ourselves,
but keep on needing address.

So, here are *The Confessions*.

Book I

1 *Great art thou, O Lord, and greatly to be praised; great is thy power, and thy wisdom is infinite.* And man wants to praise you, man who is only a small portion of what you have created and who goes about carrying with him his own mortality, the evidence of his own sin and evidence that *Thou resistest the proud.* Yet still man, this small portion of creation, wants to praise you. You stimulate him to take pleasure in praising you, because you have made us for yourself, and our hearts are restless until they can find peace in you. Grant me, O Lord, to know and understand which should come first, prayer or praise; or, indeed, whether knowledge should precede prayer. For how can one pray to you unless one knows you? If one does not know you, one may pray not to you, but to something else. Or is it rather the case that we should pray to you in order that we may come to know you? But *how shall they call on him in whom they have not believed? Or how shall they believe without a preacher?* And again, *they that seek the Lord shall praise Him;* for *they that seek shall find Him,* and they that find Him shall praise Him. Let me seek you, Lord, by praying to you and let me pray believing in you; since to us you have been preached. My faith prays to you, Lord, this faith which you gave me and with which you inspired one through the Incarnation of your Son and through the ministry of the Preacher.

2 AND HOW SHALL I pray to my God, my God and my Lord? When I pray to Him, I call Him into myself. And in me what place or room is there into which my God should come? How should God come into me, God who made heaven and earth? Can it really be so, my Lord God? Can there be in me anything capable of containing you? Can heaven and earth contain you, heaven and earth which you made and in which you made me? Or, since nothing in existence could exist without you, does it therefore follow that everything that exists must contain you? I too exist. Why then do I ask you to enter into me? For unless you were in me, I could not exist. For after all I am not in Hell—and yet you are there too. For *if I go down into Hell, Thou art there.* I could not exist therefore, my God, were it not for your existence in me. Or would it be truer to say that I could not exist unless I existed in you, *of whom are all things, by whom are all things, in whom are all things?* So it is, Lord, so it is. How can I call you when I am already in you? Or where can you come from to enter into me? Can I find a place outside heaven and earth so that there my God may come to me? My God who has said: *I fill the heaven and I fill the earth.*

3 YOU FILL the heaven and the earth. Do they therefore contain you? Or after you have filled them, is there still something of you left over, since they are unable to contain you? If so, when heaven and earth are filled with you, into what do you pour that surplus of yourself which remains over? Or is it not rather the case that you have no need to be contained by anything? You yourself contain all things and it is by containing things that you fill them. For those vessels which are full of you do not, as it were, keep you in a fixed condition; since, if they were broken, you would not be dispersed. And when you are poured out over us, it is not you who are brought low but us who are raised up, not you who are scattered but us who are brought together. You who fill everything are wholly present in everything which you fill. Or can we say that, because all things together are unable to contain you wholly, therefore each thing contains only a part of you? Does every thing contain the same part? Or are there different parts for different things in accordance with the varying sizes of the things? That would mean that some parts of you could be greater and some smaller than others. Shall we not rather say this: everywhere you are present in your entirety, and no single thing can contain you in your entirety?

4 WHAT, THEN, is my God? What, I ask, except the Lord *God? For who is Lord but the Lord? Or who is God save our God?* O highest and best, most powerful, most all-powerful, most merciful and most just, most deeply hidden and most nearly present, most beautiful and most strong, constant yet incomprehensible, changeless, yet changing all things, never new, never old, making all things new; *bringing the proud to decay and they know it not;* always acting and always at rest, still gathering yet never wanting; upholding, filling and protecting, creating, nourishing and bringing to perfection; seeking, although in need of nothing. You love, but with no storm of passion; you are jealous, but with no anxious fear; you repent, but do not grieve; in your anger calm; you change your works, but never change your plan; you take back what you find and yet have never lost; never in need, you are yet glad of gain; never greedy, yet still demanding profit on your loans; to be paid in excess, so that you may be the debtor, and yet who has anything which is not yours? You pay back debts which you never owed and cancel debts without losing anything. And in all this what have I said, my God, my Life, my holy sweetness? What does any man succeed in saying when he attempts to speak of you? Yet woe to those who do not speak of you at all, when those who speak most say nothing.

5 OH THAT I might find my rest and peace in you! Oh, that you would come into my heart and so inebriate it that I would forget my own evils and embrace my one and only good, which is you! What are you to me? Have mercy on me that I may speak. What am I to you, that you should demand to be loved by me? That you should be angry with me, if I fail to love you, and should threaten me with the utmost misery? And not to love you, is not this in itself misery enough? Oh, in the name of all your mercies, O Lord my God, tell me what you are to me! *Say unto my soul: I am thy salvation.* Speak so that I can hear. See, Lord, the ears of my heart are in front of you. Open them and *say unto my soul: I am thy salvation.* At these words I shall run and I shall take hold of you. Do not hide your face from me. Let me die, lest I should die indeed; only let me see your face.

My soul's house is narrow for you to enter; will you not make it broader? It is in a state of collapse; will you not rebuild it? It contains things which must offend your eyes; this I know and I admit. But who will make it clean? To whom, except you, shall I cry: *Lord, cleanse me from my secret faults, and spare Thy servant from the power of the enemy. I believe, and therefore do I speak.* Lord, you know this. *Have I not confessed against myself my transgressions unto Thee, and Thou, O God, has forgiven the iniquity of my heart? I contend not in judgment with Thee,* for you are Truth. And I will not deceive myself: *lest my iniquity lie unto itself.* Therefore I do not contend in judgment with you; *for if Thou should'st mark what is done amiss, O Lord, Lord, who shall abide it?*

6 YET NEVERTHELESS allow me to speak in front of your mercy. I am only dust and ashes, but allow me to speak, since, see, it is to your mercy that I am speaking and not to man, my mocker. You too may smile at me, but you will turn and have compassion on me. For what do I want to say, O Lord, except that I do not know where I came from into this mortal life or (should I say?) into this vital death. Then it was the comforts of your mercy which upheld me, as I have heard from the parents of my flesh, from where and in whom you fashioned me in time; for I myself do not remember. I was welcomed then with the comfort of woman's milk; but neither my mother nor my nurses filled their own breasts with milk; it was you who, through them, gave me the food of my infancy, according to your own ordinance and according to the way in which your riches are spread throughout the length and depth of things. You also granted me not to desire more than you supplied; and on those who suckled me you bestowed a desire to give to me what you gave to them. Their feelings were so ordered that they wanted to give me something of that abundance which they received from you. For the good that I got from them was good for them—not that this good came to me from them, but rather it came to me by means of them. Since in truth all good things, God, come from you, and *from my God is all my health.* This I came to know later, when you were crying out to me by means of all those senses and faculties, internal and external, which you bestow on us. Then all I knew was how to suck, to be content with bodily pleasure, and to be discontented with bodily pain; that was all.

Afterward I began to smile; first when I was asleep and later when awake. So, at least, I have been told and I can easily believe it, since we see the same thing in other babies. I cannot of course remember what happened in my own case. And now little by little I began to become conscious of where I was, and I wanted to express my desires to those who could satisfy them; but this was impossible, since my desires were inside me and those to whom I wished to express them were outside and could not by any sense perception of their own enter into my spirit. And so I used to jerk my limbs about and make various noises by way of indicating what I

wanted, using the limited forms of communication which
were within my capacity and which, indeed, were not
very like the real thing. And when people did not do
what I wanted, either because I could not make myself
understood or because what I wanted was bad for me,
then I would become angry with my elders for not being
subservient to me, and with responsible people for not
acting as though they were my slaves; and I would
avenge myself on them by bursting into tears. This, I
have learned, is what babies are like, so far as I have
been able to observe them; and they in their ignorance
have shown me that I myself was like this better than
my nurses who knew that I was.

And now my infancy has been long dead, while I still
live. But you, O Lord, who are always alive and in whom
nothing dies—since before the beginning of the worlds,
before anything that can be called "before," you are and
are God and Lord of all that you have created; and in
you stand the causes of all things that are unstable; in
you remain the unchanging sources of all that changes;
in you live the eternal reasons of all that is temporal
and will not submit to reason—answer my prayer, God,
and tell me, pitiable as I am, be pitiful to me and tell
me this: did I have another period of life, which died
and was succeeded by my infancy? Was this the period
which I spent inside my mother's womb? I have heard
something of this too; and of course have seen women
who were pregnant. And what about the time even before then, O God, my sweetness? Was I anywhere, or
anybody? For I have no one to tell me this. My father
and mother could not tell me, nor could the experience
of others or my own memory. Or do you smile at me for
asking such questions? Is it your will that I should
simply praise you and acknowledge you for what I do
know? Indeed I acknowledge you, Lord of heaven and
earth, and I give praise to you for my first beginnings
and for that infancy of mine which I do not remember,
for on this subject you have granted man to guess from
others about himself and to believe many things about

himself merely on the evidence of weak women. So even then I had life and being, and by the end of my infancy I was already trying to find signs by which I could make my feelings intelligible to others. From what source, O Lord, except from you could such a living creature come into existence? Can anyone design his own creation? Or can there be tapped elsewhere any other vein or source from which life and being can stream into us, except from you, Lord, in whom life and being are not two different things, since for you it is one and the same thing fully to be and fully to live? *For Thou art most high and art not changed,* and this Today does not come to an end in you; and yet it does come to an end in you, since all times are in you; for they would have no way of succeeding each other, if they were not all contained in you. And since *Thy years do not fail*, your years are Today. And how many of our years and of our fathers' years have passed through this Today of yours, receiving from it the pattern and form of the existence which they had; and more still will pass through it; also receiving their pattern and degree of existence. But *Thou art still the same,* and all things of tomorrow and after tomorrow, all things of yesterday and before yesterday, you will accomplish today and you have accomplished today. What does it matter to me if someone finds this incomprehensible? I should like him too to rejoice as he says: "What does this mean?" Yes; this is the way I should like him to rejoice, preferring to find you in his uncertainty rather than in his certainty to miss you.

7   HEAR ME, God. Alas for man's sin. So says man and you pity him; for you made him, but you did not make sin in him. Who can recall to me the sin I did in my infancy? *For in thy sight no one is clean of sin, not even the infant whose life is but one day upon earth.* Who can recall those sins to me? Surely this is done by every little child I see, since in him I can see what I do not remember in myself. What, then, was my sin? Was it that I cried for more as I hung upon the breast? If I were to do this now (not, of course, crying for the breast but for the sort of food which is suitable to me at my age), I should very rightly be laughed at and blamed. Even in my infancy, therefore, I was doing something that deserved blame, but because I could not understand anyone who blamed me, custom and reason did not allow me to be blamed. For as we grow up we root out and get rid of such childish ways, and certainly I have never seen anyone knowingly throw away what is good when he is clearing his ground. But can we say that, just for the time being, even such things as these were good: to attempt by crying to get what would do one harm if it was given? To get into a bad temper when people who are responsible and who are one's elders do not do exactly as one wants? To get angry even with one's own parents? And with many others too who were wiser than oneself, when they failed to give in to one's least whim? To strike out and do one's best to hurt when one's commands which, if they had been obeyed would have done one harm, were not obeyed? It is clear, indeed, that infants are harmless because of physical weakness, not because of any innocence of mind. I myself have seen and known a baby who was envious; it could not yet speak, but it turned pale and looked bitterly at another baby sharing its milk. All this is well known, and mothers and nurses say that they have various ways and means of dealing satisfactorily with these things. But can one really describe as "innocence" the conduct of one who, when there is a fountain of milk flowing richly and abundantly, will not allow another child to have his share of it, even though this other child is in the greatest need and indeed at this stage depends entirely on this nourishment to keep alive? As it is we put up kindly enough with this behavior, not because there is nothing wrong with it or nothing much wrong, but because it will disappear as the child grows older. This can be proved by the fact that these same faults, if found in an older person, are considered quite intolerable.

You, therefore, my Lord God, who gave me when an infant life and a body which, as we see, you have equipped with senses, fitted with limbs, adorned with its due proportion and, for its general good and safety, have implanted in it all the impulses of a living creature—you command me to praise you in these things, *to confess to Thee and to sing unto Thy name, O Thou most Highest.* For you are God, Almighty and good, even if you had done nothing else but only this, which no one else could do except you, the one alone from whom is every manner of form, you, most beautiful, the creator of beauty in all things, you who by your law lay down for all things the rule.

So then, Lord, as to this period of my life, which I cannot remember having lived, which I take on the word of others, and which, however reliable the evidence may be, is still a matter of conjecture from the behavior of other infants, I am reluctant to count it as part of this present life of mine which I live in the world; for, so far as the darkness of forgetfulness is concerned, it is just the same as the period of life which I spent in my mother's womb. But if *I was shapen in iniquity, and in sin did my mother conceive me,* where I beseech you, my God, where Lord, or when was I, your servant, ever innocent? But, see, I will pass over that time; for what have I to do now with it, considering that there is not a trace of it that I can recall?

8 EVIDENTLY I grew out of this state of infancy and reached boyhood. Or should I say that boyhood grew in me, replacing infancy? For infancy did not go away. Where could it have gone to? Nevertheless it was no longer my state. For I was no longer an infant, incapable of speech; I was now a speaking boy. This I can remember, and since then I have observed how I learned to speak. It was not that my elders provided me with words by some set method of teaching, as they did later on when it came to learning my lessons. No, I learned to speak myself by the use of that mind which you, God, gave me. By making all sorts of cries and noises, all sorts of movements of my limbs, I desired to express my inner feelings, so that people would do what I wanted; but I was incapable of expressing everything I desired to express and I was incapable of making everyone understand. Then I turned things over in my memory. When other people gave a particular name to some object and, as they spoke, turned toward this object, I saw and grasped the fact that the sound they uttered was the name given by them to the object which they wished to indicate. That they meant this object and no other one was clear from the movements of their bodies, a kind of universal language, expressed by the face, the direction of the eye, gestures of the limbs and tones of the voice, all indicating the state of feeling in the mind as it seeks, enjoys, rejects, or avoids various objects. So, by constantly hearing words placed in their proper order in various sentences, I gradually acquired the knowledge of what they meant. Then, having broken in my mouth to the pronunciation of these signs, I was at last able to use them to say what I wanted to say. So I was able to share with those about me in this language for the communication of our desires; and in this way I launched out further into the stormy intercourse of human life, though still dependent on the authority of my parents and subject to the commands of my elders.

9   O GOD, MY GOD, what misery did I experience in my boyhood, and how foolish I was made to look! I was told that, at my age, the proper thing to do was to pay due attention to those who taught me how to get on in the world, and to excel in the kind of literary and rhetorical learning which would provide me with a reputation among men and with deceitful riches. I was then sent to school to become learned, though I, poor boy, had no idea of what was the use of learning. Nevertheless if I failed to work hard at my studies, I was

beaten. This kind of discipline was considered very good by our ancestors, and many people before us, who had gone through this way of life, had already organized wearisome courses of study along which we were compelled to go; the trouble was multiplied and so was the sorrow upon the sons of Adam.

But we saw, God, how men prayed to you and, with our limited capacities, we formed an impression of you as of someone great, who was able, even when not present to our senses, to hear us and to help us. For when still a boy I began to call upon you, my Help and my Refuge, and in praying to you I broke through the knots of language; I was small, but it was with no small earnestness that I prayed to you that I should not be beaten at school. And when you did not answer my prayer (thus not encouraging my foolishness), the beatings I had, which were then the great misery of my days, became subjects for merriment among my elders and even among my parents who, of course, wished me no evil at all.

When I think, Lord, of how our parents used to laugh at the torments with which we boys were afflicted by our masters, I wonder whether anyone exists with so great a spirit, with so deep and fast an affection for you (for the same result can be produced by a kind of stupidity)—can there be anyone, I say, so devoutly and closely united to you in feeling who can look at the racks and hooks and different forms of torture, in terror of which people pray to you all over the world that they may be spared the anguish, and can consider these things so unimportant that he can just be amused by those who are so keenly terrified of them, as our parents were by us in our schooldays? For we were just as frightened of our torments and prayed just as earnestly that we might escape them. Yet still we sinned by doing less than was demanded of us in writing or reading or studying literature. It was not, Lord, that we were deficient in memory or intelligence: you were pleased to grant us, considering our age, enough of these. But what we liked to do was to play, and for this we were punished by those who were themselves behaving in just the same way. But the amusements of older people are called "business," and when children indulge in their own amusements, these older people punish them for it. And no one is sorry for the children; no one is sorry for the older people; no one is sorry for both of them. I doubt whether any good judge of things would say that it was a good thing for me, as a boy, to be beaten for playing some ball game simply on the grounds that by playing this game I was impeded in my studies, the point of which was that I should be able to perform, when I grew older, in some game more unbecoming still. For this was the behavior of the teacher who beat me. If he was defeated on some trifling point of argument by another schoolmaster, he was far more bitter and more tortured by envy than I was if I was defeated in a game of ball by one of my playfellows.

10 AND YET I sinned, my Lord God, you who are the controller and creator of all things in nature, though of sins only the controller. I sinned in acting contrary to the commands of my parents and of those schoolmasters. For whatever purpose these preceptors of mine may have had in mind when they wanted me to learn, I could still afterward have made good use of this learning. For I was not disobedient because I was making some better choice, but only because I loved playing; I loved feeling proud when I won and I loved having my ears tickled by false stories, so that they might itch all the more. The same or an even greater curiosity sparkled in my eyes, when I looked at the shows and the games of my elders. And those who organize and pay for these games are so very greatly honored and admired for it that nearly all the spectators would wish their own little children to be like them, which does not prevent them being quite pleased to have their children beaten if, by spectacles of this sort, they are kept away from those studies which, so the parents hope, will result in their being able to produce such spectacles themselves someday. Look mercifully, Lord, on these things, and deliver us who now call upon you. Deliver also those who do not yet call upon you, so that they may call upon you and you may deliver them.

11 WHILE I WAS still a boy, then, I had heard of an eternal life promised us through the humility of our Lord God stooping to our pride. My mother had great hope in you, O God, and as soon as I came out of her womb I was marked with the sign of the Lord's cross and was salted with His salt. You saw, Lord, how, when I was still a boy, I was suddenly taken ill with a pain in the stomach and seemed likely to die. You saw, my God, since you were already my Keeper, with what deep emotion and with what faith I turned to the goodness of my mother and of your church, the mother of us all, and begged for the baptism of your Christ, my God and Lord. And the mother of my flesh was greatly moved (since, with her heart pure in your faith, she more lovingly still *travailed in the birth* of my eternal salvation) and she was already hastening on with the preparations for me to be initiated and cleansed in your health-giving sacraments, confessing you, Lord Jesus, for the remission of sins; and so I would then have been baptized, if I had not suddenly recovered. As a result of my recovery my cleansing was deferred, the argument being that, if I went on living, I should become still more defiled, because the guilt incurred in the filth of sin would be greater and more perilous after that washing than before. At that time I already believed; so did my mother and our whole household, except for my father. Yet, though he did not yet believe in Christ, he did not break the hold over me of my mother's goodness and did not stop me believing. For she earnestly endeavored, my God, that you rather than he should be my father, and in this you aided her and helped her to overcome her husband, to whom, though she was the better of the two,

she was still obedient because this is your command and
in this she was obedient to you.

I ask you, my God (for I would like to know, if you
would like to tell me), what was the reason that my
baptism was put off at that time? Was it for my own
good that I was given, as it were, more free rein to sin?
Or was I not given more free rein? How is it that even
now one is constantly and everywhere hearing it said of
one person or another: "Leave him alone; let him do as
he likes; he is not baptized yet?" But when it is a question of physical health, we do not say: "Let him have a
few more wounds: he is not well yet." How much better,
therefore, would it have been, if I had been made well
at once and then, by my own care and that of my friends,
had managed to bring it about that the recovered health
of my soul had been preserved in your keeping, who
gave it to me! Surely this would have been better. Yet
wave after great wave of temptation seemed to be hanging over me after my boyhood. My mother could see
them coming and she preferred to expose to them the
mere clay out of which I might afterward be reshaped,
rather than the express image itself.

12   LESS APPREHENSION, then, was felt about me in
boyhood than in adolescence. Yet in this period
of boyhood I did not enjoy my lessons, and I hated being
forced to do them. However I was forced to do them,
and this was a good thing for me, though it was not I
who did the good for myself; for I would never learn,
unless under compulsion; and no one can act well against
his will, even if what he does happens to be good. Nor
were those who forced me to learn acting well; the good
that was done to me was from you, my God. For my
teachers had no idea of how I was to use the education
which they forced upon me except for satisfying the insatia-
ble desires of that wealth which is poverty and of that
glory which is shame. But you, *by whom the very hairs of
our head are numbered,* used for my good the errors of all

those who kept forcing me to learn, and as to me, who was so unwilling to learn, you made use of my error in order to punish me, and I richly deserved it, I, so small a boy and so great a sinner. Thus by means of people who were not themselves acting well, you acted well toward me, and for my own sin you punished me as I deserved. For you have commanded it to be so, and so it is, that every inordinate affection should be its own punishment.

13 BUT I STILL cannot quite understand why I hated the Greek which I had to study as a boy. For I was very fond of Latin, not the elementary grammar but the literature. As to the rudiments—reading, writing, and arithmetic—I found these just as boring and troublesome as all my Greek studies. And how can this be explained except from the sin and vanity of life, because I *was flesh, and a breath that passeth away and cometh not again?* For by means of these rudiments I acquired and still retain the power to read what I find written and to write what I want to write myself; they are therefore undoubtedly better, because more reliable, than those other studies in which I was forced to learn all about the wanderings of a man called Aeneas, while quite oblivious of my own wanderings, and to weep for the death of Dido, because she killed herself for love, while all the time I could bear with dry eyes, O God my life, the fact that I myself, poor wretch, was, among these things, dying far away from you.

What indeed can be more pitiful than a wretch with no pity for himself, weeping at the death of Dido, which was caused by love for Aeneas, and not weeping at his own death, caused by lack of love for you, God, light of my heart, bread of the inner mouth of my soul, strength of my mind, and quickness of my thoughts? You I did not love. Against you I committed fornication, and in my fornication I heard all around me the words: "Well done! Well done!" *For the love of this world is fornication against Thee* and when one hears these words: "Well done! Well done!" they have the effect of making one ashamed not to be that sort of person. But this was not what I wept for; I wept for dead Dido "who by the sword pursued a way extreme," meanwhile myself following a more extreme way, that of the most extremely low of your creatures, having forsaken you, and being earth going back to earth. And if I were forbidden to read these things, I would be sad at not being allowed to read what would make me sad. And this sort of madness is considered a superior and richer form of learning than learning how to read and write!

But now let my God cry out in my soul; let your truth speak to me and say: "Not so, not so at all. Those first studies were very much better." For obviously I would rather forget about the wanderings of Aeneas and everything of that sort than how to read and write. True enough that curtains are hung at the doors of Schools of Literature. Why? Rather as a covering for error than as a mark of the distinction of some special knowledge. These professors of literature, of whom I am no longer afraid, need not cry out against me as I confess to you, my God, what my soul wishes to confess and as I find rest in the condemnation of my evil ways in order that I may love those good ways of yours. There is no need for either the buyers or sellers of literary knowledge to cry out against me. For suppose I were to ask them: "Is it really true that, as the poet says, Aeneas came at some time to Carthage?" the more ignorant ones will reply: "We don't know," and the more learned: "No, it is not true." But if I ask: "What is the correct spelling of the name 'Aeneas,'" all who have learned it will give me the correct answer, an answer in accordance with the general agreement which men have made among themselves for the use of these signs. And again if I were to ask: "Which would have the worse effect on man's life; to forget how to read and write, or to forget all these imaginary stories of the poets?" is it not obvious what everyone not quite out of his mind would reply? I sinned, therefore, in my boyhood when I showed greater affection for these empty studies than for the others that were more useful; or, it would be truer to say, I loved the former and I hated the latter. At that time "One and one make two; two and two make four" was a horrible kind of singsong to me. What really delighted me were spectacles of vanity—the Wooden Horse full of armed men, the Burning of Troy, and "there the very shade of dead Creüsa."

14 BUT WHY, THEN, did I hate Greek literature, which is full of such things? For Homer too is full skillful at putting together this sort of story and there is great sweetness in his vanity; yet when I was a boy he was not to my taste. I think that Greek children must feel just the same about Vergil, when they are forced to study him as I was forced to study Homer. No doubt it was a question of difficulty; and this difficulty of mastering a foreign language was like bitter gall sprinkled over all the sweetness of Greek stories and fables. For I simply did not know the words, and strict measures were taken, punishments and cruel threats, to make me learn them. There had been a time too, of course, in my infancy, when I did not know any Latin words either; yet simply by paying attention I learned Latin without any fears or torments; I learned it in the caressing language of my nurses and in the laughter and play and kindness of those about me. In this learning I was under no pressure of punishment, and people did not have to urge me on; my own heart urged me on to give birth to the thoughts which it had conceived, and I could not do this unless I learned some words; these I learned not from instructors but from people who talked to me and in whose hearing I too was able to give birth to what I was feeling. It it clear enough from this that free curiosity is a more powerful aid to the learning of languages than a forced discipline. Yet this discipline restrains the dissipation of that freedom: and this, God, is through your laws, your laws which, from the master's cane to the martyr's trials, have the power to make a blend of healthful bitterness, calling us back to you from these deadly pleasures in the enjoyment of which we become separated from you.

15 LORD, HEAR MY PRAYER: let my soul not faint under your discipline, and let me not faint in confessing to you those acts of mercy of yours, by means of which you have drawn me from all those most evil ways of mine, so that you may become to me something sweeter than all these alluring pleasures that I used to follow, and so that I may love you with all my strength and clasp your hand with the fullest affection, and you may still draw me away from every temptation now and to the end. For see, Lord, my King and my God, I would wish everything useful which I learned as a boy to be used in your service—speaking, reading, writing, arithmetic, all. For you granted me your discipline when I was learning useless things, and you have forgiven me my sin in enjoying those things. Certainly in these studies I did learn a number of useful words: but I could have learned them just as well in studies that were not useless; and that is the safe path along which boys should go.

16 BUT HOW one must condemn the river of human custom! Who can stand firm against it? When will it ever dry up? How long will it continue to sweep the sons of Eve into that huge and fearful ocean which can scarcely be passed even by those who have the mark of the Cross upon their sails? Was it not here, in this stream of custom, that I read of Jupiter thundering at one moment and committing adultery the next? Undoubtedly he could not do both these things; but the idea was this: that a false notion of thunder should be used as a bawd to give countenance to real adultery. And which of our long-robed professors nowadays would

listen seriously to one of his own school (like Cicero)
who cried out: "These were Homer's fictions. He merely
gave human qualities to the gods. How I wish he had
given divine qualities to men!" Though in fact it is truer
to say: "Certainly these were fictions of Homer, but his
method was to give something of the divine to wicked
men, so that crimes should not be called crimes and that
whoever was guilty of such things might appear to be
following in the footsteps, not of abandoned men, but
of the heavenly gods."

Nevertheless into this hellish river of custom the sons
of men are hurled, and much money is spent on acquiring this learning; a great thing is made of it when it is
advertised in the forum and laws are there written down
for men to see which fix extra salaries for the teachers
in excess of the normal scholar's fees, and this river of
custom dashes against the rocks and roars out: "This is
where you can learn words. This is where you can learn
that art of eloquence which is so essential for gaining
your own ends and for expressing your own opinions."
As though we should never have learned such words as
"shower" and "golden" and "lap" and "beguile" and
"temples of the sky" and the others which occur in the
passage I am thinking of, if it had not been for the fact
that Terence had put into one of his plays a worthless
young man who regards Jupiter as an example to himself
of how to seduce people. He is looking at a painted
fresco

> Which told how Love descended in a golden shower
> to Danaë's lap and so a woman was beguiled.

And then observe how he excites himself to lust, as
though he had an example for it among the gods.

> What God? Why, he who shakes the temples of the
> sky with his own thunder. Am not I, mere man, al-
> lowed to do the same? I did; and I enjoyed it too.

Most certainly this disgraceful sentiment does not make
the words any easier to learn; it is rather the case that
by means of such words disgraceful actions are committed with more confidence. Not that I blame the words
themselves; they are like choice and valuable vessels.
What I blame is the wine of error which is put into them;
and then our drunken teachers raise their glasses to us
and, if we do not drink to them too, we get beaten for
it, without any chance of appealing to any sober judge.
Yet, my God (in whose sight I may now safely recall all
this), I myself (poor wretch) took easily to these studies
and indeed was delighted with them and for that reason
was considered a most promising boy.

17 ALLOW ME, my God, to say something of my
intelligence, which was your gift to me, and of
how I wasted it on mere stupidities. I remember how I
was set some work, which was troublesome enough to
my spirit, but it was a matter which would be rewarded
either by praise or by disgrace, and indeed one might
have to fear a beating too. The work set was that I
should declaim a speech supposed to be made by Juno
when she was sad and indignant at the fact that she
was unable

From Italy to turn the Trojan King.

I had been told that Juno in fact had never uttered these
words, but we were forced to go wandering ourselves in
the tracks of these poetic fictions, and to turn into prose
for declamation what the poet had expressed in verse.
And the declaimer who won most applause was the one
who, while preserving the dignity of the character he
was representing, gave in his performance the best imitation of the passions of anger and grief and found the
most appropriate words to express his meaning. What
was all this to me, my God and my true life? What did
it matter that when I declaimed I won more praise for

it than so many others of my own age and class? Is not all this mere smoke and wind? And was there really no other subject on which I could have employed my tongue and exercised my intelligence? Indeed there was. I might have praised you, Lord, and your praises through your Scriptures could have supported the tender shoot of my spirit, so that it would not have draggled shamefully on the ground among these empty trifles, a prey to the birds of the air. For there is more than one way to sacrifice to the fallen angels.

18 HOWEVER, considering the kind of men who were set up as models for me to imitate, it is no wonder that I was swept away into vanities and that I went out of your presence, my God. These men would be thought little of and would be thoroughly abashed if, while relating some of their own actions which were not at all bad, they made use of some solecism or barbarism of speech; but if they told the story of their lusts in a neat, well-decorated style and with an apt use of words, they would be praised for it by others and would take pride in it themselves. You see these things, Lord, and you remain silent, *long-suffering, and plenteous in mercy and in truth.* But will you always be silent? And even now you will draw out of this horrible pit the soul that seeks for you and that thirsts for your pleasures, *whose heart saith unto Thee: I have sought Thy face; Thy face, Lord, will I seek.* For to be in a darkness of affection is to be far from you. We do not go from you or return to you on foot or by spatial measurement. Nor did that younger son in the Gospel get horses for himself or chariots or ships; he did not fly away on any visible wings or travel by any motion of the limbs in order that in a far country he might waste in riotous living what you gave him at his departure. A loving father you were to him by your gifts, and more loving still when he returned empty-handed. In lust, therefore, that is to say, in the darkness of affection, is the real distance from your face.

Look down, my Lord God, and, as you always do, look down with patience on how the sons of men most carefully observe the agreed rules of letters and syllables which they received from those who spoke before them and yet pay no attention to the eternal covenant of everlasting salvation which they received from you. Indeed it is true that a teacher and learner of these traditional rules of pronunciation would cause more offense if he were to break the grammarians' laws and say " 'uman being," without the aspirate, than if, being a human being himself, he were to break your laws and hate another human being. As if one could suffer more harm from any enemy than one suffers from the hatred which one feels against him; or as if one could do more harm to an enemy by any kind of persecution than one does to one's own soul by the mere act of hating. Certainly no kind of literary learning comes so close to one as does this verdict of conscience: "You are doing to someone else what you would not like to have done to you." How secret you are, dwelling silently in the Highest, God only great, whose never-flagging justice scatters the punishment of blindnesses over unlawful desires! A man who is trying to win a reputation as a good speaker will, in front of a human judge and surrounded by a crowd of human beings, attack his opponent with the utmost fury and hatred, and he will take great care to see that by some slip of the tongue he does not mispronounce the word "human"; but he will not be concerned as to whether his rage and fury may have the effect of utterly destroying a real human being.

19 IT WAS ON the verge of this sort of life that I, poor wretch, stayed dotingly in my boyhood; this was my field of exercise and ambition, one where I was more frightened of committing a barbarism than I was careful to avoid, once I had committed one, envying those who had not. I tell you these things, my God, in my confession, and these were the things for which I was praised by people whose good opinion then meant to me the same thing as living a good and proper life. For I could not see the foul abyss into which, far from your eyes, I had been cast out. And in your eyes what could be more disgusting than I was—I who was disapproved of even by people like myself, because of the innumerable lies I told to deceive my tutor and my masters and my parents: all for love of play, eagerness to watch worthless shows, and a restless hankering to imitate them?

I also was a thief, stealing things from my parents' larder or table, either out of sheer gluttony or in order to have something to give to the other boys, who liked being paid to play with me, though they enjoyed the play just as much as I did. In these games too I often used to try to overcome my rivals by cheating, all the time being overcome myself by the empty desire to be thought the best. But if I caught someone else cheating me, I simply could not abide it and would attack him in the most savage language for doing just what I had been doing to others. And if I was caught cheating myself and blamed for it in the same way, I preferred to get into a rage rather than to yield and submit.

Is this what is called "the innocence of boyhood"? Not so, Lord, not so. I beg your leave, my God. For it is just these same sins which, as the years pass by, become related no longer to tutors, schoolmasters, footballs, nuts, and pet sparrows, but to magistrates and kings, gold, estates, and slaves; just as in later years punishments are more severe than the schoolmaster's cane. It must, therefore, have been the low stature of children, O our King, which you used as a sign of humility and commended in the words: *of such is the Kingdom of Heaven.*

20 YET, LORD, even if it had been your will for me to have advanced no further than boyhood, my thanks would still be due to you, our God, most excellent and most good, Creator and Governor of the universe. For even then I had a being; I lived and I felt; I took care for my own security (which is a sign of that mysterious Unity from which I had my being); by my inward sense I watched over the integrity of my outer senses; even in these little things and in my thoughts about these little things truth delighted me. I hated to be deceived; I had a vigorous memory; I was educated in speech; and I was made tractable by kindness. I avoided pain, meanness, ignorance. How wonderful and how praiseworthy are all these things in such a little living creature? But all these things are the gifts of my God; it was not I who gave them to myself, and they are good and all of them together am I. Good, therefore, is He who made me, and He is my good, and in Him I rejoice for all those good things which even as a boy I had. For my sin was in this—that I looked for pleasures, exaltations, truths not in God Himself but in His creatures (myself and the rest), and so I fell straight into sorrows, confusions, and mistakes. I thank you, my sweetness and my glory and my confidence, my God, I thank you for your gifts. But I pray you to preserve them for me; so you will preserve me and those things which you gave me will be increased and brought to perfection, and I myself shall be with you; for my very being is your gift.

Book II

1 I WANT TO call back to mind my past impurities and the carnal corruptions of my soul, not because I love them; but so that I may love you, my God. It is for the love of your love that I do it, going back over those most wicked ways of mine in the bitterness of my recollection so that the bitterness may be replaced by the sweetness of you, O unfailing sweetness, happy sweetness and secure! And gathering myself together from the scattered fragments into which I was broken and dissipated during all that time when, being turned away from you, the One, I lost myself in the distractions of the Many.

For in that youth of mine I was on fire to take my fill of hell. Outrageously in all my shady loves I began to revert to a state of savagery: *my beauty consumed away* and I stank in your sight; pleasing myself and being anxious to please in the eyes of men.

2 AND WHAT was it that delighted me? Only this—to love and be loved. But I could not keep that true measure of love, from one mind to another mind, which marks the bright and glad area of friendship. Instead I was among the foggy exhalations which proceed from the muddy cravings of the flesh and the bubblings of first manhood. These so clouded over my heart and darkened it that I was unable to distinguish between the clear calm of love and the swirling mists of lust. I was storm-tossed by a confused mixture of the two and, in my weak unstable age, swept over the precipices of desire and thrust into the whirlpools of vice. Your wrath had gathered above me, and I was not aware of it. I had grown deaf through the clanking of the chain of my mortality. This was your punishment for my soul's pride. I was going further and further from you, and you let me be. I was tossed here and there, spilled on the ground, scattered abroad; I boiled over in my fornications. And still you were silent, O my joy so slow in coming! Then you were silent, and I went on going, further from you and further, making my way into more and more of these sterile plantations of sorrow, arrogant in my dejection and still restless in my weariness.

How I wish that there had been someone at that time to put a measure on my disorder and to turn to good use the fleeting beauties of these new temptations and to put limits to their delights. Then the waves of my youth might at last have spent themselves on the shore of marriage, if tranquility could not be found simply in the purposeful begetting of children, as your law, Lord, prescribes; for you shape even the offspring of our mortality and are able with a gentle hand to blunt the thorns which were excluded from your paradise. And not far from us is your omnipotence, even when we are far from you. Or certainly I ought to have listened with greater heed to the voice from those clouds of yours: *Nevertheless such shall have trouble in the flesh, but I spare you.* And, *it is good for a man not to touch a woman.* And, *he that is without a wife thinketh of the things of God, how he may please God; but he that is married thinketh of the things of the world, how he may please his wife.* I should have listened more carefully to words such as these and should have become a *eunuch for the kingdom of heaven's sake,* so in greater happiness awaiting your embraces.

But I, poor wretch, boiled up and ran troubled along the course of my own stream, forsaking you. I broke through all the boundaries of your law but did not escape your chastisement. What mortal can? For you were always with me, angered against me in your mercy, scat-

tering the most bitter discontent over all my illicit pleasures, so that thus I might seek for pleasure in which
there was no discontent and be unable to find such a
thing except in you, Lord, except in you, who shape
sorrow to be an instructor, who give wounds in order to
heal, who kill us lest we should die away from you.
Where was I, and how far was I banished from the delights of your house in that sixteenth year of my flesh
when the madness of lust (forbidden by your laws but
too much countenanced by human shamelessness) held
complete sway over me and to this madness I surrend-
ered myself entirely! And those about me took no care
to save me from falling by getting me married; their one
aim was that I should learn how to make a good speech
and become an orator capable of swaying his audience.

3   IN THIS YEAR there was a break in my studies. I
came back home from Madaura, the nearby city
to which I had gone to learn the beginnings of literature
and rhetoric, and now money was being provided for me
to go further afield, to Carthage. This was rather because
my father had big ideas than because he was rich. He
was only a poor citizen of Tagaste. But to whom am I
relating this? Not to you, my God. But I am telling these
things in your presence to my own kind, to that portion
of mankind, however small it may be, which may chance
to read these writings of mine. And my object in doing
so is simply this: that both I myself and whoever reads
what I have written may think *out of what depths we are
to cry unto Thee.* For nothing comes nearer to your ears
than a confessing heart and a life of faith.

At that time, then, people on all sides praised my father for spending more money than his means really allowed so that his son could be equipped with what was
necessary for a long journey and be able to continue his
studies. Many citizens much richer than my father did
no such a thing for their children. And yet this father of
mine was not at all interested in how I was growing up

in relation to you or how chaste I was. The only idea
was that I should become "cultured," though this "culture" really meant a lack of cultivation from you, God,
the one true and good landlord and farmer of this field
of yours, my heart.

But in this sixteenth year of my age when, because of
our straitened circumstances, I had a period of leisure,
living at home with my parents and not doing any
schoolwork at all, the brambles of lust grew up right
over my head, and there was no hand to tear them up
by the roots. In fact when my father saw me at the baths
and noticed that I was growing toward manhood and
showing the signs of the burgeoning of youth he told my
mother of it with great pleasure, as though he were already confident of having grandchildren; but his pleasure
proceeded from that kind of drunkenness in which the
world forgets you, its creator, and falls in love with your
creature instead of with you; so drugged it is with the
invisible wine of a perverse self-will, bent upon the lowest objects. But in my mother's breast you had already
begun to build your temple and had laid the foundation
for your holy dwelling place. My father was still a catechumen, and had only been a catechumen for a short
time. My mother, therefore, was seized with a holy fear
and trembling; even though I was not yet baptized, she
was alarmed for me, fearing those crooked ways which
are trodden by those who turn their backs to you and
not their face.

How bitter this is to me! And do I dare to say that
you, my God, kept silent while I was going further and
further from you? Did you really say nothing to me
then? Whose words were they except yours which, by
the means of my mother, your devoted servant, you kept
crying in my ears? Not that any of them sank down into
my heart and made me act in accordance with them. For
it was her wish, and I remember how privately and with
what great anxiety she warned me not to commit fornication and especially not to commit adultery with an-

other man's wife. And these warnings seemed to me merely the sort of things which one might expect from a woman and which it would be a shame for me to follow. But, though I did not know it, these warnings came from you. I thought that you were silent and that it was my mother who was speaking; but you were not silent; you spoke to me through her, and in despising her I was despising you, I, her son, the son of your handmaid, I, your servant. But I did not know. I went headlong on my way, so blind that among people of my own age I was ashamed to be more modest than they were. I heard them boasting of their acts of vice (and the worse these were, the more they boasted), and so I enjoyed the pleasure not only of the act but also of the praise one got for having committed it.

What deserves censure except vice? I, to avoid censure, made myself more vicious than I was, and when, in fact, I had not committed a sin that would put me on a level with the worst sinners, I used to pretend that I had committed it, so that I might not be despised for my greater degree of innocence or thought less of for a comparative chastity. With what companions did I walk the streets of Babylon and wallow in its mire as though I lay in a bed of spices and precious ointments! And, so that I should stick the closer to the very center of it, the invisible enemy trod me underfoot and seduced me, since I was easy to seduce. And as to the mother of my flesh (who had herself already *fled out of the center of Babylon,* yet still lingered in the outskirts), she had certainly advised me to be chaste; but she did not give the attention she might have given to what she heard about me from her husband; she thought that if my desires could not be, as it were, cut off at the root, it would be unhealthy for the moment and dangerous for the future to restrain them within the bounds of the affections of marriage. The reason why she was against my getting married was that she feared that a wife would be a handicap to me in my hopes for the future, and these hopes were not those which my mother had of a future life in you; they were merely hopes that I might attain proficiency in literature. In these hopes both of my parents indulged too much — my father, because he hardly thought of you at all and only thought in the most trivial way about me; my mother, because, in her view, these usual courses of learning would be, not only no hindrance, but an actual help to me in attaining you. So at least I conjecture when I recollect to the best of my ability what the characters of my parents were. Meanwhile, the reins were loosened; I was given free play with no kind of severity to control me and was allowed to dissipate myself in all kinds of ways. In all of these was a mist cutting me off, my God, from the pure brightness of your truth, and *mine iniquity burst out as from my fatness.*

4   CERTAINLY, Lord, your law punishes theft; indeed there is a law written in men's hearts which not iniquity itself can erase; for no thief will submit to being robbed by another; even a rich thief will not tolerate another man who is forced to steal by poverty. Yet I both wanted to steal and did steal, and I was not forced to it by any kind of want; it was only that I lacked and despised proper feeling and was stuffed with iniquity. For I stole something of which I had plenty myself, and much better than what I stole. I had no wish to enjoy what I tried to get by theft; all my enjoyment was in the theft itself and in the sin.

Near our vineyard there was a pear tree, loaded with fruit, though the fruit was not particularly attractive either in color or taste. I and some other wretched youths conceived the idea of shaking the pears off this tree and carrying them away. We set out late at night (having, as we usually did in our depraved way, gone on playing in the streets till that hour) and stole all the fruit that we could carry. And this was not to feed ourselves; we may have tasted a few, but then we threw the rest to the pigs. Our real pleasure was simply in doing something that was not allowed. Such was my heart, God, such was my heart which you had pity on when it was at the very bottom of the abyss. And now let my heart tell you what it was looking for there, that I became evil for nothing, with no reason for wrongdoing except the wrongdoing itself. The evil was foul, and I loved it; I loved destroying myself; I loved my sin—not the thing for which I had committed the sin, but the sin itself. How base a soul, falling back from your firmament to sheer destruction, not seeking some object by shameful means, but seeking shame for itself!

5   CERTAINLY the eye is pleased by beautiful bodies, by gold, and silver and all such things, and in the sense of touch a great part is played by a kind of reciprocity. All the other senses too have their own proper modulations with regard to their particular objects. Worldly honor also has its own grace and the power to command and prevail over others (from which comes too the eagerness to assert one's own rights); yet in following all these things, we must not depart from you, Lord, or transgress your law. The life too, which we live here, has its own enchantment because of a certain measure in its own grace and a correspondence with all these beautiful things of this world. And human friendship, knotted in affection, is a sweet thing because of the unity between many different souls which it expresses. Yet for all these things and all things of this sort sin is committed. For there are goods of the lowest order, and we sin if, while following them with too great an affection, we neglect those goods which are better and higher—you, our Lord God, and your truth and your law. Certainly these lower things have their delights, but not like my God, who made all things, *for in Him doth the righteous delight, and He is the joy of the upright in heart.*

So, when we inquire into why any particular crime was committed, the only motives which, as a rule, we regard as credible are when it appears that there might have been either a desire for gaining or a fear of losing some of these goods which we have described as "lower." For they certainly are objects of beauty and worth, although they are low and mean enough when compared with those higher goods which confer real happiness. Suppose a man has committed murder. Why did he do it? Perhaps he was in love with the other man's wife, or with his estate; or he wanted to rob him of his money in order to live himself; or he was afraid that the other man might despoil him of one of these things; or he had been injured and was eager to revenge himself. Certainly a man does not commit murder for no reason at all, simply for the pleasure of doing the deed. No one could believe such a thing. Even in the case of that brutal and savage man of whom it was said that he was evil and cruel just for the sake of evil and cruelty, there is still a reason given for it. It was (says Sallust) "to prevent his hand and heart from growing slow through inactivity." And why was that? Why indeed? Obviously the point of this exercise in crime was that, after having seized Rome, he might obtain honors, commands, and riches and, in his poverty and guilty knowledge of his own evil deeds, might be freed from all fear of the law and all financial difficulties. Even Catiline, therefore, did not love his own crimes; what he loved was something else, for the sake of which he committed them.

6   AND WHAT DID I, wretched I, love in you, you theft of mine, you sin in the night committed by me in my sixteenth year? There was nothing beautiful about you, because you were merely theft. But are you in fact anything, for me to speak to you like this? Certainly the pears that we stole were beautiful since they were of your creation, yours, most beautiful of all, Creator of all, good God, God supremely good, and my true good. The pears certainly were beautiful, but it was not

the pears that my miserable soul desired. I had plenty of better pears of my own; I only took these ones in order that I might be a thief. Once I had taken them I threw them away, and all I tasted in them was my own iniquity, which I enjoyed very much. For if I did put any of these pears into my mouth, what made it sweet to me was my sin. And now, my Lord God, I inquire what it was that delighted me in that act of theft. Clearly there is no beauty about it at all. I am not speaking about the beauty that is to be found in justice and wisdom; nor of that which is in the mind and memory and senses and animal life of man; nor of the stars, which, set in their places, are beautiful and glorious; nor the earth and the sea, which is full of new life constantly being born to replace what passes away; no, it has not even got that incomplete and shadowy beauty which we find in deceiving vices.

Pride too strives to appear as though it was high and lofty, whereas you alone are God high over all. Ambition's one aim is honor and glory, whereas you alone and before all else are to be honored and are glorious forever and ever. Great men in their anger wish to inspire fear; but who is to be feared except God alone? From His power what can be withdrawn or subtracted? And where, or when, or whither, or by whom? The tender endearments of passion aim at provoking love. But nothing can be more tender and more dear than your charity, and nothing can be loved more healthfully than your truth, that truth which is beautiful and brilliant above all things. Curiosity puts on the appearance of a zeal for knowledge, while you, in the highest degree, know everything. Even ignorance and mere foolishness go under the names of simplicity and innocence, because there is nothing more simple than you; and what can be more innocent than you, since what brings hurt to the wicked is their own actions? And laziness seems to be looking for rest; but what sure rest is there except in the Lord? Luxury would like to be called plenty and abundance; but you are the fullness and the unfailing supply of a sweetness that is incorruptible. Prodigality shows, as it were, the shadow of liberality; but you are the most supremely rich bestower of all good things. Avarice wishes to possess much: you possess everything. Envy disputes for the first place; what place is higher than yours? Anger seeks requital; what requital is more just than yours? Fear shows its agitation in the presence of what is unusual or sudden and endangering to things that are loved, and it tries to secure their safety. But to you nothing is unusual, nothing is sudden. No one can take away from you the thing which you love, and nowhere except with you is there real safety. Grief pines away at the loss of things in which the desire delighted; this is because it would like nothing to be taken away, just as nothing can be taken away from you.

So the soul commits fornication when she turns away from you and tries to find outside you things which, unless she returns to you, cannot be found in their true and pure state. So all men who put themselves far from you and set themselves up against you are in fact attempting awkwardly to be like you. And even in this imitating of you they declare you to be the creator of everything in existence and that consequently there can be no place in which one can in any way withdraw oneself from you.

What then was it that I loved in that theft of mine? In what way, awkwardly and perversely, did I imitate my Lord? Did I find it pleasant to break your law and prefer to break it by stealth, since I could not break it by any real power? And was I thus, though a prisoner, making a show of a kind of truncated liberty, doing unpunished what I was not allowed to do and so producing a darkened image of omnipotence? What a sight! A servant running away from his master and following a shadow! What rottenness! What monstrosity of life and what abyss of death! Could I enjoy what was forbidden for no other reason except that it was forbidden?

7   *What shall I render unto the Lord* because, while my memory recalls these things, my soul is not terrified at them? *I will love Thee, O Lord, and thank Thee and confess unto Thy name,* because you have forgiven me these great sins and these evil doings of mine. To your grace I owe it, and to your mercy, that you have melted away my sins like ice. And to your grace too I owe the not doing of whatever evil I have not done. For what evil might I not have done, I who loved crime simply for crime's sake? Yes, I own it: all these evils have been forgiven me—both those which I committed of my own will and those which, because of your guidance, I did not commit.

No man who considers his own weakness can dare to say that it is because of his own virtue that he is chaste or innocent, and so love you less, as though he had less need of your mercy, by which you remit the sins of those that turn to you. And if a man has heard your voice and followed it and not committed those sins which he reads of in this recollection and confession of mine, he ought not to laugh at me, who was sick and then cured by the Physician owing to whose care he himself avoided sickness or rather was not so sick; for this he should love you just as much, or rather much more; he sees that I have recovered from the great weakness and depression of my sins, and he sees that my recovery was due to that same Physician who preserved him from being the victim of the same weakness and depression.

8   WHAT ADVANTAGE did I gain then, poor wretch, from these things which I now blush to remember? And in particular what advantage did I get from that act of theft, in which the only thing that I loved was just the act of theft itself, and it too was nothing, and I, therefore, who loved it, still more of a wretch. And yet I would not have done it by myself; for I can remember what I was like then; no, I would certainly never have done it by myself. Then in the act of theft I

must have loved something else too, namely the company of those with whom I committed it. And so I did not love nothing except the theft itself; yet, no; indeed there was nothing else, since this fact of having accomplices is also nothing. What is the real truth of the matter? Who can teach me, except he who sheds his light into my heart and scatters the shadows that are within it? And what is it which makes me indulge in all this inquiry and discussion and consideration? For if I then loved the pears which I stole and desired to enjoy them, I could have committed the theft by myself, supposing that I merely had to do this in order to get what I wanted to enjoy; there was no need to raise the pruriency of my desire by the excitement of having others to share the guilt. No, it was in the sin itself and not in those pears that my pleasure lay—a pleasure occasioned by the company of others who were sinning with me.

9   NOW WHAT exactly was this feeling? Certainly it was a very bad one and a disgrace to me, who had it. But what exactly was it? *Who can understand his errors?* We laughed at it, as though our hearts were tickled at the thought that we were deceiving people who had no idea of what we were doing and who would have strongly disapproved of it. Why, then, was my pleasure of such a kind that still I did not do the act by myself? Was it because people do not generally laugh by themselves? Generally they do not; but nevertheless there are times when, if something really ridiculous occur to the mind or is presented to the senses, people, even quite alone by themselves, will be overcome by laughter. But I would not have done that alone; no, certainly, I would not.

See, my God, in front of you this vivid memory of my soul. By myself I would not have committed that theft in which what pleased me was not what I stole, but that I stole; nor would I have got any pleasure out of it by myself, nor would I have done it at all by myself. What an unfriendly friendship is this! What a seduction of the soul and how difficult to track! That out of mere fun and play should proceed an eagerness to hurt and an appetite to do harm to others and with no sort of a desire either to avenge myself or to gain anything for myself! It has only to be said: "Come on, let's do it," and we become ashamed at not being shameless.

10 WHO CAN DISENTANGLE this most twisted and most inextricable knottiness? It is revolting; I hate to think of it; I hate to look at it. It is you that I desire, O justice and innocence, you who, to the eyes of the pure, are beauty and honesty, you, O plenteous unsating satisfaction. With you is true peace and life imperturbable. He who enters into you *enters into the joy of his Lord;* he shall have no fear; he shall be well indeed in him who is best of all. I slipped from you and went astray, my God, in my youth, wandering too far from my upholder and my stay, and I became to myself a wasteland.

Book III

1   I CAME TO Carthage, and all around me in my
ears were the sizzling and frying of unholy loves.
I was not yet in love, but I loved the idea of love, and
from a hidden want I hated myself for not wanting more.
Being in love with love I looked for something to love; I
hated security and a path without snares. I was starved
inside me for inner food (for you yourself, my God), yet
this starvation did not make me hungry. I had no desire
for the food that is incorruptible, and this was not because
I was filled with it; no, the emptier I was, the more my
stomach turned against it. And for this reason my soul
was in poor health; it burst out into feverish spots which
brought the wretched longing to be scratched by contact
with the objects of sense. Yet if these had no soul, they
could certainly not be loved. It was a sweet thing to me
both to love and to be loved, and more sweet still when
I was able to enjoy the body of my lover.

And so I muddied the clear spring of friendship with
the dirt of physical desire and clouded over its brightness
with the dark hell of lust. And still, foul and low as I
was, I would, in the exorbitance of my vanity, give myself the airs of a fine man of fashion. Desiring to be
captivated in this way, I fell headlong into love. My God
and my mercy, how good you were to me in sprinkling
so much bitterness over that sweetness! For I was loved
myself, and I reached the point where we met together
to enjoy our love, and there I was fettered happily in
bonds of misery so that I might be beaten with rods of
red-hot iron—the rods of jealousy and suspicions, and
fears and angers and quarrels.

2   I WAS CARRIED away too by plays on the stage in which I found plenty of examples of my own miseries and plenty of fuel for my own fire. Why is it, I wonder, that people want to feel sad at miserable and tragic happenings which they certainly would not like to suffer themselves? Yet as spectators they do want to suffer the sadness and indeed their whole pleasure is just in this. What a wretched sort of madness! For if one is oneself subject to the kind of emotions one sees on the stage, one is all the more moved by them. Yet when one suffers in real life, this is described as "misery," and when one feels for others, we call it "compassion." But there can be no real compassion for fictions on the stage. A man listening to a play is not called upon to help the sufferer; he is merely invited to feel sad. And the sadder he feels, the higher is his opinion of the actor of this fantasy. If the disasters which happen to people on the stage (disasters which either took place in the remote past or else are pure inventions) are represented in such a way that the spectator does not feel sad, he will go out of the theater in disgust and speak disparagingly of the performance; but so long as he feels sad, he will stay fixed in his place, enjoying every moment.

Are we to say, then, that tears and sufferings are things which we love? Undoubtedly what every man wants is to be glad. Or is it that, while no one wants to be miserable, one still does want to have compassion, and, since one cannot feel compassion without feeling suffering, this and this alone is the reason why sufferings are loved?

This also springs from that vein and source of friendship. But in what direction does it flow? Why is it that it runs into that torrent of pitch which boils and swells with the high tides of foul lust, changing itself into them and of its own will altering its own nature from a heavenly clearness into a precipitation of depravity? Is compassion, then, to be cast out? Certainly not. We must therefore allow ourselves sometimes to love sufferings. But beware of uncleanness, my soul. Stay in the keeping of my God, the *God of our fathers, who is to be praised and exalted above all forever.* Beware of uncleanness.

I have not ceased to feel compassion now. But in those days in the theaters I used to sympathize with the joys of lovers, when they wickedly enjoyed each other, even though all this was purely imaginary and just a stage show, and when they were separated from one another, I used to sympathize with their misery, as though I felt real pity for them; yet I was thoroughly enjoying it in both cases. But now I feel more pity for someone who rejoices in his wickedness than for someone who is supposed to be suffering great hardships because of the lack of some harmful pleasure or the loss of some miserable felicity. This certainly is a truer form of compassion, but the pain in it does not give one pleasure. To feel grief for another's misery is a sign and work of charity and is therefore to be commended; but it is still true that a man who is genuinely compassionate would rather that there was nothing for him to feel grief about. Only if good will could will evil (which is impossible) could there be a man really and truly compassionate who would wish some people to be unhappy so that they could be objects for his compassion. Some sorrow, therefore, may be approved of, but none loved. For this, Lord God, is your way. You are wounded by no sorrow, yet you love souls far more deeply than we can, and your compassion is more lasting and indestructible than ours. *And who is sufficient for these things?*

But I, poor wretch, at that time loved to feel sad and went looking for something to feel sad about; in someone else's sorrow, which was purely fictitious and acted. I was best pleased and most strongly attracted by the performance of an actor who brought tears to my eyes. Unhappy sheep that I was, straying from your flock and impatient of your keeping! No wonder that I became infected with a foul disease, and this was the origin of my love for sorrows—not sorrows that really affected me deeply, for I did not like to suffer in my own person the things which I liked to see represented on the stage, but only those imaginary sorrows the hearing of which had, as it were, the effect of scratching the surface of my skin. And, as happens after the scratching of poisoned nails, what came next were feverish swellings, abscesses, and running sores. Such was the life I led. Was this, my God, a life at all?

3 AND ABOVE ME hovered your mercy, faithful however far I strayed. I wasted myself away in great sins. I followed in the path of sacrilegious curiosity, allowing it to lead me, in my desertion of you, down to the depths of infidelity and the beguiling service of devils, to whom I made my own evil deeds a sacrifice, and in all these things you beat me with your rod. Once when your solemnities were being celebrated within the walls of your Church, I actually dared to desire and then to bring to a conclusion a business which deserved death for its reward. For this you lashed me with punishments that were heavy, but nothing in comparison with my fault, O you infinite mercy, my God, my refuge from those terrible destroyers, among whom I wandered with a stiff neck on my path further and further away from you, loving my own ways and not yours, loving the liberty of a runaway.

Those studies of mine also, which were considered perfectly respectable, were designed to fit me for the law so that I might gain a great name in a profession where those who deceive most people have the biggest reputations. Such is the blindness of men, that blindness should become an actual source of pride! And by now I was a senior student in the School of Rhetoric and very pleased with myself and proud and swelling with arrogance, although, as you know, Lord, I was a quieter character and indeed entirely without any share in the subversive behavior of the "Subverters"—this being the savage and diabolical name which was used as a kind of badge or mark of a "man of the world." However, I kept company with these Subverters and felt a kind of shameless shame for not being like them. I went about with them and there were times when I enjoyed their friendship, though I always hated their actions—that is to say, their "subvertings," which were a kind of wanton persecution of the modesty of ordinary unknown people, a persecution carried out for no reason at all except that by jeering and mocking they were able to give themselves a malicious amusement. Nothing can be more like the behavior of devils than this. "Subverters," therefore, was a very good name for them. Most clearly they themselves were first subverted and entirely perverted, and on those occasions when they took pleasure in mocking and deceiving others, there were hidden within themselves deceiving spirits, laughing at them and leading them astray.

4   AMONG SUCH companions in this unsettled age of mine I pursued my studies of the books of eloquence, a subject in which I longed to make a name for myself, though my reason for this was damnable and mere wind, being simply joy in human vanity. In the normal course of study I came across a book by Cicero, a man whose style, though not his heart, is almost universally admired. This book of his contains an exhortation to philosophy; it is called *Hortensius*. Now it was this book which altered my way of feeling, turned my prayers to you, Lord, yourself, and gave me different ambitions and desires. Every vain hope suddenly became worthless to me; my spirit was filled with an extraordinary and burning desire for the immortality of wisdom, and now I began to rise, so that I might return to you. I was in my nineteenth year (my father having died two years previously), and I might be assumed to be spending the money my mother sent me on sharpening my tongue; but it was not for the purpose of sharpening my tongue that I had used this book of Cicero's; what moved me was not the style, but the matter.

I was on fire then, my God, I was on fire to leave earthly things behind and fly back to you, nor did I know what you would do with me; for with you is wisdom. But that book inflamed me with the love of wisdom (which is called "philosophy" in Greek). There are some who lead us astray by means of philosophy and who use that great and pleasant and honorable name as a disguise or artificial coloring for their own errors, and nearly all such people, both of Cicero's time and before, are noted in that book and censured. There too is clearly stated that wholesome advice given to us by your good and faithful servant: *"Beware lest any man spoil you through philosophy and vain deceit, after the tradition of men, after the rudiments of the world, and not after Christ. For in Him dwelleth all the fullness of the Godhead bodily."* And as to me at that time (you know this, O light of my heart), I was still unacquainted with the Apostolic Scriptures. Yet the one thing in that exhortation which delighted me was this: I was not encouraged by this work of Cicero's to join this or that sect; instead I was urged on and inflamed with a passionate zeal to love and seek and obtain and embrace and hold fast wisdom itself, whatever it might be. And in my ardent desire only one thing held me back, which was that the name of Christ was not there; for this name, Lord, this name of my Saviour, your son, had been with my mother's milk drunk in devoutly by my tender heart, where it remained deeply treasured. So I could not be entirely swept away by anything, however learned or well written or true, which made no mention of this name.

5   I THEREFORE decided to give my attention to the study of the Holy Scriptures and to see what they were like. And what I saw was something that is not discovered by the proud and is not laid open to children; the way in is low and humble, but inside the vault is high and veiled in mysteries, and I lacked the qualities which would make me fit to enter in or stoop my neck to follow the pathway. For when I studied the Scriptures then I did not feel as I am writing about them now. They seemed to me unworthy of comparison with the grand style of Cicero. For my pride shrank from their modesty, and my sharp eye was not penetrating

enough to see into their depths. Yet these Scriptures
would grow up together with a little child; I, however,
thought too highly of myself to become a little child;
swollen with pride, I was, in my own eyes, grown-up.

6 AND SO I fell in with a sort of people who were
arrogant in their madness, too fond of the flesh
and too fond of talking, in whose words were the snares
of the devil and a kind of birdlime compounded out of
a mixture of the syllables of your name and that of the
Lord Jesus Christ and of the Holy Ghost, the Comforter.
These names were never out of their mouths, but only
so far as the sound went and the pronunciation of the
words; in their hearts there was no truth whatever. And
they kept on saying: "Truth, Truth"; they were forever
dinning it in my ears, and *the truth was not in them*.
What they said was false, and not only false about you
but false about the elements of this world, your creation.
And even those philosophers who speak the truth of
such things ought to have been disregarded by me for
the love of you, my Father and my highest good, O
beauty of all things beautiful. O Truth, Truth, how I
panted for you even then deep down in the marrow of
my soul, when they were constantly and in all kinds of
ways making use of the sound of your name—by voice
and in their many books and huge tomes. On these
dishes there was set before me, in my hunger for you,
the sun and the moon, beautiful creations of yours, but
nevertheless creations of yours and not you yourself, nor
indeed the first of your creations. For your spiritual creations are before these physical creations, heavenly and
shining as they are. But it was not even for these first
creations of yours that I was hungry and thirsty; it was
for you yourself, Truth, *in whom is no variableness neither shadow of turning*. But they in those dishes of theirs
kept on putting before me glittering fantasies, and it
would be better to love the actual sun, which is real to
our sight at least, than those false fantasies which make

use of the sight to deceive the mind. Nevertheless, since I thought that these were you, I fed on them, not with any great eagerness (for the taste in my mouth was not the real taste of you, just as you were not these empty fictions), and, so far from being nourished by them, I became the weaker. The food we dream about is very like the food we see in waking life; yet in our dreams we are not fed; we are, in fact, asleep. But (as you have since said to me) those things were not like you in any way; they were fantasies made out of physical objects, false objects, since we can place more reliance in those real objects which we see, whether on earth or in the sky, with our fleshly sight; animals and birds perceive these objects just as we do, and they are more real when we see them than when we imagine them. And again we can have more confidence in our imagination of them than in conjectures made from them as to other greater and infinite objects which in fact do not exist at all.

It was on such things as these that at this time I was fed—fed without being nourished. But you, my love, for whom I faint that I may become strong, are not those objects which we see, though they are in heaven, nor are you those objects which we do not see there; for all these things are your creations, and you do not regard them as among the chief of your creations. How far then are you from those fantasies of mine, fantasies of objects which do not exist at all! More real than these are fantasies of objects that do exist, and the objects themselves are still more real; yet you are not they. Nor are you the soul, which is the life of bodies, and of course the life of bodies is better and more real than the bodies themselves. But you are the life of souls, the life of lives, the very living life; nor is there change in you, life of my soul. For me, then, at that time, where were you? How far away? Far indeed was I straying from you, debarred even from the husks of the swine whom I fed with husks. For even the stories of the poets and the masters of literature are better than these deceitful traps. Verses, poems, and "Medea flying through the air" are undoubtedly of more use to one than the Five Elements, variously tricked out to correspond with the Five Dens of Darkness—all of which have no existence at all and are death to the believer. For I can turn verses and poems into true nourishment, and if I declaimed "Medea flying," I was not asserting a fact, nor, if I heard someone else declaiming the lines, did I believe them to be true. But those other doctrines I did believe. And miserable indeed I feel now when I think of the steps by which I was brought down to the depths of hell. For want of truth I toiled and I tossed, for I was seeking for you, my God (this I confess to you who had pity on me even before I made my confession), not by means of the intellect and reason (which, according to your will, set us above the beasts), but by means of the bodily senses. But you were inside me, deeper than the deepest recesses of my heart, and you were above me, higher than the highest I could reach. I had fallen in with that bold woman in the allegory of Solomon who, *knowing nothing, sits at her door and says: Eat ye bread of secrecies willingly, and drink ye stolen waters which are sweet.* She it was who seduced me, for she found my soul dwelling out of doors, in the eye of my flesh, and chewing over in myself the cud of what I had eaten through that eye.

7 FOR I DID NOT know that other reality which truly is, and it was as though my own sharpness of intelligence was persuading me to agree with those stupid deceivers when they put forward their questions: "What is the origin of evil?" and "Can we imagine a God bounded by any physical shape and having hair and nails?" and "Should we consider good those who had many wives at the same time, who killed men and made animal sacrifices?" In my ignorance I was much disturbed by these questions, and, as I went further from the truth, I had the impression that I was drawing nearer to it. This was because I did not yet know that evil is nothing but a privation of good, which can continue to

the point where a thing ceases to exist altogether. And how could I see this, when my eyesight could reach no further than bodies and the sight of my mind no further than a fantasy? I did not know that God is a spirit and not one with parts extended in length and breadth, nor one of whose being can be used such words as "size," "weight," "bulk." For every thing of that kind must have parts which are less than the whole, and even if it is infinite there will be less of it in a part defined by a fixed space than in its total infinitude, and so it cannot be wholly everywhere, as Spirit is, as God is. Then too I was ignorant of what in us is the principle of our existence and what is meant by the words of Scripture *"after the image of God"*—as to that I was entirely ignorant.

I was ignorant also of that true and inward goodness which makes its judgments not from convention but from the most right and undeviating law of God Almighty. By this law the customs of different times and places are formed as is right for those times and those places, while the law is the same always and everywhere, not one thing in one place and one in another. According to this Abraham and Isaac and Moses and David and all those men praised by the mouth of God were good men, and to deny that they were good is a mark of ignorance, for it is to judge merely out of man's judgment and to measure the whole moral structure of the human race by one's own particular and partial standard of morality. It is as if someone who knew nothing about armor or what piece of armor was made for each limb were to try to put a shin guard on his head or a helmet on his foot and were then to complain that they fitted badly: or as if, when there was a public holiday in the afternoon, a shopkeeper were to object to not being allowed to keep his shop open then, because he had been allowed to keep it open in the morning; or when in a house one sees one servant handling something or other which the man who carries around the wine would not be allowed to handle; or something done behind the stables which would be forbidden in the dining room; or as

if one should be indignant that in one house and one
family there is not exactly the same system of distribu-
tion to everyone. All this is like the behavior of those
who are offended when they hear that good men were
allowed to do something in former ages which good men
are not allowed to do today; or that, for reasons connected with time, God's commands to those in former
times were not the same as his commands are to men
of today; yet both in the past and in the present it is the
same goodness to which obedience is due. And yet they
can see in one man and one day and one household
examples of different things being suited to different
members, of one thing allowed at one time and not allowed an hour later, or of something permitted or commanded to be done in one corner which is forbidden
under pain of punishment to be done in the next corner.
Does this mean that justice is something which changes
and varies? No, it does not; but the times, over which
Justice presides, do not pass by evenly; for they are
times. Men however, whose *days are few upon the earth,*
cannot by the use of their senses find in previous ages
and in other nations of which they have no experience
the same relations of cause and effect which they observe in times and peoples of which they have experience. In the case of one body or one day or one house
they can easily see what is fitting for each particular
member and time and part and person. This argument
is convincing, while the more remote argument is often
a stumbling block.

At that time I was ignorant of these things and unaware of them. On all sides they were striking me in the
eye, but still I did not see them. For instance, when I
wrote poetry, I was not allowed to use every kind of
foot wherever I liked; different feet had to be used in
different meters, and even in the same meter one could
not use the same foot in every part of the line. Yet the
art of poetry, in accordance with which I wrote, did not
have different principles for different occasions; it comprised all the rules together in itself. And I still could

not see that the rule of righteousness, followed by these good and holy men, comprised, in a much more lofty and sublime sense, all its precepts together, and that in itself it never varied at all, although at various times, instead of prescribing everything at once, it laid down rules and principles proper for each occasion. So in my blindness I blamed these holy Fathers who not only behaved in their own times as God commanded and inspired them, but also foretold future times as revealed by God.

8 CAN IT at any time or in any place be wrong *to love God with all one's heart, with all one's soul, and with all one's mind; and one's neighbor as oneself?* Therefore, those crimes which are against nature must everywhere and always be detested and punished. The crimes of the men of Sodom are of this kind, and if all nations in the world committed them they would all stand guilty of the same crime against the Law of God, which did not design men so that they should use each other in this way. Indeed even that bond which should exist between God and us is violated when the same nature, of which God is the author, is polluted by the perversity of lust. On the other hand in avoiding those actions which are offenses against the customs of men we must take due consideration of the diversity of customs. What has been laid down as a general rule, either by custom or by law, in any city or nation must not be violated simply for the lawless pleasure of anyone, whether citizen or foreigner. For there is faultiness and deficiency in every part that does not fit in with the whole, of which it is a part.

But when God commands that something should be done which is against the customs or institutions of any people, it must be done, even if it has never been done there before; if it is something that has fallen out of use, then it must be brought back into use, and if it was never a legal obligation, then it must now be made one.

We know that it is lawful for a king in the state which he rules over to give an order which has never been given previously either by any of his predecessors or by himself, and that it is not against the general good of the state for him to be obeyed—or rather it would be against the general good if he was not obeyed, since there is a universal agreement in human society that obedience is due to kings. Then how much more unhesitatingly ought we to obey God, the Ruler of all creation, in everything which He commands! For, as in our human societies there are gradations of power, the greater being able to command more obedience than the lesser, so God is set over all.

One may also consider the various cases of sin, when there is a wish to hurt another person, either by insulting him or by injuring him. The motive may be either revenge, as in the case of one enemy against another; or to gain something which belongs to someone else, as with highwaymen against travelers; or to avoid trouble, as when one attacks someone whom one fears; or envy, as when the less fortunate turns against the more fortunate, or when the man who has been successful in something fears the prospect or is angry at the fact of having an equal; or simply the pleasure of seeing others suffer, as in the cases of those who watch gladiators or who mock and make fun of other people. Such sins fall under these headings and they spring from the lust of power, the lust of the eye, the lust of feeling—sometimes from one of these, sometimes from two, sometimes from all three. And so men live badly, against the Three and the Seven, that psaltery of ten strings, your Ten Commandments, O God most high and most sweet. But how can men's insults touch you, who are undefiled? Or what injury can be committed against you, who cannot be hurt? But your vengeance is in that which men do against themselves, because when they sin against you; they are acting wickedly against their own souls, and *iniquity gives itself the lie.* It may be by the corruption or perversion of their own nature, created and ordained by you, or in the immoderate use of things that are allowed, or in the burning lust for things not allowed and for that enjoyment which is against nature; or they may be found guilty of raging against you in their minds and in their words, *kicking against the pricks;* or when they take pleasure in the collapse of the standards of human society and brazenly set up, according to their own likes and dislikes, their private combinations or factions.

And these things are done when you are forsaken O fountain of life, who are the only and the true creator and ruler of the universe, and they proceed from the private and arrogant self-will which falsely attributes unity to a part and loves it. So then the way back to you is through humility and devoutness, and you cleanse us from our evil habits and look mercifully on the sins of those who confess them to you; you hear the groaning of the prisoners and you free us from those fetters which we have made for ourselves—so long as we do not raise against you the standards of an unreal liberty and, in desire for more, risk the loss of everything by setting our love more upon our own private good than upon you, the good of all things.

9   AMONG THE VICES and crimes and the many iniquities that there are must be counted the sins of those who are still making progress. These, if judged aright, will be condemned from the point of view of the rule of perfection, but may be commended if they show hope of future fruit, as is the green blade of the growing corn. And there are some actions which look vicious and criminal and yet are not sins because they are not offenses either against you, our Lord God, or against human society. For example material goods necessary for maintaining life or for some special occasion may be accumulated, and we do not know whether or not the motive was the lust of possession; or, in a zeal for improvement, punishments may be inflicted by the proper authority, but we cannot be sure whether the real motive

was or was not a desire to inflict pain. Many actions, therefore, which seem disreputable to men are, according to your testimony, to be approved, and many actions that are praised by men are, in your sight, to be condemned. The appearance of the act, the mind of the person who does the act, and the secret promptings of the occasion are all capable of great variations. But when you suddenly command that something unaccustomed and unforeseen should be done—even if this is something which at one time you forbade, and however much you may hide for the time being the reason for your command and however much it may run contrary to the convention of any particular human society—no one can doubt that this command of yours must be obeyed; since the only just society of men is the society which does your will. But happy are those who recognize your commands! For all the acts of your servants were done either to indicate something which needed showing in their own times, or else to foretell what was to come in the future.

10 I WAS IGNORANT of this, and so I used to mock at those holy servants and prophets of yours. And all my mocking of them meant nothing except that I myself was being mocked by you. Gradually and insensibly I was led on to believe a lot of nonsense, such as that a fig wept when it was picked and that the fig tree, its mother, shed milk-white tears. But if this fig were to be eaten by some Manichaean saint (always assuming that the picking of it was someone else's and not his guilt), it would be digested and then at the end of the process this saint would breathe out from the fig angels, or rather actual particles of God, at every groan or sigh in his prayer, and these particles of the most high and true God would have remained bound up in the fruit if they had not been set free in this way by the mastication and digestion of some sainted "elect." Poor fool that I was, I believed that more mercy ought to be shown to the fruits of the earth than to men, for whom these fruits were created. For supposing some hungry person, not a Manichee, was to ask for a bit and were to be given it, the morsel given would be considered to be as it were condemned to capital punishment.

11 AND YOU stretched out your hand from on high and drew my soul out of that deep darkness. My mother, your faithful servant, was weeping for me to you, weeping more than mothers weep for the bodily deaths of their sons. For she, by that faith and spirit which she had from you, saw the death in which I lay, and you, Lord, heard her prayer. You heard her and you did not despise her tears which fell streaming and watered the ground beneath her eyes in every place where she prayed; indeed you heard her. How otherwise can one explain that dream of hers by which you comforted her and as a result of which she allowed me to live with her and eat at the same table in the house, a thing which she had begun to avoid, since she shrank from and detested the blasphemies of my error? For in her dream she was standing on a sort of wooden ruler, and there came to her a very beautiful young man with a happy face, smiling at her, though she herself was sad and overcome with her sorrow. He then asked her (his purpose being, as is usual in these visions, to instruct her rather than to be instructed) why it was that she was so sad, and she replied that she was weeping for my perdition. Then he told her to have no fear and instructed her to look carefully and see "that where she was, I was too," and when she did look she saw me standing close by her on the same ruler.

Now how could she have dreamed this unless your ears had been open to her heart, O omnipotent Good, you who care for each one of us as though he was your only care and who cares for all of us as though we were all just one person? And how too can this be explained? For when my mother told me her dream, I tried to twist it to a different meaning, namely, that it was she who need not despair of being one day what I was. But she at once and without the slightest hesitation said: "No; for what was told me was not, 'Where he is, you are too.' It was 'Where you are, he is too.'" I confess to you, Lord, that, to the best of my recollection (and I have often spoken of this), I was more moved by this reply given by you through my mother than I was by the dream itself. For my false interpretation was so plausible, yet she was not perplexed by it, and she saw so quickly what was to be seen and what I myself had certainly not perceived before she spoke. So for the consolation of her present distress, joy in the future was promised to this holy woman. And the prediction was made long before the event. For nearly nine years after this I wallowed in the mud of the pit and in the darkness of falsehood, often trying to rise and then being plunged back again all the more violently. Yet all this time that chaste widow, holy and sober (such as you love), though she had now more hope to cheer her, never slackened in her weeping and her lamentations, never ceased in all hours of her prayer to weep to you about me, and her prayers entered into your presence, and yet you still allowed me to roll over and over in that darkness.

12 AND IN THE meantime you gave her another answer, which I remember. For I am leaving out much, since I am hurrying on to those things which I want especially to confess to you, and also there is much that I have forgotten. You did then give her another answer through a priest of yours, a bishop who had been brought up in your Church and was well versed in your books. My mother asked this bishop to be so kind as to discuss things with me, to expose my mistakes, to unteach me what was bad, and to teach me what was good; for he used to do this, if he found suitable people for his instruction. However, he refused to do so in my case, and very sensibly too, as I realized later. He told my

mother that I was not yet fit to be taught, because I was
full of self-conceit with the novelty of that heresy and
had already, as she had told him, been disturbing the
minds of people who were not skilled in argument by
my captious questions. "But," he said, "let him alone
for a while. Only pray to the Lord for him; he himself
will find out by his reading what his mistake is and how
great is its impiety." And at the same time he told her
that he himself, when a small boy, had been handed over
to the Manichees by his mother, who had been led astray
by them; he had not only read nearly all their books but
had actually copied them out, and (with no one to argue
with him or attempt to convince him) it had become
clear to him that that sect ought to be entirely avoided,
and so he had left it. But when he had said this to her,
my mother still refused to be satisfied. She kept on begging and praying him, weeping many tears, that he would
see me and discuss matters with me. In the end he became somewhat annoyed and said: "Now go away and
leave me. As you live, it is impossible that the son of
these tears should perish."

And this answer (as she has often mentioned to me
in our conversations) she took as though the words had
sounded from heaven.

Book IV

1 SO FOR THE SPACE of nine years (from my nineteenth to my twenty-eighth year) I lived a life
in which I was seduced and seducing, deceived and deceiving, the prey of various desires. My public life was that of
a teacher of what are called "the liberal arts." In private
I went under cover of a false kind of religion. I was arrogant in the one sphere, superstitious in the other, and vain
and empty from all points of view. On the one hand I
and my friends would be hunting after the empty show
of popularity—theatrical applause from the audience, verse
competitions, contests for crowns of straw, the vanity of
the stage, immoderate lusts—and on the other hand we
would be trying to get clean of all this filth by carrying
food to those people who were called "the elect" and "the
holy ones," so that in the factory of their own stomachs
they could turn this food into angels and gods, by whose
aid we should be liberated. This was my way of life and
these were the things I did, I and my friends, who were
deceived through me and with me. Let proud-hearted men
laugh at me, and those who have not yet, for their own
health, been struck down and crushed by you, my God. I
shall still confess to you the story of my shame, since it is
to your glory. Allow me this, I beg, and grant me the
power to survey to my memory now all those wanderings
of my error in the past and *to offer unto Thee the sacrifice
of rejoicing.* For without you what am I to myself except
a guide to my own downfall? Or what am I, even at the
best, except an infant sucking the milk you give and feeding upon you, the food that is imperishable? And what

sort of a man is any man one can name, seeing that he is only a man. So let the strong and the powerful laugh at us; but let us, weak and needy as we are, make our confession to you.

2 In those years I taught the art of rhetoric. Overcome myself by a desire for gain, I took money for instructing my pupils how to overcome other people by speechmaking. Nevertheless, Lord, as you know, I preferred to have honest pupils (as honesty is reckoned nowadays); without deceit I taught them the arts of deception, to be used not against the life of any innocent man, though sometimes to save the life of the guilty. And, God, from afar you saw me stumbling in that slippery way and in all that smoke showing just a spark of honor; for in my teaching I did act honorably toward those who loved vanity and sought after a lie, being indeed their companion. In those years I lived with a woman who was not bound to me by lawful marriage; she was one who had come my way because of my wandering desires and my lack of considered judgment; nevertheless, I had only this one woman and I was faithful to her. And with her I learned by my own experience how great a difference there is between the self-restraint of the marriage covenant which is entered into for the sake of having children, and the mere pact made between two people whose love is lustful and who do not want to have children—even though, if children are born, they compel us to love them.

I remember too that once when I had decided to go in for a competition in poetry to be recited on the stage, some magician or other came to me and asked how much I would give him to be assured of winning the competition, but I loathed and detested the filthy ceremonies of these people, and I told him that, even if the crown to be won were golden and immortal, I would not allow a fly to be kited in order to give me the victory. For his intention was to kill some living creatures in the

sacrifices he was going to make and it seemed to me
that he meant to try to secure for me the favor of devils
by honoring them in this way. Yet in rejecting this evil
thing, I was not, O God of my heart, acting out of any
pure feeling toward you. I did not know how to love
you. I did not know how to think except in terms of a
kind of corporeal splendor. And a soul that pants for
such figments of the imagination is surely committing
fornication against you, is putting its trust in falsity and
feeding upon the winds. There was I not allowing this
magician to sacrifice to devils on my behalf; yet all the
time I was, in that superstition of mind, sacrificing myself
to them. For surely to feed them is to feed the winds,
and we do this when by our own errors we become objects for their laughter and contempt.

3   THUS I WAS ready enough to consult those im-
posters called astrologers, my reason being that
they made no sacrifices and addressed no prayers to any
spirit to assist them in their divinations. Yet true Christian piety must necessarily reject and condemn their art.
For *it is a good thing to confess unto Thee,* and to say,
*Have mercy upon me, heal my soul, for I have sinned
against Thee,* and not to misuse your mercy so as to
make it a license for sinning, but to remember the Lord's
words: *Behold, thou art made whole, sin no more lest a
worse thing happen to thee.* But the astrologers try to do
away with all this wholesome truth when they say: "The
cause of your sin is inevitably determined by the stars"
and "Venus was responsible here, or Saturn or Mars."
As though man, who is flesh and blood and proud corruption, should be guiltless and the guilt should be laid
upon the creator and the ruler of heaven and of the
stars—you, our God, sweetness and fount of justice, *who
shall render to every man according to his works,* and *a
broken and a contrite heart wilt Thou not despise.*

The governor of the province at that time was a wise
man who had a great knowledge of medicine and was

very widely known for his skill. He it was who put on my fevered head the crown which I won in the poetry contest. But here he was not acting as a doctor for my fever. That disease can only be cured by you, *who resist the proud and give grace to the humble.* Nevertheless you did not fail to help me by means of this old man, nor did you let slip the opportunity of doing good to my soul. I grew to know him better and I used to listen eagerly and intently to what he said. His talk had no great literary pretensions but was delightful to listen to and also very much worth hearing because of the liveliness and force of his opinions. When in the course of conversation he discovered that I was an eager student of the books of those who make horoscopes, he spoke to me in a most kind and fatherly way, urging me to throw away these books and not to waste on pure nonsense the care and attention that should be devoted to something useful. He told me that he himself had in his youth studied astrology with the idea of adopting it as the profession by which he would make his living. "And if," he said, "I could understand Hippocrates, there would certainly be no difficulty in mastering that subject." Nevertheless he had abandoned astrology and pursued his study of medicine, simply because he had discovered that astrology was a false science, and, being an honest man, he had no wish to make his living by deceiving other people. "But you," he said, "have a profession, the profession of rhetoric, to support yourself by. You are giving your time to this astrological nonsense of your own free will and not for any reason of financial necessity. So you ought to be all the more ready to believe what I say; for I worked hard to gain a really thorough knowledge of the subject, with a view to making it my one source of income." I asked him why it was then that a number of true predictions were made by astrology, and he, within the limits of his knowledge, replied that this was due to the force of chance which was, as it were, distributed through everything in nature. Often, for instance, while turning over haphazardly the pages of a book of poetry, one may come upon a line which is extraordinarily appropriate to some matter which is in one's own mind, though the poet himself had no thought of such a thing when he was writing. So, he said, there was no reason to be surprised if a man's soul, while quite unconscious of what was going on inside it, should be acted upon by some higher instinct and should, by chance and not by any kind of skill, produce an answer that would fit in well with the affairs or the doings of the inquirer.

This too, either by him or through him, you did for me, and it was you who traced in my memory the lines along which I was later to follow up the inquiry by myself. But at the time neither he nor my dear friend Nebridius (a really good and a really pure young man, who used to laugh at the whole business of divination) could persuade me to give up these studies. I was still too much impressed by the authority of the astrological writers, and I had not yet found the certain proof that I was looking for, which would make it clear to me beyond all doubt that when these men were consulted and gave a true answer this was by luck or by chance and not from a real science of stargazing.

4   IN THE TIME when I first began to teach rhetoric in the town where I was born, I had found a very dear friend who was following the same studies. We were both of the same age, now at the beginning of manhood; he had grown up with me as a child and we had gone to school together and played together. But he was not in those early days, nor even in this later time, a friend in the true meaning of friendship, because there can be no true friendship unless those who cling to each other are welded together by you in that love which is spread throughout our hearts by the holy spirit which is given to us. But still this friendship was something very sweet to us and had ripened in the enthusiasm of the studies which we had pursued together. For I had turned him away from the true faith (in which, being so young, he was not soundly or thoroughly grounded) and had led

him into that deadly superstitious folly of my own, which had so saddened my mother. His mind was wandering astray with mine, and my soul could not be without him. But you were there, you who are always close upon the heels of those who run away from you, you who are at the same time the God of vengeance and the fountain of mercy and who turn us to yourself in ways that are wonderful. You were there, and you took him away from this life, when he had scarcely had a year of this friendship with me, a friendship that was sweeter to me than all sweetnesses that in this life I had ever known.

Who can recount your praises? Who can recount the praises due for what he personally has experienced in himself? What was it, my God, that you did then? And how unsearchable is the abyss of your judgments! For a long time my friend suffered from a high fever and lay unconscious in a sweat that looked like death. When they despaired of his recovery, he was baptized. He knew nothing of this himself, and I paid little attention to the fact of his baptism. I assumed that his soul would retain what it had learned from me and would not be affected by something done to his body while he was unconscious. But it turned out very differently. For he got better and came back to life again, and, as soon as I could speak to him—which was as soon as he could speak to me, since I never left his side and indeed we depended too much on each other—I began to make jokes with him, assuming that he would join in, about the baptism which he had received when he could neither feel nor know what was being done, and yet had now been told that he had received it. But he shrunk back from me as though I were an enemy. With a sudden confident authority which took me aback he told me that, if I wanted to be a friend of his, I must give up talking to him in this way. I was astonished and amazed, and I put off telling him what was in my mind until he should get well again and should be strong enough in health for me to be able to discuss things with him as I wished. But he was taken away beyond the reach of my folly, so that with you he might be

kept safe for my comfort. A few days later, when I was
not there, his fever returned and he died.

My heart was darkened over with sorrow, and whatever I looked at was death. My own country was a torment to me, my own home was a strange unhappiness.
All those things which we had done and said together
became, now that he was gone, sheer torture to me. My
eyes looked for him everywhere and could not find him.
And as to the places where we used to meet I hated all
of them for not containing him; nor were they able to
say to me now, "Look, he will soon come," as they used
to say when he was alive and away from me. I had become a great riddle to myself and I used to ask my soul
why it was sad and why it disquieted me so sorely. And
my soul did not know what to answer. If I said, "Trust
in God," she very rightly did not obey me, because the
man whom she had lost, my dearest friend, was more
real and better than the fantastic god in whom she was
asked to trust. Only tears were sweet to me, and tears
had taken the place of my friend in my heart's love.

5   AND NOW, LORD, all that has passed and time
has dulled my pain. May I learn from you, who
are Truth, and may I put close to your mouth the ear
of my heart so that you can tell me why it is that tears
are sweet to us when we are unhappy? Or have you, in
spite of the fact that you are present everywhere, put
our unhappiness far from you? You abide in yourself,
while we are tossed about from one trial to another.
And yet if we could not speak our misery into your ears,
there would be nothing at all left to us of hope. How is
it, then, that from the bitterness of life we can pluck
such sweet fruit in mourning and weeping and sighing
and lamentation? Is the sweetness simply in the fact that
we hope that you are listening to us? This is certainly
so in the case of our prayers, since our prayers have a
longing to reach you. But is it also so in the case of that
sorrow and grief felt for something lost, in which I was

overwhelmed at that time? For I had no hope that he would come back to life again, and this was not what I begged for with my tears; I merely felt sad and I wept; for I was in misery and I had lost my joy. Or is weeping really a bitter thing, and is it only pleasant to us at the moment when we are shrinking back from the things we once enjoyed and can scarcely bear to think of them?

6   BUT WHY am I saying all this? It is not the time now to be asking questions but for making my confession to you. I was unhappy and so is every soul unhappy which is tied to its love for mortal things; when it loses them, it is torn in pieces, and it is then that it comes to realize the unhappiness which was there even before it lost them. Such was I at that time, and I wept most bitterly, and I found repose in bitterness. Indeed I was unhappy; yet this unhappy life of mine was dearer to me than the friend whom I had lost. Certainly I would have liked to change my life, but not to part with it; I would prefer rather to part with my friend. And I doubt whether I would have parted with it even for his sake—as in the story, or fable, of Orestes and Pylades, who both wanted to die together, each for each, at the same time, since not to live together was worse to them than death. But I had a strange kind of feeling, which was just the opposite of theirs: I was at the same time thoroughly tired of living and extremely frightened of dying. The fact was, I think, that the more I loved my friend, the more I hated and feared death which, like a cruel enemy, had taken him away from me, and I imagined that, since it had been able to destroy him, it would quickly and suddenly destroy all men living. Yes; I remember it well; this was how I thought. Look, my God, into my heart; look inside it; see, because I remember, O my hope, you who cleanse me from the uncleanness of such affections, directing *mine eyes toward Thee and plucking my feet out of the snare.* I was surprised that other mortals could remain alive when the man, whom I had loved as though he would never die,

was dead. And I was still more surprised that, when he was dead, I, who was his other self, should still live. I agree with the poet who called his friend "the half of his own soul." For I felt that my soul and my friend's had been one soul in two bodies, and that was why I had a horror of living, because I did not want to live as a half being, and perhaps too that was why I feared to die, because I did not want him, whom I had loved so much, to die wholly and completely.

7   WHAT MADNESS it is not to know how to love men as they should be loved! And how foolish man is to be violent and impatient with the lot of man. Mad and foolish I was at that time. I raged and sighed and wept and worried, I could not rest, I could not think intelligently. For I was carrying about with me my soul all broken and bleeding and not wanting to be carried by me; yet I did not know where to put it down. There was no rest for it anywhere—not in pleasant groves, not in games and singing, not in sweet-smelling gardens, not in fine banquets, not in the pleasures of the bed, not in the reading of books, nor in poetry. I loathed everything, even the light itself, and everything that was not he seemed to me painful and wearisome, except for my tears and my laments; for in these alone I did find a little peace. But as soon as my soul was distracted from weeping, I became overwhelmed by a great load of unhappiness. It was a load which I should have brought to you, Lord, for you to lighten. I knew this but I neither would nor could—all the more so because, when I thought of you, I was not thinking of something firm and solid. For it was not you yourself who were my God; my god was an empty fantasy, a creation of my own error. If I tried to lay down my burden there, that it might rest, it slipped through the void and came tumbling back upon me again. And myself to myself had become a place of misery, a place where I could not bear to be and from which I could not go. For my heart could not flee away from my heart,

nor could I escape from myself, since wherever I ran, I should be following. Nevertheless I did flee from my native place; for my eyes did not search for him so much in places where they were not accustomed to see him. So I left the town of Tagaste and came to Carthage.

8 TIME IS NOT inactive. So far from passing through our senses without doing anything, it performs wonders in our minds. So now time came and went from one day to another, and in its coming and going it gave me other things to hope for and other things to remember, and gradually patched me up again with the sort of pleasures which I had known before. To these pleasures my great sorrow began to give way. But, though its place was not taken by other sorrows, it was taken by things which could cause other sorrows. For the reason why that great sorrow of mine had pierced into me so easily and so deeply was simply this: I had poured out my soul like water onto sand by loving a man who was bound to die just as if he were an immortal. Now certainly what did me most good and helped most to cure me was the comfort I found in other friends, in whose company I loved all the things which, after this, I did love. And this was one huge fable, one long lie; by its adulterous caressing, my mind, which lay itching in my ears, was corrupted. Nor, if one of my friends died, would that fable die out in me. There were other things which more fully took up my mind in their company—to talk and laugh and do kindnesses to each other; to read pleasant books together; to make jokes together and then talk seriously together; sometimes to disagree, but without any ill feeling, just as one may disagree with oneself, and to find that these very rare disagreements made our general agreement all the sweeter; to be sometimes teaching and sometimes learning; to long impatiently for the absent and to welcome them with joy when they returned to us. These and other similar expressions of feeling, which proceed from the hearts of those who love and are loved

in return, and are revealed in the face, the voice, the eyes, and in a thousand charming ways, were like a kindling fire to melt our souls together and out of many to make us one.

9 IT IS THIS which we love in our friends, and we love it so much that a man's conscience will condemn him if he fails to give or accept friendship when it is sought for or offered; nor will he expect anything else of a physical nature from his friend except these demonstrations of good feeling. It is for this that we feel such sorrow if a friend dies, such darkness of pain, the heart steeped in tears, all sweetness turned to bitterness, and for us a kind of living death because we have lost in death one who was alive. Blessed is the man who loves you, who loves his friend in you, and his enemy because of you. He alone loses no one dear to him, for they are all dear to him in one who is not lost. And who is this except our God, the God who made heaven and earth and who fills them, because it was by filling them that He created them? No one loses you, except one who voluntarily leaves you. And if he leaves you, where can he go, or where can he escape from you? He can only run from your kindness to your anger. Everywhere in his own punishment he will encounter your law. And your law is truth, and truth is you.

10 *Turn us, O God of hosts, show us thy countenance and we shall be whole.* For wherever man's soul turns, except toward you, it is fixed to sorrows, even if it fixes itself on things of beauty outside you and outside itself. These things of beauty would have no existence at all unless they were from you. They rise and set; in their rising they begin, as it were, to exist; they develop so as to reach their perfection, and after that they grow old and die; not all grow old, but all die. So, when they rise and reach their way into existence, the quicker they are to grow into being, the more they hurry toward ceasing to be. That is their law. So much you have given them, namely to be parts of a structure in which the parts are not all in existence at the same time; instead, by fading and by replacing each other, they all together constitute the universe of which they are parts. Our own speech too, which is constructed out of meaningful sounds, follows the same principles. There could never be a complete sentence unless one word, as soon as the syllables had been sounded, ceased to be in order to make room for the next. In these things let my soul praise you, God, creator of all things, yet let it not be stuck and glued too close to them in love through the senses of the body. For these things go along their path toward nonexistence, and they tear and wound the soul with terrible longings, since the soul itself desires to be and to find rest in what it loves. But on those things there is no place to rest, since they do not stay. They pass away and no one can follow them with his bodily senses. Nor can anyone grasp them tight even while they are present and in front of him.

Our bodily sense is slow because it is bodily sense and is bounded by the physical. It is sufficient for the purpose for which it was made, but it is quite incapable of grasping and holding things as they run on their appointed way from their beginnings to their endings. For in your word, by which they are created, they hear their decree: "From this point; and not beyond that."

11 DO NOT BE FOOLISH, my soul, and do not let the ear of your heart be deafened by the din of your folly. Listen now. The Word itself calls you to come back; and there is the plate of peace that is imperturbable, where love cannot be forsaken unless it first forsakes. See how things pass away so that other things may take their places and that so this lower universe may be established in all its parts. "But do I ever depart," says the Word of God, "and is there any place to which I could depart?" There fix your dwelling place, my soul, and there store up everything which you have received from there. Do it now at least, tired out as you are with falsities. Entrust to truth whatever truth has given you, and you will lose nothing. What is withered in you will flower again, and all your illnesses will be made well, and all that was flowing and wasting from you will regain shape and substance and will form part of you again, and they will not lay you down in the place where they themselves descend, but will stand fast with you and abide with you forever before God who stands and abides forever.

Why then be perverse, my soul, and why follow your own flesh? Will you not rather turn and let your flesh follow you? Whatever you perceive through the flesh you perceive only in part, and you are ignorant of the whole, of which these are parts; yet still these parts delight you. But if your bodily sense were capable of comprehending the whole—instead of being, for your punishment, justly restricted itself to a part of the universe—you would wish that everything in existence at the present moment would pass and go on, so that you might have the greater pleasure of perceiving the entirety of things. For these words we speak are perceived by you through your bodily sense, and you certainly do not want to hear the same syllables forever; you want them to pass away so that others may come and so that you may hear the whole sentence. And this is always the case when one thing is made up of many parts and all the parts do not exist together at the same time. To perceive all the parts together at once would give more pleasure than to perceive each individual part separately. But far better than these is He who made all things, and He is our God. And He does not pass away, because there is nothing to take His place.

12   IF BODIES PLEASE YOU, praise God for them and turn your love back from them to their maker, lest you should displease Him in being pleased by them. If souls please you, love them in God, because by themselves they are subject to change, but in Him they are established firm; without Him they would pass away and be no more. So you must love them in Him and take with you to Him as many souls as you can and say, to them: "It is He whom we must love; He made all this and He is not far off." For He did not make things and then go away; things are from Him and also in Him. See where He is: He is everywhere where there is the least trace of truth. He is right inside the heart, but the heart has wandered away from Him. Return, sinners, to your own heart and cling to Him who made you. Stand in Him, and you shall stand fast; rest in Him, and you shall find peace. Where are you going to over those rough paths? Where are you going? The good that you love is from Him; but its goodness and sweetness is only because you are looking toward Him; it will rightly turn to bitterness if what is from Him is wrongly loved, He Himself being left out of the account. What are you aiming at, then, by going on and on walking along these difficult and tiring ways? There is no rest to be found; here you are looking for it. Seek what you seek, but it is not there where you are seeking. You seek a happy life in the country of death. It is not there. For how can life be happy, where there is no life?

But our Life came down to us and suffered our death and destroyed death by the abundance of His own life: and He thundered, calling us to return to Him into that secret place from which He came out to us—coming first into the Virgin's womb, where humanity was married to Him, our mortal flesh, that it might not be forever mortal, and from there *like a bridegroom coming out of His chamber, rejoicing as a giant to run His course.* For He was not slow; He ran, crying aloud in His words, in His deeds, in His death, in His life, in His descent, in His ascension, crying and calling us to return to Him. And He withdrew Himself from our eyes so that we might return to our heart and find Him. He went away, and, look, He is here. He did not want to be with us long, and He has not left us. He went back to a place which He had never left, since the world was made by Him

and He was in this world, and He came into this world
to save sinners. It is to Him that my soul makes confession, and He heals my soul, for it has sinned against
Him. Sons of men, how long will you be so slow and
heavy of heart? Now that Life has come down to you,
will you not raise yourselves and live? But how can you
raise yourselves, when you are already high in the air
and have *set your mouth against the heavens?* Come
down, so that you may go up and go up toward God.
For in climbing up against God, you fell. Say this to the
souls you love. Tell them to weep in this valley of tears,
and so carry them up with you to God, because it is by
His spirit that you are saying this to them, if, while you
say it, you are burning with the fire of charity.

13 AT THAT TIME I did not know this and I loved
these lower beauties and I was sinking down to
the depths. I used to say to my friends, "Do we love
anything except what is beautiful? What, then, is the
beautiful? And what is beauty? What is it that attracts
us and wins our affection for the things we love? For
unless there were grace and beauty in them, they could not
possibly draw us to them." And, observing things closely, I
saw that in bodies themselves there was one sort of beauty
which comes from a thing constituting a whole, and another sort of grace which comes from the right and apt
relationship of one thing to another, such as one part of
a body to the whole body, or a shoe to the foot, and so
on. This idea sprang up into my mind from the depths
of my heart, and I wrote some books on "The Beautiful
and the Fitting"—two or three books, I think. You
know, God, for I cannot remember. I no longer have
the books. Somehow or other they have disappeared.

14 WHY WAS IT, Lord my God, that I decided to
dedicate these books to Hiereus, who was an
orator at Rome? I had never seen the man, but I had

come to love him because of his very great reputation
for learning, and I had heard and very much admired
some of the things he had said. But the greater part of
my admiration came from the fact that others admired
him. He was praised to the skies and people were astonished that he, a Syrian who was brought up as a master
of Greek oratory, should later become such a wonderful
speaker in Latin and should also possess such a wide
knowledge of philosophy. So he was praised and, without
ever having been seen, was loved. Does this kind of love
come into the heart of the hearer straight from the words
of praise which he hears? Not at all. What happens is that
love is kindled by love. We only love someone whom we
hear praised when we believe that the praise comes from
a sincere heart, that is to say, when the man who gives the
praise loves the man whom he is praising.

So at that time I loved men on the strength of the
judgment of other men—not on your judgment, my God,
in whom no one is deceived. Yet my feeling was not like
that which one may have for a famous charioteer or a
fighter with wild beasts in the theater who is the idol of
the crowd. My feelings were different and more serious,
and I admired others as I would have liked to be admired myself. For I would not have wanted to be praised
and loved as actors are, though I myself would certainly
praise and love actors. But I would rather have been
quite unknown than known in that way, rather have
been hated than loved like that. How does it come about
that the weights and impulses toward all these different
kinds of love are distributed in one soul? Why is it that
I love some quality in another man and yet would appear to hate it too, since I should reject it and detest it
in myself? We are both of us human; the actor and I
share the same nature, so one cannot compare my feeling about him with the feeling of a man who loves a
good horse but would not like to be a horse, even if he
could. How is it then that I love in a human being something which I should hate in myself, though I also am a
human being? Man himself is a great deep, and you,

Lord, number the very hairs of his head and in your sight they are not lost. Yet the hairs of man's head are easier to number than are his affections and the impulses of his heart.

That orator, however, whom I loved so much, was the kind of man that I would have wished to be myself. And I erred through swelling pride; I was tossed about by every wind, and it was too difficult for me to feel your steering hand. Why is it that I know now, and can confess it to you confidently, that I loved that man more because of the love of those who praised him than because of the actual qualities for which he was praised? The fact is that if the same people, instead of praising him, had abused him and had said just the same things about him in an abusive and contemptuous spirit, I should not have been so set on fire with admiration for him; yet his qualities would have been just the same; the man himself would have been no different; the only differences would have been in the feelings of the speakers. See how abject and helpless the soul is before it learns to cling to the solidity of truth! As the winds of speech blow from the hearts of those who hold their varying opinions, so the soul is carried this way and that, changing its course now here, now there; its light is clouded over, and it cannot see the truth. And there is the truth, right in front of us. And to me it was a matter of great importance for my style and my work to become known to that famous orator, and if he liked them, I should be all the more ardent about him; though if he thought little of them, then my vain heart, quite empty of your solidity, would be wounded. Yet still I enjoyed my meditations on "The Beautiful and the Fitting," which I dedicated to him, and, if there was no one else to admire the work, I thought it very good myself.

15 BUT, ALMIGHTY, I did not yet see that all this great matter has its hinge in your workmanship; for you alone make wonders, and my mind was ranging over corporeal forms. I defined and distinguished the beautiful as being that which is beautiful in itself and the fitting as being that which derives its grace from its appropriateness to something else, and I used corporeal examples in support of my argument. I also considered the nature of the mind, but the false view I had of spiritual things prevented me from seeing the truth. And the very force of truth itself was staring me in the face, but I turned my panting mind away from what was incorporeal and concentrated on line and color and swelling magnitudes, and because I could not see these in my mind, I concluded that I could not see my mind. And as in virtue I loved peace and in vice I hated discord, so I noted the unity in the one and the division, as it were, in the other, and it seemed to me that in the unity lay the rational mind and the nature of truth and the supreme good; but in the division I was wretched enough to imagine that I saw some sort of substance of the irrational life and a nature of the supreme evil, which was not only substance but actually life—yet not proceeding from you, my God, from whom proceed all things. I called the first a Monad, conceiving of it as a mind without any sex, and I called the other a Dyad—anger as in deeds of violence, and lust as in sins of impurity. I was talking ignorantly. I did not know and I had not yet been taught that evil is not a substance at all nor is our soul that supreme and unchangeable good.

For just as acts of violence are done if the emotion, in which lies the impulse to act, is vicious and aggressive and muddled, and just as sins of impurity are done if the affection of the soul from which carnal pleasures are derived is uncontrolled, so errors and false opinions contaminate life if the rational soul itself is corrupted. And so it was with me at that time, when I did not know that my soul needed to be illumined by another light, if it was to be a partaker of truth, since it is not itself the essence of truth. *For Thou shalt light my candle, O Lord my God, Thou shalt enlighten my darkness:* and *of Thy fullness have we all received, for Thou art the true light*

*that lighteth every man that cometh into the world; for in
Thee there is no variableness, neither shadow of change.*

But I was aiming to reach you and at the same time
was being forced back from you, so that I might taste
death; for *Thou resistest the proud.* And how could anything be more proud than to assert, as I did in my incredible folly, that I was by nature what you are? For,
being subject to change myself (as was obvious from the
mere fact that I wanted to become wise and so proceed
from worse to better), I preferred to think that you also
were subject to change rather than I was not what you
are. And so I was forced back from you and you resisted
my vain stiff-neckedness, and I imagined corporeal forms,
and, being myself flesh, I accused the flesh, and, being
a wayfaring spirit, I did not return to you, but went on
and on wandering into fancies which have no existence
either in you or in me or in the body and, so far from
being created for me by your truth, were figments constructed by my imagination out of corporeal things. And
I used to speak to the little ones of your faith—my own
fellow citizens, though I, without knowing it, was in exile
from them—and, like a talkative ass, I used to say,
"How is it, then, that the soul makes a mistake if it was
created by God?" But I would not allow myself to be
asked, "How is it, then, that God makes a mistake?"
And I preferred to maintain that your unchangeable substance went astray under compulsion, rather than admit
that my own changeable substance had deviated of its
own accord and for its punishment had fallen into error.

I was about twenty-six or twenty-seven when I wrote
those books. As I wrote them I turned over in my mind
all those corporeal fictions which made such a noise that
the ears of my heart were deafened. Yet, sweet truth, I
was straining these ears to try to hear your inner melody,
as I meditated upon "The Beautiful and the Fitting";
and I longed to stand and hear you and rejoice with joy
at the voice of the bridegroom; but I could not. I was
being dragged out and away by the voices of my own
error, and I was sinking down to the depths under the

weight of my own pride. You did not *make me to hear joy and gladness* nor did *the bones exult which were not yet humbled.*

16 AND WHAT GOOD did it do me that at about the age of twenty I was able to read and understand without any help that book of Aristotle's called *The Ten Categories* when it came into my hands? My rhetoric master at Carthage and others too with a reputation for learning would puff out their cheeks with pride whenever they mentioned this book, and so I was looking forward to it eagerly as though it was something wonderful and inspired. Later I compared notes with people who told me that they had had the greatest difficulty in understanding this book, even with the help of most learned commentators who had explained matters not only in words but by diagrams drawn in the sand. However they could tell me no more about the book than what I had discovered by reading it myself. Indeed the book seemed to me to deal very clearly with substances, such as "man," and with their qualities, such as the figure of a man; what sort of man he is; his height, how many feet; his family relationships, whose brother he is; where he is placed; when he was born; whether he is standing or sitting; whether he is wearing shoes or armor; whether he is doing something or having something done to him—and all the other innumerable things that can be put either in these nine categories of which I have given examples, or else in the main category of substance.

All this, so far from doing me any good, actually did me harm. For, imagining that everything in existence could be placed under these ten categories. I attempted by this method to understand you, my God, in your wonderful simplicity and changelessness, as though you were a substance with the qualities of your own greatness or your own beauty, as we find qualities in a body. But you yourself are your greatness and your beauty, but a body is not great or beautiful simply by the fact of being a body, since it would still be a body if it were less great or less beautiful. My thoughts of you were falsehood and not truth, fictions of my misery and not the realities of your blessedness. You gave the order, and so it was done in me, that the *earth should bring forth briars and thorns to me* and that *in the sweat of my brows I should eat my bread.*

And what good did it do me that I, at a time when I was the vile slave of evil desires, read and understood for myself every book that I could lay my hands on which dealt with what are called the liberal arts? I enjoyed these books and did not know the source of whatever in them was true and certain: For I had my back to the light and my face to the things on which the light shone; so the eyes in my face saw things in the light, but on my face itself no light fell. I could understand quite easily and without the aid of an instructor every work on rhetoric or logic, geometry, music, and arithmetic. This you know, my Lord God, since quickness of intelligence and precision in understanding are your gifts. But I did not use these gifts by making an offering of them to you. And so it all turned more to my destruction than to my profit, because I labored to secure so good a portion of my substance in my own power, and, instead of preserving my strength for you, I went away from you into a far country to waste my substance upon false and prostitute desires. For what good could my good abilities do me if I did not use them well? I never realized that even hardworking and talented people find these arts very difficult to understand until I began to try to explain them to others; then I found that the real experts in them were the ones who could follow my explanations reasonably quickly.

But what good was all this to me, holding, as I did, that you, Lord God and Truth, were a vast luminous body and that I was a sort of piece broken off from this body? What an extraordinary perversity I showed! Yet this was what I was then. And now, my God, I do not

blush to confess to you the mercies which you have
shown me and to call upon you—I who did not blush
then, when I was professing my blasphemies before men
and raising my barking voice against you. What good to
me then was that intelligence of mine, so quick and nim-
ble in those arts and sciences? What good to me were
all those knotty volumes which I unraveled without the
aid of any human teacher, when all the time I was so
disgracefully, so sacrilegiously, and so foully wrong in
the doctrine of piety? Or what great harm was it to your
little ones, if they had a far slower intelligence than
mine, since they did not go far from you, and so were
able safely to become fledged in the nest of your Church
and nourish the wings of charity on the food of a
sound faith?

O Lord our God, *under the shadow of Thy wings let
us hope.* Protect us and bear us up. You will bear us up,
yes, from our infancy until our gray hairs you will bear
us up. For our strength, when it is from you, is strength
indeed; but when it is our own, it is weakness. With you
our good is ever living, and when we turn our backs on
it, then we are perverse. Let us return now to you, Lord,
so that we may not be overturned, because our good is
with you, living and without any defect, since you yourself are our good. And we need not be afraid of having
no place to which we may return. We of our own accord
fell from that place. And our home, which is your eternity, does not fall down when we are away from it.

Book V

1 ACCEPT THE SACRIFICE of my confessions which my tongue sets before you. You formed the tongue and moved it to make confession to your name. *Heal Thou all my bones, and let them say, O Lord, who is like unto Thee.* When we confess to you, we do not inform you of what is happening inside us; for the closed heart does not shut out your eye, and man's hardness cannot resist your hand. You dissolve it at your pleasure, either in pity or in punishment, and *nothing can hide itself from Thy heat.* But let my soul praise you so that it may love you, and let it confess to you your acts of mercy, so that it may praise you. Your whole creation is never silent and never ceases to praise you. The spirit of every man utters its praises in words directed to you; animals and material bodies praise you through the mouth of those who meditate upon them, so that our soul may rise out of its weariness toward you, first supporting itself upon the things which you created, and then passing on to you yourself who made them marvelously. And there is refreshment and true strength.

2 LET THE WICKED and the restless go from you and run away. Yet still you see them, piercing through their shadows and all about them things are beautiful and they themselves are deformed. And what harm have they done you or in what respect have they brought dishonor on your government which from the heavens down to the lowest things of earth is just and perfect? For where did they run, when they ran from your face? Is there anywhere where you do not find them? In fact they ran away so as not to see you, though all the time you saw them, and that, in their blindness, they might stumble on you (since *Thou forsakest nothing Thou hast made), that in their injustice they might stumble on you and by your justice they might suffer for it, withdrawing themselves from your gentleness and stumbling on your uprightness and falling into your anger. Little do they know that you are everywhere, that it is impossible to draw a line of circumscription about you, and that you alone are always present even to those who have put themselves furthest from you. Let them turn, then, and seek for you, since you have not deserted your creation in the same way as they have deserted their creator. Let them turn and see, you are there, you are in their hearts, in the hearts of those who confess to you and who throw themselves upon your mercy and weep upon your breast after the difficult ways which they have trod. And you in your gentleness wipe the tears from their eyes, and they weep the more and rejoice in their weeping, since it is you, Lord, and not any man of flesh and blood, but you, Lord, their creator, who are giving them refreshment and consolation. And where was I when I was seeking for you? You were there, in front of me; but I had gone away even from myself. I could not even find myself, much less find you.

3   I NOW SET DOWN in the sight of my God the story of my twenty-ninth year. At this time there had come to Carthage a Manichaean bishop called Faustus. He was a great snare of the devil and many were caught in the snare. What charmed people was the smoothness of his language, and I certainly admired this myself; but I was able to distinguish between it and the truth, about those matters which I was so eager to learn; I was interested not so much in the dish and adornment of a fine style as in the substance of the knowledge which this celebrated Fau-

stus of theirs was setting before me. For his reputation had
preceded him, and I had been told that he was a really
remarkable scholar in all branches of learning and particularly learned in the liberal sciences.

Now I had read a lot of philosophy, and I retained in
my memory a great deal of what I had read. I began to
compare some of the things said by the philosophers
with those interminable fables of the Manichees, and it
seemed to me that what the philosophers said was the
more probable, even though their powers were limited
to the investigation of this world and they could not
possibly discover its Lord and Master. *For Thou art
great, O Lord, and hast respect unto the humble, but the
proud Thou beholdest afar off.* Nor do you draw near
except to the contrite in heart. The proud cannot find
you, however deep and curious their knowledge, not
even if they could count the stars and the grains of sand,
or measure the constellations in the sky and track down
the paths of the stars. Into all these things they look
with the mind and understanding which you gave them;
they have discovered much and many years in advance
of the event have predicted eclipses of the sun and
moon, setting down the day, the hour, and the extent of
these eclipses. Their calculations have been proved correct; everything took place as they had foretold; they put
into writing the rules which they had discovered, and
these rules are read today; on the basis of these rules
one can foretell the year, the month, the day, and the
hour when there will be an eclipse of the sun or moon
and whether the eclipse will be total or partial. And
everything will take place as predicted. And men who
are ignorant of the subject are full of astonishment and
admiration, while those who know will boast of their
knowledge and will be praised for it, thus turning away
from you in their evil pride and losing the light that
comes to them from you. They can see an eclipse of the
sun long before it happens, but cannot see their own
eclipse when it is actually taking place. For they do not
approach the matter in a religious spirit and ask what is

the source of the intelligence which they use to inquire into all this, and then, finding that it is you who made them, they do not give themselves up to you for you to preserve what you have made; nor do they sacrifice to you what they have made of themselves; nor do they slaughter their flighty imaginations like birds, and their inquisitivenesses, by which they wander through the secret paths of the abyss, like the fish of the sea, and their lusts like the beasts of the field, so that you, God, the consuming fire, may burn up those dead cares of theirs and recreate the men themselves immortally.

But they do not know the way, which is your word, and by your word you made the things which they number and themselves who do the numbering and the sense by which they see what they number and the understanding from which comes the ability to number, *and of Thy wisdom there is no number*. But the Only Begotten is Himself *made unto us wisdom, and righteousness and sanctification,* and was numbered among us, and *paid tribute to Caesar*. They do not know this way, the way to descend from themselves to Him, and by Him ascend to Him. They do not know this way; they fancy that they are high up and shining with the stars, and in fact they have fallen to the ground and *their foolish heart is darkened*.

Much that they say about what is created is true; but they do not seek religiously for the truth which is the maker of creation, and therefore they do not find Him, or, if they do find Him and know Him to be God, they do not honor Him as God and give Him thanks; instead they become vain in their imaginations and consider themselves to be wise; they attribute to themselves what is yours, and in this way, such is the perversity of their blindness, they actually attribute their own qualities to you, making you, who are Truth, responsible for their own falsehoods, and *changing the glory of the uncorruptible God into an image made like corruptible man, and to birds, and four-footed beasts, and creeping things, changing Thy truth into a lie, and worshiping and serving the creature more than the Creator.*

Nevertheless, I could remember many true things which the philosophers have said about this created world, and I could see the reason for what they said calculation, in the order of time, and in the visible evidence of the stars. I compared their views with those of Manes, who, drawing on a rich vein of pure fantasy, has had a lot to say on these subjects. I found in him no reason given for the solstices and the equinoxes or the eclipses, of the sun and moon or anything else of this kind which I had learned in the books of secular philosophy. I was told to believe in these views of Manes; but they did not correspond with what had been established by mathematics and my own eyesight; in fact they were widely divergent.

4   BUT, LORD GOD of truth, does a man please you by knowing all these things? For the man who knows them all, but does not know you, is unhappy, and happy is the man who knows you, even if he does not know these other things. And he who knows both you and them is not the happier because of them but is only happy because of you, if *knowing Thee, he glorifies Thee as God, and is thankful* and becomes not vain in his imaginations. The man who consciously owns a tree and knows how to use it and gives you thanks for it may not know its exact height or how widely the branches spread; but he is better off than the man who, while he has measured the tree and counted all its branches, neither owns it nor knows and loves its creator. In just the same way a faithful servant of yours, who has the whole world of wealth and who though apparently possessing nothing yet possesses everything because he clings to you, whom all things serve, may not even know about the circles of the Great Bear; but it would be absurd to doubt that he is better off than the man who, though he can measure the heaven and count the stars and weigh the elements, is forgetful of you, who have *made all things in number, weight, and measure.*

5   What then was the point of this Manes writing on these subjects, which are not necessary for the learning of goodness and piety? For you have said to man: *Behold, piety is wisdom.* And Manes, even if he had known all these subjects perfectly, might still have been without wisdom; but in impudently presuming to teach them, when he did not know them, he certainly revealed an incapacity for piety. For the profession of these subjects, even when one knows them, is worldly vanity; confession to you is piety. So he had gone astray, and all he achieved by his numerous statements on these matters was this: he was shown up by people who had an accurate knowledge of them, and it was thus made perfectly plain how much reliance could be placed on his understanding of other more abstruse matters. He certainly did not wish to be thought little of; for he made it his business to persuade people that the Holy Ghost, the comforter and enricher of your faithful ones, was personally and with plenary authority resident in himself. And so when he was caught out making false statements about the heaven and the stars and the movements of the sun and moon, even though these things are not an integral part of religious doctrine, yet it was clear enough that his presumption was sacrilegious: he was talking about things he did not know; he was making false statements about them, and so mad was the vanity of his pride that he attempted to have these statements attributed to him as though he were a divine person.

Now whenever I come across any Christian brother, whoever it may be, who is ignorant of these sciences and has mistaken views on them, I can listen to him patiently enough as he delivers his opinions. So long as he does not hold any unworthy beliefs about you, Lord and Creator of all things, I cannot see that it does him any harm if he is rather ignorant about the situation or conditions of material objects. But it does do him harm if he imagines that this scientific knowledge is an integral part of the structure of the doctrine of piety, and then has the audacity to make overconfident assertions on subjects of which he knows nothing. Yet even such weakness as this is borne patiently by our mother Charity while a man's faith is in its infancy until the new man rises up into the perfect man, so as not to be carried about with every wind of doctrine. Manes, however, set himself up as the teacher, the first authority, the leader, and the guide of his disciples, and he did it in such a way that his followers imagined that they were following not a mere man, but your Holy Spirit. Obviously, once he was convicted of having made false statements, one must consider this extraordinary madness of his as something detestable and something which ought to be utterly rejected. Nevertheless I had not as yet reached a firm conclusion as to whether or not it might be possible to explain the changes in the lengths of days and nights, the alternation of night and day, eclipses of sun and moon and other such things of which I had read in a manner that would be consistent with the doctrines of Manes. If it were possible, then it would still be an open question to me whether his solution was correct; yet, because of his reputation for sanctity, I would still prefer to trust in him as an authority.

6 FOR ABOUT NINE YEARS, in my mental aberration, I was a disciple of the Manichees, and for nearly all of this time I had been waiting with a kind of boundless longing for the coming of this man Faustus. For the other Manichees whom I met and who failed to produce any answers to the questions I was raising on these subjects were always putting forward his name and promising me that as soon as Faustus arrived and I was able to discuss matters with him, all these difficulties of mine, together with any more weighty questions that I might care to ask, would be very easily dealt with and very lucidly explained. Well, he did arrive, and I found him a charming man with a very pleasant choice of words; he came out with exactly the same things as the others are always saying, but he did it much more elegantly.

However, my thirst could not be relieved by expensive drinking vessels and a well-dressed waiter. My ears were full already of this stuff, and the arguments themselves did not appear to me to be any better simply because they were better expressed; eloquence did not make them true; nor could I consider the soul wise because the face was attractive and the words well chosen. And as to those who promised me so much of him, they were not good judges of things. Their reason for thinking him wise and intelligent was simply that his way of speaking gave them pleasure.

I have had experience too of a quite different kind of person, the sort who will bring truth itself into suspicion and refuse to assent to it, if it is expressed in a good and ordered style. But you, my God, had already taught me in wonderful and hidden ways, and I believe that it was you who taught me because it is the truth and apart from you there is no other teacher of the truth, wherever or however it may be revealed. I had now learned this from you: that a thing is not necessarily true for being expressed eloquently, nor necessarily false if the sounds made by the lips are imperfectly pronounced; nor, on the other hand, is a thing true simply because it is expressed in a rough and ready way, nor false because it is uttered in a fine style. For with wisdom and folly the same thing holds good as with wholesome and unwholesome food. You can have silver or earthenware dishes on the table, just as you can have a decorated or undecorated use of language; either kind of food can be served in either kind of dish.

So those eager feelings of mine, with which I had so long been waiting for this man, were certainly gratified when I saw the way he carried himself and the way he behaved in a discussion, and when I saw how readily he found just the right words for expressing his thought I was delighted, and with many others, indeed more than most, I praised him and spoke highly of him. But I was upset when I found that, with all his disciples around him, I was not allowed to put a question to him and communicate to him the perplexities which troubled me by talking to him as man to man with each of us speaking in turn. In the end I did get a chance to do this and, with some friends of mine, was able to engage his attention at a time when it was not incorrect for him to discuss matters by means of question and answer. I put forward some of the things which were disturbing me and at once discovered that this man was not educated in any of the liberal sciences except literature, and even here his learning was of a very conventional kind. He had read some of Cicero's speeches, a very few books by Seneca, some poetry, and those volumes written by people of his own persuasion which were in Latin and were neatly constructed; he also had daily practice in making speeches, and all this was the source of his eloquence, which was made the more agreeable and charming by being directed by a good intelligence and expressed with a kind of grace which was natural to the man.

Is it not so, as I remember it, Lord my God, judge of my conscience? My heart and my memory are open before you, and you in the hidden secrecy of your providence were working upon me then and setting in front of my face those shameful errors of mine, so that I might see them and hate them.

7   FOR AFTER IT became quite clear to me that he was ignorant of those subjects in which I had thought him to be so particularly learned, I began to lose hope in his being able to solve my perplexities and explain to me the questions that troubled me—though, as I see now, he could have been ignorant of all this and still held the truth of piety, if only he had not been a Manichee. The books of the Manichees are indeed full of lengthy fables about the heavens and the stars and the sun and the moon, and I now thought that he could not possibly give me a reasoned answer to what I wanted to know, which was whether, after comparing all this with the calculations I had read of elsewhere, the facts were as stated in the books of Manes, or if, at any rate, some explanation equally good could be discovered in these books. When I put forward this question as something to be considered and discussed he behaved with great modesty and would not venture to take up the

burden. He knew that he was ignorant of these things and was not ashamed to admit it. He was not one of those talkative people (I had had to put up with a great many of them) who attempted to instruct me in these subjects but had no instruction to give. Indeed he had a heart which, while not right toward you, was quite well prepared to look after himself. He was not altogether ignorant of his own ignorance, and he had no wish to get rashly involved in a controversy which he could not possibly win and from which he would find it difficult to retire. For this too I liked him all the better; for there is more beauty in the modesty of a mind that admits its faults than in the knowledge that I was seeking for. So I found him too when it came to all the more difficult and subtle questions.

As a result of this I lost the enthusiasm which I had had for the writings of Manes, and I had all the less confidence in the other Manichaean teachers after I found that the famous Faustus had shown up so badly in many of the questions which perplexed me. However I began to spend much time with him because of his own kind of enthusiasm, which was for literature, and it was literature which I, as professor, was at that time teaching to the young at Carthage. I used to read with him what he wanted to have read or what I considered right for his kind of intelligence. But all the ambition I had had to go far in that sect simply collapsed once I had got to know the man. Not that I broke completely with the Manichees. It was simply that, not being able to find anything better than the course on which I had somehow or other become set, I had decided to stay as I was for the time being, unless something else should happen to appear which seemed preferable. So this Faustus, who to many people had been a real snare of death, now began, without willing it or knowing it, to unloosen the snare in which I had been caught. Your hands, my God, in the secrecy of your providence never abandoned my soul; from the blood of my mother's heart, by the tears which she shed day and night, sacrifice for me was

offered to you, and in wonderful ways you dealt with
me. It was your doing, my God: for *the steps of a man
are ordered by the Lord, and He shall dispose his way.*
Or how shall we find salvation except by your hand's
remaking what you made?

8 YOU ACTED UPON ME in such a way that I was
persuaded to set out for Rome to teach there
the same subjects as I had been teaching in Carthage.
How it was that I came to be persuaded to do this must
not be passed over in my confession to you; here too I
must ponder over and openly declare the deep secrecy of
your ways and your mercy which is always so close to us.
I wanted to go to Rome not only because of the higher
earnings and the greater reputation which my friends, who
persuaded me to go, thought I would get there, though
these reasons did have some weight with me at that time;
in fact, however, my main and almost my only reason for
going was that I heard that in Rome the young men followed their studies in a more orderly manner and were
controlled by a stricter discipline. They were not allowed,
for instance, insolently and at their own pleasure, to come
rushing into the school of a man who was not their own
teacher; in fact they were not allowed to enter the school
at all without the master's permission.

At Carthage, on the other hand, the students are disgracefully out of control. They come breaking into a
class in the most unmannerly way and, behaving almost
like madmen, disturb the order which the master has
established for the good of his pupils. They commit a
number of disorderly acts which show an incredible stupidity and which ought to be punished by law. However,
custom protects them, and this is a fact which makes
their state even more wretched, because the things they
do appear to them permissible, though by your eternal
law such things can never be permitted, and they imagine that they are getting away scot-free with what they
do, whereas the very blindness with which they act is

their punishment, and the harm which they do to themselves is incomparably worse than what they do to others. When I was a student myself I refused to become one of those who behaved in this way, though when I became a teacher I had to put up with this behavior from other people, and so the reason why I wanted to go to Rome was that all who knew about it told me that there these things were not done. But you, my hope and my portion in the land of the living, were urging me to change countries for the salvation of my soul. In Carthage you prepared goads for me, so that I should be driven from the place, and at Rome you provided attractions which would draw me there, and in both cases you made use of men who were in love with this deathly life; on the one side were people acting like lunatics and on the other people who promised me mere vanities. So, to reform my ways, you secretly made use both of their perversity and of my own. For those who were disturbing my peace were blinded by a disgraceful frenzy, and those who urged me to go elsewhere savored of earth. And I, hating my real misery in Carthage, looked for a false happiness in Rome.

But you, God, knew why it was that I was going from the one place to the other, and you did not reveal the reason either to me or to my mother, who was most bitterly distressed at my going away and who followed me right down to the seacoast. She clung to me with all her force, begging me either to return or to take her with me, but I deceived her and pretended that I had a friend whom I did not want to leave until the wind was right for him to set sail. So I told a lie to her, my mother, and such a mother, and I got away from her. And this too you have mercifully forgiven me. You saved me, full as I was with the most execrable uncleanness, from the waters of the sea and brought me to the water of your grace, so that, when I was washed in this water, the rivers that flowed from my mother's eyes, tears daily shed for me that watered the ground below her downcast looks, should be dried up. Still she refused to go home without me, and I had much difficulty in persuading her

to stay that night in a place near the ship where there
was an oratory in memory of St. Cyprian. That night I
stole away, leaving her behind; she stayed there weeping
and praying. And the whole purport, my God, of the
prayers which she addressed to you with so many tears
was that you would not allow me to sail. But your coun-
sels are deep; you granted what was the key point of
her prayer and did not do what she was asking for at
that moment so that you might make me what she always wanted me to be. The wind blew and filled our
sails; we lost sight of the land where, that morning, my
mother was frantic with grief and filled your ears with
her lamentations and complaints, and you seemed not
to hear her, yet all the time you were dragging me away
by the force of my own desires in order that these desires might be brought to an end, and you were justly
punishing her with the whip of sorrow for an affection
that was too much of the flesh. For she loved having me
with her, as all mothers do, only she much more than
most, and she did not know what great joys you were
preparing for her by my going away. This she did not
know, and so she wept and cried aloud and by all this
agony she showed in herself the heritage of Eve, seeking
in sorrow what in sorrow she had brought forth. Nevertheless, after accusing me of treachery and cruelty, she
turned once more to her prayers to you for me. She
went home and I went on my way to Rome.

9   THERE THE FIRST THING that happened to me
was that I was struck down by a sickness of the
body, and I very nearly went to hell, carrying with me
all the sins I had committed against you and against
myself and against others. Many and grievous they were,
over and above the bond of original sin whereby we all
die in Adam. For you had not yet forgiven me any of
them in Christ, nor had He abolished by His cross the
enmity which by my sins I had incurred with you. Indeed
how could He do so by the cross of a phantom, which

was how I thought of Him? Just as the death of His flesh seemed to me not true, so true was the death of my soul, and just as the death of His flesh was true, so false was the life of my soul, which did not believe in it. My fever grew worse and worse. I was very nearly gone and very nearly lost. For, if I had gone then, where should I have gone except to the fire and the torments which in the truth of your ordinance my deeds deserved? My mother knew nothing of my illness, yet, though she was far away, she continued to pray for me. But you, who are present everywhere, heard her where she was and pitied me where I was, so that I regained my bodily health, though I was still sick enough in my sacrilegious heart. For even in this great danger I did not long for your baptism. Indeed I was better when I was a boy and begged for this from my mother's piety, as I have already recalled in my confession. But I had grown up into my own shame; I madly mocked at the medicine prescribed by you, who would not allow me in my present state to die a double death. If I had so died and my mother's heart had been struck with that wound, it would never have been cured again. For I cannot express how she loved me and how she labored with much greater pain to give me birth in the spirit than she had suffered when giving birth to me in the flesh. So I cannot see how she could have been cured, if I had died a death like this and the very core of her love for me had been pierced through by it. And where then would have been all those prayers of hers which she uttered day and night without ceasing? Nowhere but with you. But would you, God of mercies, despise the contrite and humbled heart of that chaste and good widow, who was so constant in almsgiving, so willing and ready in the service of your saints, who never let a day pass without making her oblation at your altar, who used to go twice a day, without any exception, in the morning and in the evening, to your Church, not to listen to idle gossip and old wives' tales, but that she might listen to you in the sermons preached and that you might listen to her as she prayed?

Could you refuse your help to her or despise her tears with which she asked from you, not gold or silver or any mutable and transitory good, but the salvation of her son's soul—for it was by your grace that she was like this? No, Lord, you could not. It is certain that you were with her and heard her and that you were doing everything in the order which you had predestined. It would be impossible that you should deceive her in the visions and answers which you gave her—both those which I have mentioned and others, all of which she laid up in her faithful heart and would constantly bring them forward to you in your prayers, as though they were promises written in your own handwriting. For you (since your mercy endures forever) will deign to become by your promises actually the debtor of those whose debt of sin you have entirely forgiven.

10 So you brought me back from that illness, and you gave the son of our handmaid his bodily health at that time, so that he might live for you to give him a better and a more certain health. Even then, in Rome, I associated myself with those false and deceiving "saints," not only with the "hearers" (one of whom was the man in whose house I had been ill and had recovered), but also with the ones whom they call "the elect." For I was still of the opinion that it is not we ourselves who sin, but some other nature which is in us; it gratified my pride to think that I was blameless and, if I did something wrong, not to confess that I had done it, so that you might heal my soul, because my soul had sinned against you. Instead I liked to excuse myself and accuse something else—something that was in me, but was not really I. But in fact I was wholly I and it was my impiety which had divided one me from another me. My sin was all the more incurable because I imagined that I was not a sinner, and it was most execrable wickedness in me that I preferred that you, you, Almighty God, should be overcome in me to my destruction rather than that I should be overcome by you for my salvation.

You had not yet *set a watch before my mouth and a door of safekeeping around my lips, that my heart might not turn aside to wicked speeches, to make excuses of sins, with men that work iniquity.* And for this reason I was still in the fellowship of their Elect. However, I saw no prospect of being able to go far in that false doctrine, and I began to have less and less interest in and enthusiasm for even those principles of theirs with which I had decided to be content, if I could find nothing better.

The thought occurred to me that those philosophers who are called the Academics were wiser than the rest, because they held that everything should be considered doubtful and had come to the conclusion that no truth could be comprehended by man. For it seemed to me quite clear that this (as is the general belief) was the view they held, though in fact I had not yet even grasped what they were driving at. Certainly I quite openly persuaded this man in whose house I was staying not to have such excessive faith, which I could see that he had, in all those fables of which the books of Manes are full. Yet I still lived on more friendly terms with the Manichees than with others not of that heresy. I was no longer defending it with my old fervor, but my friendship with those people (and Rome shelters a great many of them) made me slower to look for some other belief, especially since, Lord of heaven and earth, Creator of all things visible and invisible, I had no hope of finding the truth in your Church. For they had turned me against it, and I thought it most unseemly to believe that you had the shape of our human flesh and were bounded by the bodily outlines of our limbs. When I wanted to think of my God, I did not know how to think of him except as a mass of bodies, for it seemed to me that what was not this was nothing. And this was the chief, indeed almost the only, cause of my inevitable error.

Because of this I believed that evil also was some such a kind of substance, with its own foul and hideous bulk, which might be either gross (which they called earth) or thin and subtle like the body of air; for they imagine it to be a kind of malignant mind creeping through the earth. And because this strange form of piety of mine led me to believe that a good God had never created any evil nature, I came to the conclusion that there were two masses in opposition to each other, both infinite, but the evil one more contracted and the good one more expansive. And from this pestilent beginning other sacrilegious notions followed naturally.

When my mind tried to revert to the Catholic faith, it was driven back again, because I had a false idea of what the Catholic faith really was. It seemed to me more reverent to believe that you, God (to whom I now confess your mercies done in me), were infinite in all parts except one—for I should be forced to confess that you were finite in respect to that part where the mass of evil was set in opposition to you—rather than to hold the view that you were in all your parts finitely contained in the shape of a human body. And it seemed better to believe that you had created no evil than to believe that what I conceived to be the nature of evil was from you, and evil seemed to me in my ignorance to be not only a substance, but actually a physical substance; for I could not even think of mind except as a rarefied form of body with extension in space. And I thought of our Saviour Himself, your Only-begotten Son, as if He were for our salvation stretched out to us, as it were, from the mass of your bright and shining substance, and as a result I could believe nothing of Him except what would fit in with my empty imagination. I considered that such a nature could not possibly be born of the Virgin Mary, unless it were mingled with her flesh, and I could not see how the nature which I had imagined to myself could be mingled without being defiled. Thus I was afraid to believe that He was born in the flesh lest I should be forced to believe that He was defiled by the flesh. I know that your spiritual ones will be smiling at me, though kindly and lovingly, if they read the story of these confusions of mind. But this was what I was like at that time.

11 THEN TOO I thought that some of the Manichaean criticisms of your Scriptures were unanswerable. Yet there were times when I certainly would have liked to discuss each point separately with someone really learned in those books and to find out what he thought about it. Even at Carthage I had begun to be disturbed by listening to a man called Elpidius who spoke and argued openly against the Manichees and produced evidence from the Scriptures which was not easy to resist. And the answer which they did give seemed to me a very feeble one; indeed they preferred not to give it at all in public, but only in private gatherings of ourselves. What they said was that the Scriptures of the New Testament had been corrupted by people who wanted to insert the Jewish law into the Christian faith; yet they themselves could not produce any copies that had not been corrupted. But, as I still thought only in terms of bodies, it was chiefly these "masses" which held me down a prisoner and were practically stifling me; under their weight I panted for the fresh air of your truth, but was unable to breathe it pure and untainted.

12 I STARTED AT ONCE to do what I had come to do, namely to teach rhetoric at Rome. First of all I collected a few pupils at my house and by means of them I began to become known. I soon found out that things went on in Rome which I had not had to put up with in Africa. True enough I discovered that in Rome there was none of that subversive behavior which I knew on the part of the worst types of young men; but, so I was told, "in order to avoid paying their fees to the professor, a number of young men form a conspiracy and suddenly go off to study under another professor, thus breaking their pledged words and showing that

to them justice is cheap compared with the love of
money." I hated them too in my heart, though the hatred I felt was not a perfect hatred. I think that I hated
them more because of what I was likely to suffer from
them personally than because of the wrong they did to
everyone concerned. Such people, however, are certainly
vile characters; they fornicate against you in loving the
fleeting mockeries of time and the filthy lucre which soils
the hand that holds it and in embracing this fleeting
world and in despising you who abide and who call them
back to you and who give pardon to the adulterous soul
of man when it returns to you. I still hate wicked and
depraved people of this sort, though I love the thought
of their being corrected and taught to love learning more
than money and to love you, God, the truth and fullness
of certain good, and the purest peace, more than learning. But at that time I was more anxious not to have to
put up with their evil ways for my own sake than that
they should learn good for your sake.

13 So when the prefect of the city in Rome received
a message from Milan, asking him to provide
them with a professor of rhetoric and promising to pay the
expenses of his journey out of public funds, I applied for
the post myself. My application was supported by these
very people who were intoxicated with the vanities of Man-
ichaeism, and it was just to be rid of these people that I
was going—though neither they nor I realized the fact. So
I had the opportunity to make a speech on a set subject;
Symmachus, who was then prefect, approved of it, and I
was sent to Milan. And at Milan I came to Bishop Ambrose, who had a worldwide reputation, was a devout servant of yours and a man whose eloquence in those days
gave abundantly to *Thy people the fatness of Thy wheat,
the gladness of Thy oil and the sober intoxication of Thy
wine.* Though I did not realize it, I was led to him by you
so that, with full realization, I might be led to you by him.
That man of God welcomed me as a father and, in his

capacity of bishop, was kind enough to approve of my coming there. I began to love him at first not as a teacher of the truth (for I had quite despaired of finding it in your Church) but simply as a man who was kind and generous to me. I used to listen eagerly when he preached to the people, but my intention was not what it should have been; I was, as it were, putting his eloquence on trial to see whether it came up to his reputation, or whether its flow was greater or less than I had been told. So I hung intently on his words, but I was not interested in what he was really saying and stood aside from this in contempt. I was much pleased by the charm of his style, which, although it was more learned, was still, so far as the manner of delivery was concerned, not so warm and winning as the style of Faustus. With regard to the actual matter there was, of course, no comparison. Faustus was merely roving around among Manichaean fallacies, while Ambrose was healthily teaching salvation. But salvation is far from sinners of the kind that I was then. Yet, though I did not realize it, I was drawing gradually nearer.

14 FOR ALTHOUGH my concern was not to learn what he said but only to hear how he said it (this empty interest being all that remained to me, now that I had despaired of man's being able to find his way to you), nevertheless, together with the language, which I admired, the subject matter also, to which I was indifferent, began to enter into my mind. Indeed I could not separate the one from the other. And as I opened my heart in order to recognize how eloquently he was speaking it occurred to me at the same time (though this idea came gradually) how truly he was speaking. First I began to see that the points which he made were capable of being defended. I had thought that nothing could be said for the Catholic faith in the face of the objections raised by the Manichees, but it now appeared to me that this faith could be maintained on reasonable grounds— especially when I had heard one or two passages in the

Old Testament explained, usually in a figurative way, which, when I had taken them literally, had been a cause of death to me. So, after a number of these passages had been explained to me in their spiritual sense, I began to blame that despairing attitude of mine which had led me to believe that the Law and the Prophets could not possibly stand up to hostile and mocking criticism. However; I did not feel that I ought to take the way of the Catholics simply because they too could produce learned men to maintain their belief and to answer objections skillfully and without absurdity; nor did I think that the faith which I held should be condemned simply because the Catholics were just as well able to defend theirs. So, though the Catholic cause did not seem to me defeated, it did not yet seem to me to have won.

Then indeed I began to bend my mind earnestly to the question: Could I find any sure proofs by which to convict the Manichees of falsehood? If only I had been able to form the idea of a substance that was spiritual, all their strongholds would have collapsed at once and been thrown out of my mind. But I could not.

However, with regard to the body of this world and the whole of nature that is within the reach of our bodily senses, I considered, after much consideration and frequent comparisons, that very many of the philosophers held views which were much more probable than those of the Manichees. So, in what is assumed to be the manner of the Academics, while doubting everything and wavering between one thing and another, I did at least decide that I must leave the Manichees. For even in this period of doubt, I did not consider that I ought to remain in that sect when I already thought more highly of some of the philosophers than of the Manichees. Though still I absolutely refused to allow these philosophers to take care of my sick soul, because they were without the saving name of Christ. I decided, therefore, to be for the time being a catechumen in the Catholic Church (the Church which my parents had encouraged me to join) until I should see some certain light by which to steer my course.

Book VI

1 HOPE OF MINE from my youth, where were you and where had you gone from me? Was it not you who had created me and distinguished me from the beasts of the field and made me wiser than the birds of the air? Yet I walked through shadows and on slippery ways, and I searched for you outside me and did not find the God of my heart. I had come to the depths of the sea, and I had no confidence or hope of discovering the truth.

By this time my mother had joined me. Her piety had given her strength and she had followed me over land and sea, confident in you throughout all dangers. In the perils of the sea it was she who put fresh heart into the sailors although as a rule it is for the sailors to reassure the passengers who are inexperienced on the high seas. But she promised them that they would get safely to land because you had promised this to her in a vision. She found me in grave danger indeed, my danger being that of despairing of ever discovering the truth. I told her that, though I was not yet a Catholic Christian, I was certainly no longer a Manichaean; but she showed no great signs of delight, as though at some unexpected piece of news, because she already felt at ease regarding that particular aspect of my misery; she bewailed me as one dead, certainly, but as one who would be raised up again by you; she was in her mind laying me before you on the bier so that you might say to the widow's son: *"Young man, I say unto thee, Arise,"* and he should revive and begin to speak and you should give him to his mother. So her heart was shaken by no storm of exulta-

tion when she heard that what she had daily begged you
with her tears should happen had in so large a part taken
place—that I was now rescued from falsehood, even
though I had not yet attained the truth. She was indeed
quite certain that you, who had promised her the whole,
would give her the part that remained, and she replied to
me very calmly and with a heart full of confidence that
she believed in Christ that, before she departed from this
life, she would see me a true Catholic. So much she said
to me. But to you, fountain of mercies, she poured out her
prayers and her tears more copiously than before, begging
you to hasten your help and to lighten my darkness, and
she would hurry more eagerly than ever to church and
hang upon the words of Ambrose, praying for *the fountain
of that water, which springeth up into life everlasting.* For
she loved that man as though he were an angel of God,
because she knew that it was through him that I had been
brought for the time being to this doubtful wavering state
of mind, and she was perfectly certain that I would pass
through this from sickness to health, though before then I
should be exposed to a more serious attack, like that which
doctors call "the crisis."

2   THERE WAS an occasion when my mother had
brought, as was her custom in Africa, cakes and
bread and wine to some of the chapels built in memory
of the saints and was forbidden to do this by the door-
keeper. When she found that it was the bishop who had
forbidden this practice, she accepted his ban so devoutly
and so willingly that I myself was amazed to see how
much more readily now she would condemn her own
practice of the past than dispute the bishop's prohibition.
For her soul was not a victim to the craving for wine, and
no liking for wine stimulated her into a hatred for
the truth—a thing which happens to many people of
both sexes who are just as disgusted by a hymn of sobri-
ety as drunkards are if their wine is mixed with water.
But when my mother brought her basket with the usual

sorts of food, which were first to be tasted by her and then given away, she never took more than one small cup well watered down to suit her sober taste, and this was just for the sake of courtesy. And if there were many memorial chapels which she thought ought to be honored in this way, she still carried this same cup around with her to be used at each place; in the end it would be not only nearly all water, but also lukewarm, and she would share this out in small sips with those around her; for she came then to look for piety, not for pleasure. But when she found that that famous preacher and that great example of piety had forbidden the practice even to those who used it soberly—so that drunkards should not be given an occasion for excess and also because this kind of anniversary funeral feast is very much like the superstitious ceremony of the pagans—she most willingly gave up her old habit. Instead of a basket filled with the fruits of the earth, she had learned to bring to the chapels of the Martyrs a breast full of something much purer, her prayers. So she was able to give what she could spare to the poor, and so the communion of the Lord's body might be celebrated in those places where, in imitation of His passion, the martyrs had lost their lives and won their crowns.

And yet it seems to me, my Lord God—and on this matter my heart lies open in your sight—that in abandoning this old custom of hers my mother might possibly not have given way so easily if the prohibition had come from someone else whom she did not love as she loved Ambrose. For she loved him very greatly on account of my salvation, and he loved her for her religious way of life; for she was always doing good works, was fervent in spirit, and constantly at church. So that when he saw me he often used to burst forth in her praises, congratulating me on having such a mother, though he was unaware of what sort of a son she had in me—one who was in doubt on all these matters and who thought that there was no possibility of finding the way of life.

3   I WAS NOT YET groaning in prayer for you to help me. My mind was intent on inquiry and restless in dispute. I considered Ambrose himself, who was honored by people of such importance, a lucky man by worldly standards; only his celibacy seemed to me rather a burden to bear. But I could neither guess nor tell from my own experience what hope he had within him, what were his struggles against the temptations of his exalted position, what solace he found in adversity; nor could I tell of that hidden mouth of his (the mouth of his heart), what joys it tasted in the rumination of your bread. And he on his side did not know of the turmoil in which I was or the deep pit of danger before my feet. I was not able to ask him the questions I wanted to ask in the way I wanted to ask them, because I was prevented from having an intimate conversation with him by the crowds of people, all of whom had some business with him and to whose infirmities he was a servant. And for the very short periods of time when he was not with them, he was either refreshing his body with necessary food or his mind with reading. When he was reading, his eyes went over the pages and his heart looked into the sense, but voice and tongue were resting. Often when we came to him (for no one was forbidden to come in, and it was not customary for visitors even to be announced) we found him reading, always to himself and never otherwise; we would sit in silence for a long time, not venturing to interrupt him in his intense concentration on his task, and then we would go away again. We guessed that in the very small time which he was able to set aside for mental refreshment he wanted to be free from the disturbance of other people's business and would not like to have his attention distracted; also we thought that he might be taking precautions in case, if he read aloud in the presence of some eager and interested person, he might have to give a lecture on the obscure points in the author whom he was reading, or enter into a discussion on the questions of difficulty, with the result that, after he had spent time on this, he would

not be able to read as many books as he wanted to read. Though perhaps a more likely reason for his reading to himself was that he wanted to preserve his voice, which grew tired very easily. But whatever his reason was for acting in this way it would certainly be a good one.

Anyhow, I was given no chance of making the inquiries I wished to make from that holy oracle of yours, his breast. I could only ask things that would not take long in the hearing. But I needed to find him with plenty of time to spare if I was to pour out to him the full flood of agitation boiling up inside me, and I could never find him like this. Yet every Sunday I listened to him rightly preaching to the people the word of truth, and I became more and more sure that all those knots of cunning calumny which, in their attacks on the holy books, my deceivers had tied could be unraveled. In particular I discovered that the phrase "man, created by Thee, after Thine own image" was not understood by your spiritual children, whom you have made to be born again by grace through the Catholic mother, in such a way as to mean that you are bounded by the shape of a human body. And although I had not the faintest or most shadowy notion about what a spiritual substance could be, nevertheless with a kind of pleasant shame I blushed to think of how for all these years I had been barking not against the Catholic faith but against figments of carnal imaginations. And indeed I had been rash and impious; for I had spoken in condemnation of things which I ought to have taken the trouble to find out about. But you, the highest, and the nearest, most hidden and most present, have no limbs or parts greater and smaller; you are everywhere in your entirety, yet limited by no particular space; you are not of any bodily form, yet you made man "after your own image" and, see, man is in space from head to foot.

4 BEING IGNORANT, then, of how this image of yours could subsist, I ought to have knocked at the door and asked in what sense the doctrine was to be believed, instead of insulting and attacking what I assumed to be the accepted doctrine. And so my anxiety as to what I could hold for certain gnawed at my inmost heart all the more keenly as I felt the more ashamed of myself for having been so long deluded and deceived by the promise of certainties and then having, with a quite childish inaccuracy and enthusiasm, gone on and on proclaiming uncertainties as though they were truths. That they were actual falsehoods only became clear to me later. What was certain was that they were uncertain and that I for some time had accepted them as certainties when, in my blind zeal for contention, I was attacking your Catholic Church. I had not yet discovered that this Church was teaching the truth, but at least I now knew that it was not teaching the things which I had so vigorously attacked. So I was both confounded and converted, and I was glad, my God, that your only Church, the body of your only son—that Church in which the name of Christ had been put upon me as an infant—was not flavored with this childish nonsense and did not, in her healthy doctrine, maintain the view that you, the Creator of all things, could be, in the form of a human body, packed into a definite space which, however mighty and large, must still be bounded on all sides.

I was glad too that the old Scriptures of the Law and the Prophets were set before me in such a way that I could now read in a different spirit from that which I had had before, when I used to criticize your holy ones for holding various views which, plainly, they never held at all. And I was happy when I heard Ambrose in his sermons, as I often did, recommend most emphatically to his congregation this text as a rule to go by: *The letter killeth, but the spirit giveth life.* So he would draw aside the veil of mystery and explain in a spiritual sense the meanings of things which, if understood literally, appeared to be teaching what was wrong. And I could raise no objections to what he said, even though I was still not sure whether what he said was true or not. I held my heart back from positively accepting anything, since

I was afraid of another fall, and in this condition of suspense I was being all the more killed. I wanted to be just as certain about things which I could not see as I was certain that seven and three make ten. For I was not quite mad enough as to think that even this proposition is beyond our comprehension; but I did demand the same degree of certainty with regard to other things, whether they were material things not present to my senses or spiritual things, of which I could form no conception except in material terms. By believing I might have been cured, so that the sight of my mind would be clearer and might be somehow or other directed toward your truth which is the same forever and in no point fails. But it was the same with me as with a man who, having once had a bad doctor, is afraid of trusting himself even to a good one. So it was with the health of my soul which could not possibly be cured except by believing, but refused to be cured for fear of believing something falser. So I resisted your hands, for it was you who prepared the medicines of faith and applied them to the diseases of the world and gave them such potency.

5   FROM NOW ON, however, I began to prefer the Catholic faith. In requiring belief in what was not demonstrated (and this includes both things that cannot be proved at all and things which, though capable of being proved, cannot be proved to everyone) I felt that the Catholic faith showed more modesty and more honesty than did the Manichees, who made rash promises of certain knowledge, derided credulity, and then produced a lot of fabulous absurdities in which we were required to believe because they were not susceptible of proof. Finally it was you, Lord, who with your most tender and merciful hand gradually laid hold upon my heart and settled it in calm. I considered what a countless number of things there were which I believed though I had not seen them and had not been present when they had taken place—so many historical events,

so many facts about countries and cities which I had never seen, so many things told me by friends, by doctors, by one man or another man—and unless we believed these things, we should get nothing done at all in this life. Then in particular I considered how fixed and unalterable was the belief I held that I was the son of a particular father and mother, a thing which I could not possibly know unless I had believed it on the word of others. And so by these considerations you led me to see that the people to be blamed were not those who believed in those books of yours, which you have established with such authority in nearly every nation of the world, but those who did not believe in them, and that I ought not to pay any attention to anyone who might say to me: "How do you know that those books were bestowed on mankind by the spirit of the one true and most true God?" It was indeed just this point which in particular must be believed. Since however much I might be assaulted by calumnious questionings (and I had read much in the works of philosophers as they contradicted each other), nothing could shake these two beliefs—first, that you exist (though I did not know what your nature was), and secondly, that the government of human affairs is in your hands.

I believed this sometimes more and sometimes less strongly. Nevertheless, I always did believe that you exist and that you have a care for us, even though I did not know what to think about your substance or what way leads, or leads back, to you. So, since we were too weak to discover truth by pure reason and therefore needed the authority of Holy Writ, I now began to believe that you could not possibly have given such supreme authority to these Scriptures all over the world, unless it had been your wish that by means of them men should both believe in you and seek after you. As for the absurdities which used to offend me in Scripture, I had heard many of them explained in a convincing way and I now looked for their meanings in the depth of mystery. In fact the authority of Scripture seemed to me the more venerable and the more worthy of religious faith because, while it was easy to read for everybody, it also preserved in the more profound sense of its meaning the majesty of something secret; it offers itself to all in plain words and a very simple style of speech, yet serious thinkers have to give it their closest attention. Thus its arms are wide open to receive everyone, yet there are a few whom it draws to you along narrow ways, and these few would be fewer still if it were not for the fact that at the same time it stands on such a peak of authority and also draws crowds into its bosom because of its holy humility. These were my thoughts, and you were by me; I sighed and you heard me; I was storm tossed and you held the tiller; I was going on the broad path of this world and you did not forsake me.

6 I PANTED FOR HONORS, for money, for marriage, and you were laughing at me. I found bitterness and difficulty in following these desires, and your graciousness to me was shown in the way you would not allow me to find anything sweet which was not you. Look into my heart, Lord; for it was you who willed me to remember all this and to confess it to you. And let my soul cling to you now that you have freed it from that gripping birdlime of death! How unhappy it was then! And you pricked its wound on the quick, so that it might leave everything else and turn to you, who are above all things and without whom all things would be nothing so that it might turn to you and be cured. I was unhappy indeed, and you made me really see my unhappiness. It was on a day when I was preparing a speech to be delivered in praise of the emperor; there would be a lot of lies in the speech, and they would be applauded by those who knew that they were lies. My heart was all wrought up with the worry of it all and was boiling in a kind of fever of melting thoughts. I was going along one of the streets of Milan when I noticed a poor beggar; he was fairly drunk, I suppose, and was laughing and enjoying himself. It was a sight which depressed me, and I spoke to the friends who were with me about all the sorrows which come to us because of our own madness. I thought of how I was toiling away, spurred on by my desires and dragging after me the load of my unhappiness and making it all the heavier by dragging it, and it seemed to me that the goal of this and all such endeavors was simply to reach a state of happiness that was free from care; the beggar had reached this state before us, and we, perhaps, might never reach it at all. With the few pennies that he had managed to beg he had actually obtained what I, by so many painful turns and such devious ways, was struggling to reach namely, the joy of a temporary happiness.

No doubt the beggar's joy was not true joy; but it was a great deal truer than the joy which I, with my ambition, was seeking. And undoubtedly he was happy while I was worried; he was carefree while I was full of fears. And if I were asked which I would prefer, to be merry or to be frightened, I should reply "to be merry." But if I were asked next whether I would prefer to be a man like the beggar or a man like I then was myself, I should choose to be myself, worn out as I was with my cares and my fears. Was not this absurd? Was there any good reason for making such a choice? For I had no right to put myself in front of the beggar on the grounds that I was more learned than he, since I got no joy out of my learning. Instead I used it to give pleasure to men—not to teach them, only to please them. And therefore you were breaking my bones with the rod of your discipline.

So I will not allow my soul to listen to those who say to her: "The difference is in the source of a man's happiness. That beggar found his joy in being drunk, you were looking for your joy in winning glory." What glory, Lord? A glory that was not in you. For just as the beggar's joy was not true joy, so my glory was not true glory. Moreover it had a worse effect on my mind. The beggar would sleep off his drunkenness that very night; but I had gone to bed with mine and woken up with it day after day after day and I should go on doing so. Certainly it makes a difference what is the source of a man's happiness. I know it does. And the joy of a faithful hope is incomparably beyond all such vanity. Yes, and so was the beggar then beyond me; without any doubt he was the happier, not only because he was drenched in merriment while I eaten up with anxieties, but also because he by wishing people good luck had got some wine for himself while I by lying was seeking for an empty bubble of praise.

I said much along these lines to my intimate friends at the time, and I often noticed that it was the same with them as it was with me, and I found that things were not at all well with me, and I worried about it and by worrying made matters twice as bad, and if fortune seemed to smile on me at all, I felt too tired to grasp my opportunity, for it fled away almost before I could take hold of it.

7 ALL OF US who were friends together were depressed by these thoughts. The ones I talked to most about it were Alypius and Nebridius. Alypius was born in the same town as I, and his parents were important people there. He was younger than I. Indeed he had studied under me when I began teaching in our town and later in Carthage. He was very fond of me, because he thought me good and learned, and I was very fond of him because of his natural tendency toward virtue which was really remarkable in one so young. Nevertheless, he had been sucked into the whirlpool of Carthaginian bad habits, and in particular the empty enthusiasm for shows in the Circus. At the time when he was becoming involved in this wretched passion I had set up as a teacher of rhetoric there with a school open to the public, but he did not come to me as a pupil because of some difference which had arisen between his father and me. I had found out that he had got this fatal passion for the Circus and I was greatly disturbed about it; because it seemed to me that he was likely to throw away, if he had not thrown away already, all those high hopes we held of him. But I had no means of giving him advice or of using any kind of authority to restrain him; I could not appeal to his good will as a friend or to his duty as a pupil. For I thought that he shared his father's views about me. In fact he did not, and so, not allowing himself to be influenced by his father's quarrel, he began to greet me when we met and used to come into my school and sit listening for a time before going away.

Nevertheless, I had forgotten about any idea I might have had for trying to influence him so as to prevent the waste of such a good intelligence on a blind and head-strong enthusiasm for empty shows. But you, Lord, you, whose hand is on the helm of all that you have created, had not forgotten him who was to become one day a member of your family and a high priest of your sacra-ment. And his reform must quite clearly be attributed to you, as is shown by the fact that, though you brought it about by means of me, I did not know what I was doing. This was what happened. One day when I was sitting in my usual place with my pupils around me, Alypius came in and, after saluting me, sat down and listened to what was going on. In the course of my expo-sition of the passage of literature with which I happened to be dealing it occurred to me that I could make an apt use of a comparison taken from the games in the Circus; this would make my point clearer and more amusing, and I could combine it with some bitter sar-casm at the expense of those who were the prey of this kind of madness. You, God, know that at that time I had no thought of curing Alypius of that disease. But he took my remarks personally and believed that it was only because of him that I had made them. Another person would have taken this as a reason for being angry with me, but this fair-minded young man took it as a reason for being angry with himself and for loving me all the more. For you said long ago, and you had it put in your book: *Rebuke a wise man, and he will love thee.*

In fact I had not been rebuking him, but you make use of all men, whether or not they are aware of it, according to a method that is known to you, and that order and method is just. So out of my heart and tongue you made burning coals to cauterize and to cure that promising mind of his as it lay sick. Who can fail to praise you if he considers your mercies, mercies which I myself confess to you from the very marrow of my bones? For after those words of mine Alypius clambered out of that deep pit into which he had been glad enough to sink and in which he was being blinded by his pleasures; he took a firm hold on his mind and shook it; all the filth of the Circus fell off and he never went there again. Then he won over his father so that he might be allowed to attend my classes as a pupil. His father was unwilling enough, but gave way and gave in. Alypius was once more my pupil and became involved with me in the same superstition. He loved the Manichaean pretense of continence, considering it to be real and genuine, though in fact this kind of continence was senseless and misleading and ensnared precious souls which were not yet able to reach the depth of virtue but could easily be deceived by the superficial appearance of a virtue which was shadowy and pretended.

8   BUT THERE WAS no abandoning of the worldly career which his parents were always talking to him about. He had gone to Rome before me in order to study law and in Rome he had been quite swept away, incredibly and with a most incredible passion, by the gladiatorial shows. He was opposed to such things and detested them; but he happened to meet some of his friends and fellow pupils on their way back from dinner, and they, in spite of his protests and his vigorous resistance, used a friendly kind of violence and forced him to go along with them to the amphitheater on a day when one of these cruel and bloody shows was being presented. As he went, he said to them: "You can drag my body there, but don't imagine that you can make me turn my eyes or give my mind to the show. Though

there, I shall not be there, and so I shall have the better both of you and of the show."

After hearing this his friends were all the keener to bring him along with them. No doubt they wanted to see whether he could actually do this or not. So they came to the arena and took the seats which they could find. The whole place was seething with savage enthusiasm, but he shut the doors of his eyes and forbade his soul to go out into a scene of such evil. If only he could have blocked up his ears too! For in the course of the fight some man fell; there was a great roar from the whole mass of spectators which fell upon his ears; he was overcome by curiosity and opened his eyes, feeling perfectly prepared to treat whatever he might see with scorn and to rise above it. But he then received in his soul a worse wound than that man, whom he had wanted to see, had received in his body. His own fall was more wretched than that of the gladiator which had caused all that shouting which had entered his ears and unlocked his eyes and made an opening for the thrust which was to overthrow his soul—a soul that had been reckless rather than strong and was all the weaker because it had trusted in itself when it ought to have trusted in you. He saw the blood and he gulped down savagery. Far from turning away, he fixed his eyes on it. Without knowing what was happening, he drank in madness, he was delighted with the guilty contest, drunk with the lust of blood. He was no longer the man who had come there but was one of the crowd to which he had come, a true companion of those who had brought him.

There is no more to be said. He looked, he shouted, he raved with excitement; he took away with him a madness which would goad him to come back again, and he would not only come with those who first got him there; he would go ahead of them and he would drag others with him. Yet you, with your most strong and merciful hand, rescued him from this, and you taught him to put his trust not in himself but in you. This, however, was much later.

9   Nevertheless, this was already being stored up in his memory for his future healing. So also was something which happened to him when he was still a pupil of mine at Carthage. He was in the market place in the middle of the day, thinking over the words of a passage which in the ordinary course of his education he would have to say by heart. You then allowed him to be arrested by the market police as a thief, and, our God, I think that the only reason why you allowed this to happen was that one who was going to become such a great man should even then begin to learn that in cases of judging guilt man must not be too easily condemned by man on a basis of rash credulity. What happened was this: he was walking about by himself, with his notebooks and pen, in front of the law court, and just then a young man, also a student, who was the real thief, with an ax hidden under his clothes, got in (though Alypius did not see him) as far as the leaden gratings over the silversmiths' shops and began to cut away the lead. But the silversmiths underneath heard the sound of the ax, raised the alarm, and sent people to catch whomever they could find. Hearing their voices the thief ran away, leaving the ax behind for fear that he might be caught with it. Alypius had not seen the man coming in, but he noticed him going out and saw that he was running away fast. Wanting to know the reason for this, he went into the place, found the ax, and stood in front of it, wondering what it was doing there. At this moment the men who had been sent found him, alone and with the weapon whose noise had alarmed them and brought them there. They seized hold of him and dragged him off, boasting to the shopkeepers in the forum, who came crowding around, that they had caught the thief redhanded. And so he was led away to be handed over to justice. But his lesson stopped here. You, Lord, now came to the aid of his innocence, of which you were the only witness. For as he was being led off to prison or to torture they were met by a man who was the chief architect in charge of the public buildings. Alypius' captors

were particularly glad to meet him because they themselves were often suspected by him of making off with
property that had disappeared from the market place;
now at last, they thought, they could show him who was
really guilty. But the architect had often seen Alypius in
the house of one of the senators at which he was in the
habit of calling. He recognized him at once, took him
by the hand, got him out of the way of the mob, and
asked him what all this trouble was about. He heard
what had happened and told the crowd, who were in a
most turbulent and threatening mood, to come with him.
They went to the house of the young man who had actually committed the crime. By the door was a boy who
was too small to imagine that anything he might say
could injure his master and who was therefore likely to
tell the whole story, for he had followed his master into
the market place. Alypius recognized him and pointed
him out to the architect, who showed him the ax and
asked him whom it belonged to. The boy at once said:
"It's ours," and, after further questioning, revealed
everything. So the crime was laid at the door of that
house, much to the confusion of the crowd, who had
already begun to treat Alypius as though he were their
prisoner. He, who in the future would be a dispenser of
your word and an investigator of many cases in your
Church, went away a wiser and a more experienced man.

10 I FOUND ALYPIUS at Rome. We became very
close friends, and he came with me to Milan,
partly so as not to desert me and partly to practice the
law which he had studied—though this was rather to
please his parents than because he wanted to. He had
already sat three times as an assessor and had shown an
integrity which made others wonder at him, though he
himself was more inclined to wonder at those others who
could prefer gold to honesty. His character was also
tested not only by the lure of gain but also by the threat
of danger. At Rome he was assessor to the Count of the

Italian Treasury. There was at the time an extremely powerful senator; many people were under obligations to him, and many people were afraid of him. This man, counting upon his usual influence, wanted to get something or other past the courts which was in fact illegal. Alypius stood out against it. Bribes were offered, which he treated with contempt; threats were made and he spurned them. Everyone wondered at so rare a spirit, which neither courted the friendship nor feared the enmity of a man who was so powerful and who was so well known for having countless means of helping people on or of doing them harm. The judge himself, in whose court Alypius sat, was also against making the concession, but he would not refuse it openly; instead he made Alypius responsible, saying that it was Alypius who was preventing him; and in fact, if he had given in, Alypius would have left the court.

One thing did tempt him, and that was his love of learning. He knew that he could have books copied for him at the cheap rate allowed to praetors. But when he considered the justice of the matter, he changed his mind for the better. Equity forbade, power allowed; he chose the former as being the more valuable. A small thing, perhaps. But *he that is faithful in little, is faithful also in much.* Nor can this be an empty word which came from the mouth of your truth: *If ye have not been faithful in the unrighteous Mammon, who will commit to your trust true riches? And if ye have not been faithful in that which is another man's, who shall give you that which is your own?*

This was the sort of person that Alypius was at that time. He was my great friend and together with me he was in a state of mental confusion as to what way of life we should take.

There was Nebridius too. He had left his native place near Carthage; he had left Carthage itself, where he usually lived; he had left his rich family estate in the country, left his home, and left his mother, since she was not prepared to follow him. He had come to Milan, and his one reason for doing so was to live with me in a most ardent search for truth and wisdom. Together with me he sighed and together with me he wavered. How he burned to discover the happy life! How keen and close was his scrutiny of the most difficult questions!

So there were together the mouths of three hungry people, sighing out their wants one to another, and *waiting upon Thee that Thou mightest give them their meat in due season.* And in all the bitterness which by your mercy followed all our worldly actions, as we looked toward the end and asked ourselves why should we suffer like this, darkness came down upon us, and we turned away in sorrow saying, *How long shall these things be?* This we said often enough, yet still we did not forsake these things, because there was no dawning gleam of a certainty to which we could hold once these things had been forsaken.

11 AND I, as I looked back over my life, was quite amazed to think of how long a time had passed since my nineteenth year, when I had first become inflamed with a passion for wisdom and had resolved that, when once I found it, I would leave behind me all the empty hopes and deceitful frenzies of vain desires. And now I was in my thirtieth year, still sticking in the same mud, still greedy for the enjoyment of things present, which fled from me and wasted me away, and all the time saying: "I shall find it tomorrow. See, it will become quite clear and I shall grasp it. Now Faustus will come and explain everything. What great men the Academics are! Is it true that no certainty can possibly be comprehended for the direction of our lives? No, it cannot be. We must look into things more carefully and not give up hope. And now see, those things in the Sciptures which used to seem absurd are not absurd; they can be understood in a different and perfectly good way. I shall take my stand where my parents placed me as a child until I can see the truth plainly. But where shall I look for it? And when shall I look for it? Ambrose has no spare time; nor have I time for reading. And where can I find the books? From where can I get them and when can I get them? Can I borrow them from anybody? I must arrange fixed periods of time and set aside certain hours for the health of my soul. A great hope has dawned. The Catholic faith does not teach the things I thought it did and vainly accused it of teaching. The learned men of that faith think it quite wrong to believe that God is bounded within the shape of a human body. Why then do I hesitate to knock, so that the rest may be laid open to me? My pupils take up all my time in the morning. But what do I do for the rest of the day? Why not do this? But, if I do, how shall I find time to call on influential friends whose support will be useful to me? When shall I prepare the lessons for which my pupils pay? When shall I have time to relax and to refresh my mind from all my preoccupations?

"But these are not the thoughts I should have. I must give up all this vanity and emptiness and devote myself entirely to the search for truth. Life is a misery, death an uncertainty. Suppose it steals suddenly upon me, in what state shall I leave this world? When can I learn what I have here neglected to learn? Shall I not be punished for my negligence? Or is it true that death will cut off and put an end to all care and all feeling? This too is something to be inquired into. But no, this cannot be true. It is not for nothing, it is not meaningless that all over the world is displayed the high and towering authority of the Christian faith. Such great and wonderful things would never have been done for us by God, if the life of the soul were to end with the death of the body. Why then do I delay? Why do I not abandon my hopes of this world and devote myself entirely to the search for God and for the happy life?

"But wait. These worldly things too are sweet; the pleasure they give is not inconsiderable; we must not be too hasty about rejecting them, because it would be a shame to go back to them again. Now think: it would not be very difficult to get some high official appointment, and then what more could I want? I have quite a number of influential friends. Not to press on too fast, I could easily get a governorship. Then I should marry a wife with money, so that she would not increase my expenses. And then I should have nothing more to desire. There have been many great men, well worth imitating, who have devoted themselves to the pursuit of wisdom and have also been married."

So I used to speak and so the winds blew and shifted and drove my heart this way and that, and time went by and I was slow in turning to the Lord. My life in you I kept on putting off from one day to the next, but I did not put off the death that daily I was dying in myself. I was in love with the idea of the happy life, but I feared to find it in its true place, and I sought for it by running away from it. I thought that I should be unbearably unhappy if I were deprived of the embraces of a woman, and I never thought of your mercy as a medicine to cure that weakness, because I had never tried it. I believed that continency was something which depended on one's own strength, and I knew that I had not enough strength for it; for I was such a fool that I did not know that it is written that no one can be continent unless you give the power. And undoubtedly you would have given it to me if with the groans of my heart I had beaten upon your ears and if in settled faith I had cast my cares upon you.

12   ALYPIUS CERTAINLY kept me from marrying. He was always saying that if I did marry, it would be quite impossible for us to have the untroubled leisure in which we could live together in the love of wisdom, as we had so long wanted to do. With regard to all this he himself was even then quite extraordinarily chaste. When he was an adolescent he had had the experience of sexual intercourse, but, so far from becoming addicted to it, he had regretted the experience and despised it and ever since had lived in the greatest continence. As to me, I countered

his arguments by producing examples of men who, though married, had pursued wisdom and served God and kept their friends and loved them faithfully. In fact I myself fell far short of their grandeur of spirit; I was the prisoner of this disease of the flesh and of its deadly sweetness, and I dragged my chain about with me, dreading the idea of its being loosed, and I pushed aside the good advice of Alypius as I might push aside the hand of one coming to unchain me which had knocked against a wound.

Also it was by means of me that the serpent began to speak to Alypius himself. My tongue was used to weave sweet snares and scatter them in his path to trap his free and unsuspecting feet. He was much surprised to find that I, of whom he thought so highly, was so stuck in the glue of this kind of pleasure that I would assert, whenever we discussed the subject, that it was quite impossible for me to live a single life. I on my side, when I saw how surprised he was, would defend myself by saying that there was a great difference between that hurried and furtive experience of his—which he could now scarcely remember and could thus quite easily despise—and the delights of my normal state. If, I said, to these was added the honorable name of marriage, he could have no reason to be surprised that I was incapable of rejecting such a way of life. On hearing this Alypius began to want to get married himself, not because he lusted after that kind of pleasure, but simply for curiosity. He wanted to find out, he said, what this thing was without which my life, which seemed to him so pleasant, would be to me not worth living and indeed a torment. For his mind was free of my kind of bondage and was simply amazed at it. So from being amazed he went on to desire the experience of it. And he would have proceeded to the same experience and next might well have fallen into the same slavery as that which amazed him in me; since he wished to *make a covenant with death*, and *he that loves danger shall fall into it*. For neither of us had more than the faintest interest in the good and honorable side of marriage—the duty of a controlled association and of having children. In my case what chiefly enslaved me and kept me on tenterhooks was the habit of sating a lust that could never be satisfied; while he was being dragged into slavery simply by his amazement at my behavior. So there we were until you, most high, not forsaking our dust, but pitying our pitiful state, came to our help in secret and wonderful ways.

13 THE MOVE TO get me married went on apace. I made my proposal and the girl was promised to me. In all this my mother played a large part, for, once I was married, she wanted me to be washed in the health-giving water of baptism for which, to her joy, she saw me becoming more fit every day, so that she now felt that her own prayers and your promises were being fulfilled in my faith. It was at my request and also to satisfy her own longing that at this time she begged you every day, crying out to you from her heart, to show her in a vision something about my future marriage; but you were never willing to do so. She did have some visual experiences of a vain and fantastical nature (caused no doubt by the eagerness of a human mind to be satisfied on this particular point), but when she told me of them, she spoke slightingly of them and not with the confidence which she always had when you were really showing her something. She used to say that there was a kind of tone or savor, impossible to define in words, by which she could tell the difference between your revelations to her and the dreams that came from her own spirit. Nevertheless, plans for my marriage went ahead and the girl was asked for. She was still about two years below the marriageable age, but I liked her and was prepared to wait.

14 A GROUP OF US, all friends together, after much thought and conversation on how we hated the whole wearisome business of human life, had almost reached the conclusion that we would retire from the crowd and live a life of peace. In order to achieve this we planned to pool our resources and make one common property out of the property of all of us. So, in the sincerity of friendship, there would be no distinction between what belonged to one man or another; all our possessions should count as one piece of property, and the whole should belong to each individual and everything should belong to everybody. It appeared that there might be about ten of us in this society and among these ten were some very rich men—Romanianus in particular, who was a fellow towns-man of ours and had been a great friend of mine from childhood. He had now come to the court at Milan because of some urgent business in connection with his own affairs. He was particularly enthusiastic about the project and his voice had much weight in persuading the rest of us, since his property was much greater than anybody else's. We had decided that two of us should be, like magistrates, appointed every year to deal with the necessary provisions for life, while the rest would be left in peace. Next, how-ever, the question was raised as to whether our wives would put up with it—some of us having wives already and I being anxious to have one. And so the whole scheme, which had been so well worked out, fell to pieces in our hands and was abandoned as impracticable. We went back to our sighing and complaining and our steps continued to follow the broad and well-worn paths of the world; for we had many thoughts in our hearts, *but Thy counsel standeth forever.* And out of this counsel you laughed ours to scorn, and you were preparing for us your own things, being about *to give us meat in due season, and to open Thy hand, and to fill our souls with blessing.*

15 MEANWHILE MY SINS were being multiplied. The woman with whom I was in the habit of sleeping was torn from my side on the grounds of being an impedi-ment to my marriage, and my heart, which clung to her, was broken and wounded and dropping blood. She had returned to Africa after having made a vow to you that she would never go to bed with another man, and she had

left with me the natural son I had had by her. But I, in
my misery, could not follow the example of a woman. I
had two years to wait until I could have the girl to whom
I was engaged, and I could not bear the delay. So, since I
was not so much a lover of marriage as a slave to lust, I
found another woman for myself—not, of course, as a wife.
In this way my soul's disease was fed and kept alive so
that it might reach the domination of matrimony just as
strong as before, or stronger, and still the slave of an un-
breakable habit. Nor was the wound healed which had
been made by the cutting off of my previous mistress. It
burned, it hurt intensely, and then it festered, and if the
pain became duller, it became more desperate.

16 PRAISE TO YOU, glory to you, fountain of mercies!
As I became more unhappy, so you drew closer
to me. Your right hand was ready, it was ready to drag
me out of the mud and to wash me; but I did not know.
And there was nothing to call me back from that deeper
gulf of carnal pleasure, except the fear of death and of
judgment to come, and this, whatever the opinions I held
from time to time, never left my mind. I used to discuss
the nature of good and evil with my friends Alypius and
Nebridius, and certainly in my judgment Epicurus would
have won the palm if I had not believed (as he refused to
believe) that there was a life for the soul after death and
treatment in accordance with its deserts. And I would put
the question: "Suppose we were immortal and could live
in perpetual bodily pleasure without any fear of loss, why
should we not be happy, or what more could we want?"
And I never realized that it was just this that made me so
miserable, that in my drowned and sightless state I was
unable to form an idea of the light of honor and of a
beauty that is embraced for its own sake, which is invisible
to the eye of flesh and can only be seen by the inner soul.
I was wretched enough not to consider why and from what
source it was that I found it a pleasure to discuss these
ideas (shabby though they were) in the company of friends

and that I could not be happy, even in the way I then understood happiness, without friends, however great might be the amount of carnal pleasure I had in addition. For certainly I loved my friends for their own sake, and I knew that they too loved me for my own sake. What tortuous ways these were, and how hopeless was the plight of my foolhardy soul which hoped to have something better if it went away from you! It has turned indeed, over and over, on back and side and front, and always the bed was hard and you alone are rest. And, see, you are close to us, and you rescue us from our unhappy errors, and you set our feet in your way and speak kindly to us and say: "Run and I will hold you and I will bring you through and there also I will hold you."

Book VII

1 Now my evil abominable youth was a thing of the past. I was growing into manhood, and the older I was the more discreditable was the emptiness of my mind. I was unable to form an idea of any kind of substance other than what my eyes are accustomed to see. I did not think of you, God, in the shape of a human body. From the moment when I began to have any knowledge of wisdom I always avoided that idea, and I was glad that I had found the same view held in the faith of our spiritual mother, your Catholic Church. But how else I was to think of you, I did not know. And I, a man, and such a man too, was trying to think of you as the supreme, the only, the true God, and with all my heart I believed you to be beyond the reach of corruption and injury and change; because, though I did not know how or whence, I still saw quite plainly and with certainty that what can be corrupted is inferior to what cannot be corrupted, that what cannot be injured is undoubtedly to be preferred to what can be injured, and that what suffers no change is better than what is subject to change. My heart cried out passionately against all the phantoms I had believed in, and with this one blow I tried to beat away from the eye of my mind all those swarms of uncleanness which were buzzing around it. But they only disappeared for the flickering of an eyelid, and then they came straight back again in a mass, pressing on my sight and overclouding it, and the result was that, though I did not think of you in the shape of a human body, I was still forced to think of you as a corporeal substance occupying space, whether infused into this world or diffused through the infinite space outside the world, and this substance too I regarded as being of that incorruptible, inviolable, and changeless nature which I saw as superior to the corruptible, the violable, and the mutable. And the reason was that if I tried to imagine something as not being in space it seemed to me to be nothing, and by "nothing" I mean absolutely nothing, not even a void. For if a body is taken out of its place and the place remains empty of any kind of body, whether of earth, water, air, or sky, it will still be an empty place, a "nothing" that is nevertheless in a spatial context.

So I with my gross mind (for I was not even clearly visible to myself) considered that whatever was not extended in space, whether diffused or condensed or swelling out or having some such qualities or being capable of having them, must be, in the full sense of the word, nothing. The images in my mind were like the shapes which I was used to seeing with my eyes, and I did not realize that this very act of the mind by which I formed these images was something of a different nature altogether; yet it would not be able to form the images unless it were itself something great. So, life of my life, I thought of you as an immensity through infinite space, interfused everywhere throughout the whole mass of the universe and extending beyond it in every direction for distances without end, so that the earth should have you, the sky should have you, all things should have you, and they should be bounded in you, but you should be boundless. For just as the body of the air which is above the earth does not resist the passage of the sun's light, which goes through it without breaking or cutting it, but simply by filling it entirely, so I thought that the body not only of the heaven and the air and the sea, but also of the earth, was permeable to you and, in its greatest parts as in its least, able to be penetrated so as to receive your presence and that thus a hidden kind of inspiration from within and from without governed all things which you had created.

This was the idea I formed, because I could not think in any other way. But it was false. For according to this view a greater or a lesser part of the earth would contain a greater or a lesser part of you; all things would be full of you, but in such a way that the body of an elephant would contain more of you than the body of a sparrow to the extent that it is larger and occupies more space, and thus you would be imparting your presence piece-meal to different parts of the world—small portions of you to small parts, big portions to big parts. But this is not so. However, you had not yet enlightened my darkness.

2 AS TO THOSE deceived deceivers, those dumb talkers (dumb because they never uttered your Word), I had a perfectly good argument to oppose to them, and I had had it ever since the time when we were in Carthage. It was put forward by Nebridius, and all of us who heard it were much taken aback by it. There is in the Manichaean creed a sort of nation of darkness which is set up as a counter substance to you; now what, Nebridius asked, would this nation of darkness have done to you, if you had been unwilling to fight against it? If the reply was: "it would have done you some harm," then it would follow that you were capable of suffering injury and corruption. If, on the other hand, it was admitted that it could have done you no harm, then no reason could be produced why you should fight with it. Particularly when the fighting was of this kind: some portion or member of you or offspring of your own sub-stance was supposed to become mixed with opposite powers and natures not created by you; it was then so corrupted by them and so changed for the worse as to fall from beatitude into misery and to require help so as to be delivered and cleansed; this portion of your sub-stance was the soul, and in its state of slavery and con-tamination and corruption it was to receive the aid of your Word, which was free, pure, and entire. But that

Word was itself corruptible because it was the offspring of one and the same substance as the soul. And so if they say that you, in your real nature—that is, in your substance by which you are—are incorruptible, then all these theories of theirs must be false and execrable, and if they say that you are corruptible, that very statement in itself, as is immediately obvious, must be false and must be abominated. This argument of Nebridius was therefore all I needed against the Manichees, whom I ought to have wholly vomited up from a stomach overcharged with them; for they had no possible answer and could not defend the way in which they thought and spoke about you without the most dreadful blasphemy of heart and tongue.

3   AS TO ME, I would certainly say and I firmly believed that you—our Lord, the true God, who made not only our souls but our bodies, and not only our souls and bodies but all men and all things—were undefilable and unalterable and in no way to be changed, and yet I still could not understand clearly and distinctly what was the cause of evil. Whatever it might be, however, I did realize that my inquiry must not be carried out along lines which would lead me to believe that the immutable God was mutable; if I did that, I should become myself the very evil which I was looking for. And so I pursued the inquiry without anxiety, being quite certain that what the Manichees said was not true. I had turned against them with my whole heart, because I saw that in their inquiries into the origin of evil they were full of evil themselves; for they preferred to believe that your substance could suffer evil rather than that their substance could do evil.

And I made an effort to understand what I had heard, that free will is the cause of our doing evil and your just judgment the cause of our suffering it; but I could not grasp this clearly. And so, though I tried to raise the eyes of my mind from the pit, I fell back into it again, and as often as I tried so often did I fall back. But I was a little raised up toward your light by the fact that I was just as certain that I had a will as that I had a life. So, when I willed to do or not to do something, I was perfectly certain that the act of willing was mine and not anybody else's, and I was now getting near to the conclusion that here was the cause of my sin.

But with regard to things which I did unwillingly, it seemed to me that I was suffering rather than doing, and I considered such things to be my punishment rather than my fault; though, as I thought of you as just, I was quick to admit that I was not being punished unjustly. But then I asked: "Who made me? Was it not my God, who is not only good but goodness itself? How then could it be that I should will evil and refuse my assent to good, so that it would be just for me to be punished? Who was it who set and ingrafted in me this plant of bitterness, seeing that I was wholly made by my most sweet God? If the devil is responsible, then where did the devil come from? And if it was by his own perverse will that the devil himself, after having been a good angel, became a devil, then what was the origin in him of the evil will by which he became a devil, seeing that he was made all angel by the all-good creator?" By these thoughts I was thrust down again and choked; but I was not brought down so low as to that hell of error where no one confesses to you and where it is believed that you suffer evil rather than that man does evil.

4   So I struggled on to find out the rest in the same way as I had already discovered that the incorruptible is better than the corruptible, and therefore I was ready to confess that, whatever your nature might be, you must be incorruptible. For no soul ever has been or ever will be able to conceive of anything better than you, who are the supreme and the best good. And, since in all truth and certainty the view which I now held—that the incorruptible is to be preferred to the corrupt-

ible—was right, I should have been able, if you had not
been incorruptible, to have reached in imagination something better than my God. It was here, therefore—in
my knowledge that the incorruptible was better than the
corruptible—that I ought to have been looking for you,
and I should have gone on from here to discover where
evil is, that is to say, what is the origin of that corruption.
by which your own substance cannot possibly be affected. For there is absolutely no way in which corruption can affect our God, neither by will nor by necessity
nor by accident; because He Himself is God and what
He wills is good and He Himself is goodness; but to be
corrupted is not good. Nor are you forced toward anything against your will, for your will is not greater than
your power. But it would be greater, if you were greater
than yourself. For the will and power of God is God
Himself. And how could any accident surprise you, who
know all things? There is nothing in existence except as
a result of your knowing it. But what need is there of
more words to show that the substance which is God is
not corruptible? If it were, it would not be God.

5   I SEARCHED FOR the origin of evil and I searched
     for it in an evil way, and I did not see the evil
in the very method of my search. I put the whole creation in front of the eyes of my spirit, both what was
visible—like earth, sea, air, stars, trees, and mortal creatures—and what was invisible—like the firmament of the
heaven above and all the angels and spiritual beings
there. Though even these spiritual beings I conceived of
as bodies, each in its imagined place. And I thought
of all your creation as one great mass, distinguished in
accordance with the kinds of bodies of which it was
made up, some being real bodies, others the kind of
bodies which I imagined instead of spirits. I thought of
this mass as being of an enormous size, not the size
which it actually was (which I could not know), but the
size which seemed to me convenient; though I conceived

of it as being finite on every side. And I thought of you,
Lord, as surrounding it on every side and penetrating it,
but being in all directions infinite. It was as though there
were a sea, which everywhere and on all sides through
immensity was just one infinite sea, but which had inside
it a sponge which, though very big, was still bounded.
This sponge of course would in all its parts be completely filled with the immeasurable sea. So I thought of
your creation as finite and as filled with you, who were
infinite. And I said: "Here is God, and here is what God
has created; and God is good and is most mightily and
incomparably better than all these. Yet He, being good,
created them good, and see how He surrounds them and
fills them. Where, then, is evil? Where did it come from
and how did it creep in here? What is its root and seed?
Or does it simply not exist? In that case why do we fear
and take precautions against something that does not
exist? Or if there is no point in our fears, then our fears
themselves are an evil which goads and tortures the
heart for no good reason—and all the worse an evil if
there is nothing to be afraid of and we are still afraid.
Therefore, either there is evil which we fear or else the
fact that we do fear is evil. Where then does evil come
from, seeing that God is good and made all things good?
Certainly it was the greater and supreme Good who
made these lesser goods, yet still all are good, both the
creator and his creation. Where then did evil come
from? Or was there some evil element in the material
of creation, and did God shape and form it, yet still leave
in it something which He did not change into good? But
why? Being omnipotent, did He lack the power to
change and transform the whole so that no trace of evil
should remain? Indeed why should He choose to use
such material for making anything? Would He not
rather, with this same omnipotence, cause it not to exist
at all? Could it exist against His will? Or, supposing it
was eternal, why for so long through all the infinite
spaces of time past did He allow it to exist and then so
much later decide to make something out of it? Or, if

He did suddenly decide on some action, would not the omnipotent prefer to act in such a way that this evil material should cease to exist, and that He alone should be, the whole, true, supreme, and infinite Good? Or, since it was not good that He who was good should frame and create something not good, then why did He not take away and reduce to nothing the material that was evil and then Himself provide good material from which to create all things? For He would not be omnipotent if He could not create something good without having to rely on material which He had not Himself created."

These were the kind of thoughts which I turned over and over in my unhappy heart, a heart overburdened with those biting cares that came from my fear of death and my failure to discover the truth. Yet the faith of your Christ, our Lord and Saviour, professed in the Catholic Church, remained steadfastly fixed in my heart, even though it was on many points still unformed and swerving from the right rule of doctrine. But, nevertheless, my mind did not abandon it, but rather drank more and more deeply of it every day.

6   BY THIS TIME TOO I had rejected the fallacious forecasts and impious ravings of the astrologers. Here also, my God, let your own mercies make confession to you from the very depths of my soul. For this was entirely due to you. Who else is it who calls us back from the death of error, except the life that does not know death, and the wisdom which, needing no light, enlightens minds which are in darkness, that wisdom by which the whole world, even to the leaves of trees drifting in the wind, is governed? So it was you who dealt with that obstinate state of mind in which I was when I argued with that sharp-witted old man Vindicianus and with the young Nebridius, with his fine spiritual qualities. Vindicianus used to maintain most energetically, and Nebridius, though with rather more hesitation, often used

to say too that the supposed art of foretelling the future
was no art at all; it was rather the case that the guesses
people made had the luck of a lottery; those who made
a number of predictions would make some that turned
out true, though in making them no knowledge was
shown; it was simply a question of saying so many things
that in the course of it one was bound to stumble on
something true. And then, again by your provision, I
had a friend who was a very keen follower of the astrologers. He had no great knowledge of their literature but
was, as I said, one who showed considerable curiosity
about them. He did know something, however, which he
said had been told him by his father; but he did not
know how useful this information was for the overthrow-
ing of any belief one might have in astrology. The man's
name was Firminus; he had had a good education and
was thoroughly trained in rhetoric. As he considered me
a great friend he asked me to give him my advice about
some affairs of his which greatly concerned his worldly
ambitions, and he wanted to know what I thought about
his so-called "constellations" in the matter. By this time
I was beginning to come around to the views of Nebridius about astrology, but I did not refuse to make my
conjectures and to tell Firminus how (uncertain as I was)
things seemed to me. I added however that I was now
practically certain that all these inquiries were a ridiculous waste of time. He then told me about his father,
who had been a great student of astrology and had had
a friend who was equally enthusiastic and had joined
him in his studies. They studied zealously and compared
notes and their hearts became so much on fire with this
nonsense that they used to make careful observations of
the exact times when even the dumb animals in their
houses gave birth and they noted the position of the
heavens at these times—all in order to collect experi-
mental evidence for this presumed art. Firminus said that
his father had told him that at the time when his mother
was pregnant with him a female slave belonging to this
friend of his father's was also about to have a child. This

of course was known to the woman's master, who, even when one of his bitches was having puppies, would be most meticulously careful to find out all about it. So now in the case of this slave of his he was taking the most careful and thorough notes with regard to days, hours, and the smallest fractions of hours, while Firminus' father was doing just the same thing with regard to his wife. It happened that the two women had their babies at the same moment; so that for each newborn child the men were forced to cast exactly the same horoscope down to the last detail, one for his son, the other for the little slave. For as soon as the women's labor began each friend had let the other know what was going on in his house and they had messengers ready to send to each other as soon as it was known that one or other of the children had been born—and, since the births were taking place in their own households, they would know at once. Firminus said that the messengers sent by each met exactly halfway between the two houses, so that it was impossible for either of the men to have made any different observations from the other one with regard to the position of the stars or the precise moment of time. Yet Firminus, born to wealth in his parents' house, had one of the brighter careers in life; his riches increased and he held distinguished positions; whereas the slave had no alleviation in the burden of his condition; he continued to serve his masters. So Firminus, who knew him, told me.

After hearing this story and (since Firminus was a perfectly reliable witness) believing it, all my previous resistance gave way and collapsed. First I attempted to induce Firminus himself to give up this form of curiosity by telling him that if I had had to consult his stars in order to give him a true forecast of the future, I certainly ought to have seen in them that his parents were people of distinction, that his family was a noble one in his own city, that he was born free, and that he had had a good and liberal education. But if that slave had asked me for my opinion and I had consulted his stars, which were

exactly the same as those under which Firminus was
born, then I ought to have seen in them that his family
was of the very lowest, that he was a slave, and that in
every other respect he had a completely different lot in
life from that of Firminus. It followed, therefore, that,
after inspecting the same stars, I must, if I were to tell
the truth, say different things in the two cases, for if I
were to say the same things, it would be a falsehood,
and from this it appeared to me quite certain that anything true which may be said after casting a horoscope
is true by luck and not by skill, and anything false is
false not because of any lack of skill in the art but simply
because the luck has gone the other way.

With this approach to the subject I began to look
more deeply into the same kind of argument in case one
of those fools who make money out of astrology, and
whom I was already longing to challenge and to make
laughingstocks of, was to object by saying that what Firminus had told me or what his father had told him was
untrue. So I considered the cases of those who are born
twins. Most of them come from the womb very close to
each other, and the small interval of time between the
two births (whatever influence these people may pretend
it has in reality) simply cannot be noted by any human
method of observation so as to be put down in the tables
which the astrologer must look at in order to foretell
the truth. And of course it will not be the truth. After
looking at the same figures an astrologer would have
had to predict the same futures for Esau and for Jacob;
but in fact the same things did not happen to them.
Either, then, he would have to have made a false prediction, or else, if his prediction was true, it would have to
have been different in each case; yet each case was based
on the same figures. So, if he did tell the truth, it would
be by luck and not by skill. For you, Lord, the most just
controller of the universe, act in your own secret way so
that, while neither he who consults nor he who is consulted knows what is being done, still when a man consults he is told out of the abyss of your just judgment

what, in accordance with the secret deservings of souls, he ought to be told. Let no man say to you "What is this?" or "Why is this?" He must not, he must not say such things. For he is a man.

7   AND SO, MY HELPER, you had set me free from those chains. But still I asked: "What is the origin of evil?" and I could find no answer. Yet in all the fluctuations of my thought you did not allow me to be carried away from the faith in which I believed that you existed, that your substance was unchangeable, that you had care for men, and that you would judge them; also that in Christ your Son our Lord and in the Holy Scriptures approved by the authority of your Catholic Church you had laid down the way of man's salvation to the life which is to come after death. With these beliefs firmly and irrevocably rooted in my mind I sought, in a kind of passion, the answer to the question: "What is the origin of evil?" What agonies I suffered, what groans, my God, came from my heart in its labor! And you were listening, though I did not know it. When in silence I strongly urged my question, the quiet contrition of my soul was a great cry to your mercy. You knew what I was suffering, and no man knew it. For how little there was of it which I could put into words even for the hearing of my most intimate friends! How could they hear the tumult of my soul when I had neither time nor language sufficient to express it? Yet all of it reached your hearing, all the roarings and groanings of my heart, and my desire was in front of you and the light of my eyes was not with me. For that light was within and I was out of doors; that was not in space, but my mind was intent on things which were in space, and I could find no place there to rest, and the things of space did not welcome me so that I could say: "It is enough, it is well," nor did they let me go back to where it would have been well enough with me. For I was superior to them, but inferior to you. You are my true joy and I am

subject to you, and you have subjected to me the things
in your creation which are below me. And this was the
correct admixture, the middle way for my salvation—
that I should remain in your image and, by serving you,
be master of the body. But when I arrogantly rose up
against you and *ran upon my Lord with my neck, with
the thick bosses of my buckler,* even these inferior things
became above me and kept me under, and there was no
loosening of their hold and no chance of breathing.
When I opened my eyes they swarmed around me from
all sides in clouds, and when I tried to think, these corporeal images stood in my way and prevented me from
returning to you. It was as though they were saying:
"Where are you going to, you unworthy and unclean
creature?" All this had grown out of my wound; for you
humble the proud like one who is wounded, and I was
separated from you by the swelling of my pride. It was
as though my cheeks had swollen up so that I could not
see out of my eyes.

8   BUT YOU, LORD, abide forever, and you are not
angry with us forever because you have pity on
our dust and ashes, and it was pleasing in your sight to
reform my deformity. Inside me your good was working
on me to make me restless until you should become clear
and certain to my inward sight. Through the hidden hand
of your healing art my swelling abated and from day to
day the troubled and clouded sight of my mind grew better
through the stinging ointment of a healthy sorrow.

9   FIRST YOU WISHED to show me how *Thou resistest the proud but givest grace to the humble* and
how great was your mercy in showing to men the way
of humility in that the Word was made flesh and dwelt
among men. And so by means of a man I knew (he was
an extraordinarily conceited person) you brought to my
notice some books written by the Platonists, which had

been translated from Greek into Latin. In these books I found it stated, not of course in the same words but to precisely the same effect and with a number of different sorts of reasons, that: *In the beginning was the Word, and the Word was with God, and the Word was God: the Same was in the beginning with God: all things were made by Him, and without Him was nothing made: that which was made by Him is life, and the life was the light of men, and the light shineth in the darkness, and the darkness comprehended it not.* Also that the soul of man, though it *bears witness to the light,* yet itself *is not that light;* but the Word, God Himself, *is that true light that lighteth every man that cometh into the world.* Also that *He was in the world, and the world was made by Him, and the world knew Him not.* But I did not find in the books of the Platonists that: *He came unto His own, and His own received Him not; but as many as received Him, to them gave He power to become the sons of God, as many as believed in His name.*

I also read in these books that God the Word was *born not of flesh nor of blood, nor of the will of man, nor of the will of the flesh, but of God.* But I did not find then that *the Word was made flesh and dwelt among us.* I did discover, as I examined these books, that it was stated in a number of different ways that *the Son was in the form of the Father, and thought it not robbery to be equal with God,* because by nature He was God. But one will not find in the writings of the Platonists that *He emptied Himself, taking the form of a servant, being made in the likeness of men, and found in fashion as a man, humbled Himself, and became obedient unto death, even the death of the cross: wherefore God exalted Him from the dead, and gave Him a name above every name, that at the name of Jesus every knee should bow, of things in heaven, and things in earth, and things under the earth; and that every tongue should confess that the Lord Jesus is in the glory of God the Father.*

I did find there that your only-begotten Son was before all times and beyond all times and remains unchangeable, coeternal with you, and that *of His fullness souls receive*, that they may be blessed; also that by participation of the wisdom that abides in them they are renewed so as to become wise. But I did not find that *in due time He died for the ungodly*, or that *Thou sparedst not Thine only Son, but deliveredst Him for us all*. For *Thou hiddest these things from the wise, and revealedst them to babes;* so that they *that labor and are heavy laden might come unto Him and He refresh them*, because *He is meek and lowly in heart, and the meek He directeth in judgment, and the gentle He teacheth His ways, beholding our lowliness and trouble, and forgiving all our sins*. But those who, like actors on the stage, are raised up above the general level in their supposedly superior learning do not hear him saying: *Learn of Me, for I am meek and lowly in heart, and ye shall find rest to your souls. Although they knew God, yet they glorify Him not as God, nor are thankful, but wax vain in their thoughts, and their foolish heart is darkened; professing that they were wise, they became fools*.

I read there too that they had *changed the glory of Thy incorruptible nature* into idols and images of various kinds, *into the likeness of the image of corruptible man, and birds and beasts and creeping things*, indeed into that Egyptian food for which Esau lost his birthright, since that people which was your firstborn worshiped the head of a four-footed beast instead of you, turning in their hearts back to Egypt, and bowing down their soul, your image, in front of the image of a *calf that eateth hay*. I found these things here, but I did not feed on them. For it pleased you, Lord, to take away the reproach of inferiority from Jacob and to cause the elder to serve the younger, and you have called the Gentiles into your inheritance. I myself had come to you from the Gentiles, and I thought of the gold which you willed that your people should carry away from Egypt, since it was yours wherever it was. And you had said to the Athenians by your apostle that *in Thee we live and move and have our being, as certain of their own poets had said*, and for sure these books that I was reading came from Athens. But I did not set my mind on the idols of the Egyptians *which they served with the gold that was yours, changing the truth of God into a lie and worshiping and serving the creature more than the creator.*

10 I WAS ADMONISHED by all this to return to my own self, and, with you to guide me, I entered into the innermost part of myself, and I was able to do this because you were my helper. I entered and I saw with my soul's eye (such as it was) an unchangeable light shining above this eye of my soul and above my mind. It was not the ordinary light which is visible to all flesh, nor something of the same sort, only bigger, as though it might be our ordinary light shining much more brightly and filling everything with its greatness. No, it was not like that; it was different, entirely different from anything of the kind. Nor was it above my mind as oil floats on water or as the heaven is above the earth. It was higher than I, because it made me, and I was lower because I was made by it. He who knows truth knows that light, and he who knows that light knows eternity. Love knows it. O eternal truth and true love and beloved eternity! You are my God; to you I sigh by day and by night. And when I first knew you, you raised me up so that I could see that there was something to see and that I still lacked the ability to see it. And you beat back the weakness of my sight, blazing upon me with your rays, and I trembled in love and in dread, and I found that I was far distant from you, in a region of total unlikeness, as if I were hearing your voice from on high saying: "I am the food of grown men. Grow and you shall feed upon me. And you will not, as with the food of the body, change me into yourself, but you will be changed into me." And I learned that *Thou, for iniquity, chastenest man and Thou madest my soul to consume away like a spider.* And I said: "Is truth therefore nothing because it is not extended through any kind of space, whether finite or infinite?" And from far away you cried out to me: "I am that I am." And I heard, as one hears things in the heart, and there was no longer any reason at all for me to doubt. I would sooner doubt my own existence than the existence of that truth *which is clearly seen being understood by those things which are made.*

11 AND I CONSIDERED the other things which are below you, and I saw that, in a complete sense, they neither are nor are not in existence. They are, since they are from you; they are not, since they are not what you are. For that which truly is, is that which remains unchangeably. *It is good then for me to hold fast unto God;* because if I do not remain in Him, I shall not be able to remain in myself. But He, remaining in Himself, renews all things. And *Thou art my Lord, since Thou standest not in need of my goodness.*

12 AND IT BECAME clear to me that things which are subject to corruption are good. They would not be subject to corruption if they were either supremely good or not good at all; for, if they were supremely good, they would be incorruptible, and, if there was nothing good in them, there would be nothing which could be corrupted. For corruption does harm, and, unless what is good in a thing is diminished, no harm could be done. Therefore, either corruption does no harm (which is impossible), or (which is quite certain) all things which suffer corruption are deprived of something good in them. Supposing them to be deprived of all good, they will cease to exist altogether. For, if they continue to exist and can no longer be corrupted, they will be better than before, because they will be permanently beyond the reach of corruption. What indeed could be more monstrous than to assert that things could become better by losing all their goodness? So if they are deprived of all good, they will cease to exist altogether. Therefore, so long as they exist, they are good. Therefore, all things that are, are good, and as to that evil, the origin of which I was seeking for, it is not a substance, since, if it were a substance, it would be good. For it would either have to be an incorruptible substance (which is the highest form of goodness) or else a corruptible substance (which, unless it had good in it, could not be corruptible). So I saw plainly and clearly that you have made all things good, nor are there any substances at all which you have not made. And because you did not make all things equal, therefore they each and all have their existence; because they are good individually, and at the same time they are altogether very good, because our God *made all things very good.*

13 TO YOU, THEN, there is no such thing at all as evil. And the same is true not only of you but of your whole creation; since there is nothing outside it to break in and corrupt the order which you have imposed on it. But in some of its parts there are some things which are considered evil because they do not harmonize with other parts; yet with still other parts they do harmonize and are good and they are good in themselves. And all these things which do not fit in with each other do fit in with that lower part of creation which we call the earth, which has its own cloudy and windy sky which again is fitting to it. Far be it that I should say: "I wish these things did not exist," because even if these were the only things I saw, though certainly I should long for something better yet, still for these things alone I ought to praise you; for things from the earth show that you are to be praised—*dragons, and all deeps, fire, hail, snow, ice, and stormy wind, which fulfill Thy Word; mountains, and all hills, fruitful trees and all cedars; beasts and all cattle, creeping things and flying fowls; kings of the earth, and all people, princes and all judges of the earth; young men and maidens, old men and young, praise Thy name.* And since from the heavens these *praise Thee, praise Thee, our God, in* *the heights, all Thy angels, all Thy hosts, sun and moon, all the stars and light, the heaven of heavens, and the waters that be above the heavens, praise Thy name.* So I no longer desired better things. I had envisaged all things in their totality, and, with a sounder judgment, I realized that, while higher things are certainly better than lower things, all things together are better than the higher things by themselves.

14 IT IS THE MARK of an unsound mind to be displeased with any single thing in our creation and so it was with me, when I was displeased with many of the things which you made. And because my soul did not dare to be displeased with my God, I refused to admit that whatever did displease it was yours. And from this point it had gone on to hold the view that there are two substances, and here it found no rest and only talked perversely. And next it had gone back again and made for itself a God to fill the infinite distances of all space, and it had imagined this God to be you and had placed it in its own heart, thus again becoming the temple of its own idol, a temple abominable to you. But you, though I was not aware of it, laid your kindly hand upon my head and covered up my eyes so that they should not see vanity, and then I relaxed a little from myself, and sleep fell upon my madness. And I woke up in you and saw you infinite in a different way, and that sight was not from the eyes of the flesh.

15 AND I LOOKED AT other things and saw that they owe their existence to you and are all bounded in you, not in a spatial sense, but because your being contains everything in the hand of your truth, and all things are true insofar as they exist, and the only meaning of falsehood is when something is thought to exist when it does not. And I saw that all things fitted in not only with their places but with their times, and that you, who alone are eternal, did not begin to work after the passage of innumerable spaces of time, since all spaces of time, both past and future, could neither go nor come without your permanent presence and operation.

16 I KNEW FROM my own experience that there is nothing strange in the fact that a sick person will find uneatable the same bread which a healthy person enjoys, or that good eyes love the light and bad eyes hate it. Your justice too displeases the wicked, and even more displeasing are vipers and reptiles, though you created them good and well fitted to the lower parts of your creation, and to these lower parts of creation the wicked themselves are well fitted and become the better fitted the more they are unlike you, although in becoming more like you they will become better fitted to the higher parts of your creation. And I asked: "What is wickedness?" and found that it is not a substance but a perversity of the will turning away from you, God, the supreme substance, toward lower things—casting away, as it were, its own insides, and swelling with desire for what is outside it.

17 AND I FELT wonder at the thought that now I loved you and not a phantom instead of you. But I did not stay in the enjoyment of my God; I was swept away to you by your own beauty, and then I was torn away from you by my own weight and fell back groaning toward these lower things. Carnal habit was this weight. But there remained with me the memory of you; I knew with certainty that it was to you that I must cling, but I knew too that I was not yet capable of doing so; because *the body which is corrupted, presseth down the soul, and the earthly tabernacle weighteth down the mind that museth upon many things.* I was perfectly sure of this, *that Thy invisible works from the creation of the world are clearly seen, being understood by the things that are made, even Thy eternal power and Godhead.* For I considered how it was that I recognized the beauty of bodies, whether in the heaven or on earth, and what criterion I had to make a correct judgment of changing things and to say: "This is as it should be, this is not." So, as I considered how it was that I came to make these judgments which I did make, I had discovered that above my changing mind was the unchangeable and true eternity of truth. And so I went on by stages from bodies to the soul which perceives by means of the bodily senses, and from this to the inner power of the soul to which the bodily senses present external things. The faculties of animals extend as far as this, and from this point I went on to the faculty of reason to which sense data are referred for judgment. This also found itself in me to be something subject to change. It then, as it were, raised itself up to the level of its own understanding, freed my thought from the power of habit, and withdrew itself from those crowds of contradictory phantasms, so that it might discover what was that light with which it was illumined when, without the least hesitation, it cried out that the unchangeable is to be preferred to the changeable, and how it was that it had knowledge of the unchangeable itself: for unless it had knowledge in some way of the unchangeable, it could in no way prefer it with certainty to the changeable. And then, in the flash of a trembling glance, my mind arrived at That Which Is. Now indeed I saw your *invisible things understood by the things which are made,* but I had not the power to keep my eye steadily fixed; in my weakness I felt myself falling back and returning again to my habitual ways, carrying nothing with me except a loving memory of it and a longing for something which may be described as a kind of food of which I had perceived the fragrance but which I was not yet able to eat.

18   AND I TRIED to find a way of gaining the strength necessary for enjoying you, and I could not find it until I embraced that *Mediator betwixt God and men, the Man Christ Jesus, who is over all, God* *blessed for evermore,* calling to me and saying, *I am the way, the truth and the life,* and mingling with our flesh that food which I lacked strength to take; for *the Word was made flesh,* so that your wisdom, by which you created all things, might give its milk to our infancy.

I was not humble enough to possess Jesus in His humility as my God, nor did I know what lesson was taught by His weakness. For your Word, the eternal truth, high above the highest parts of your creation, raises up to Itself those who are subdued; but in this lower world He built for Himself a humble dwelling out of our clay, by means of which He might detach from themselves those who were to be subdued and bring them over to Himself, healing the swelling of their pride and fostering their love; so that instead of going further in their own self-confidence they should put on weakness, seeing at their feet divinity in the weakness that it had put on by wearing our "coat of skin"; and then, weary, they should cast themselves down upon that divinity which, rising, would bear them up aloft.

19 But this was not the way I thought then. I thought of my Lord Christ simply as a man of the very highest wisdom, whom no one could equal; and in particular it seemed to me that His miraculous birth from a virgin—an example of how temporal things should be despised for the sake of obtaining immortality—showed such divine care for us that He deserved full authority over us as a master. But I had not the faintest notion of the mystery contained in "The Word was made flesh." All that I had gathered from the written tradition about Him (accounts of how He ate, drank, slept, walked, was glad, was sad, preached) led me to believe that His flesh had only become united with your Word by means of a human soul and a human mind. This must be known to everyone who knows the immutability of your Word, and I, within the limits of my capacity, did now know this without having any doubt

about it at all. For to be now moving and now not moving
the limbs of the body by an act of will, to be now feeling
some emotion and now not feeling it; to be at one moment
uttering wisdom by means of the signs of speech and at
the next moment to be silent—these are all marks of a
soul and a mind which are mutable. And if the written
tradition about Him were false on these points, all the rest
too would come under suspicion of falsehood, and there
would be no sure faith in Scripture left for mankind. And
so, since what is written in Scripture is true, I recognized
in Christ a complete man; not merely with a man's body
or with the body and soul of a man and not a man's mind,
but altogether a man, and I thought that He was to be
preferred to others, not because He was Truth in person,
but because of the exceptional qualities of His human
nature and His more perfect participation in wisdom.

Alypius, on the other hand, thought that the Catholic
belief in a God clothed in flesh meant that in Christ
there were God and the flesh, but not the soul; he did
not think that they ascribed to Him a human mind. And
since he was convinced that the actions recorded of
Christ could only have been done by a vital and rational
creature, his way toward the Christian faith itself was all
the more laborious. Later he realized that this was the
error of the Apollinarian heretics and he came over joyfully to the Catholic faith. As to me, I must admit that
it was only some time afterward that I learned how in
the understanding of "The Word was made flesh" Catholic truth is distinguished from the false view of Photi-
nus. Indeed by proving heretics to be wrong we bring
into clearer light what your Church believes and what
sound doctrine is. *For there must also be heresies, that
the approved may be made manifest among the weak.*

20 BUT THEN, after reading these books of the Platonists which taught me to seek for a truth
which was incorporeal, I came to see your *invisible
things, understood by those things which are made.* I fell

back again from this point, but still I had an apprehension of what, through the darkness of my mind, I was not able to contemplate; I was certain that you are and that you are infinite, yet not in the sense of being diffuse through space whether infinite or finite: that you truly are, and are always the same, not in any part or by any motion different or otherwise: also that all other things are from you, as is proved most certainly by the mere fact that they exist. On all these points I was perfectly certain, but I was still too weak to be able to enjoy you. I talked away as if I were a finished scholar; but, if I had not sought the way to you in Christ our Saviour, what would have been finished would have been my soul. For I had begun to want to have the reputation of a wise man; my punishment was within me, but I did not weep; I was merely puffed up with my knowledge. Where was that charity which builds from the foundation of humility, the foundation which is Christ Jesus? Humility was not a subject which those books would ever have taught me. Yet I believe that you wanted me to come upon these books before I made a study of your Scriptures. You wanted the impression made by them on me to be printed in my memory, so that when later I had become, as it were, tamed by your books (your fingers dressing my wounds), I should be able to see clearly what the difference is between presumption and confession, between those who see their goal without seeing how to get there and those who see the way which leads to that happy country which is there for us not only to perceive but to live in. For if I had been first trained in your Scriptures and by my familiarity with them had found you growing sweet to me, and had then afterward come upon these books of the Platonists, it is possible that they might have swept me away from the solid basis of piety; or, even if I had held firmly to that healthy disposition which I had imbibed, I might have thought that the same disposition could be acquired by someone who had read only the Platonic books.

21 So I MOST GREEDILY seized upon the venerable writings of your spirit and in particular the works of the apostle Paul. In the past it had sometimes seemed to me that he contradicted himself and that what he said conflicted with the testimonies of the law and the prophets; but all these difficulties had now disappeared; I saw one and the same face of pure eloquence and learned *to rejoice with trembling.* Having begun, I discovered that everything in the Platonists which I had found true was expressed here, but it was expressed to the glory of your grace; so that whoever sees should not *so glory as if he had not received*—received, indeed, not only what he sees but also the power to see it; for *what hath he, which he hath not received.* I found too that one is not only instructed so as to see you, who are the same forever, but also so as to grow strong enough to lay hold on you, and he who cannot see you for the distance, may yet walk along the road by which he will arrive and see you and lay hold on you. For, though a man *be delighted with the law of God after the inner man,* what shall he do about that *other law in his members which warreth against the law of his mind, and bringeth him into captivity to the law of sin, which is in his members?* For, *Thou art righteous, O Lord, but we have sinned and committed iniquity, and have done wickedly,* and your hand has grown heavy upon us, and we have justly been handed over to that ancient sinner, the president of death; because he persuaded our will to be like his will, whereby he did not stand in your truth. *What shall wretched man do? Who shall deliver him from the body of this death, but only Thy Grace,* through Jesus *Christ, our Lord,* whom you have begotten coeternal and *formedst in the beginning of Thy ways, in whom the prince of this world found nothing worthy of death,* yet killed him, and *the handwriting, which was contrary to us, was blotted out.*

None of this is to be found in the books of the Platonists. Their pages make no mention of the face and look of pity, the tears of confession, your *sacrifice—a troubled spirit, a broken and a contrite heart,* the salvation of the people, *the bridal city, the earnest of the Holy Ghost, the cup of our redemption.* No one sings there, *Shall not my soul be submitted unto God? For of Him cometh my salvation. For He is my God and my salvation, my guardian, I shall no more be moved.* No one there hears him call, *Come unto Me all ye that labor.* They are too proud to *learn of Him; because He is meek and lowly of heart; for these things hast Thou hid from the wise and prudent, and hast revealed them unto babes.* It is one thing to see from a mountaintop in the forests the land of peace in the distance and not to find the way to it and to struggle in vain along impassable tracks, ambushed and beset on all sides by fugitive deserters under their chief *the Lion and the Dragon,* and it is another thing to hold to the way that leads there, a road built and guarded by our heavenly General, where no banditry is committed by deserters from the celestial army; for they avoid it like the plague. In marvelous ways these things grew and fixed themselves in the depths of my being as I read that *least of Thy apostles,* and had meditated upon your works and had trembled.

Book VIII

1 MY GOD, let me remember with thanks and let me confess to you your mercies done to me. Let my bones be penetrated with your love and let them say: *Who is like unto Thee, O Lord? Thou hast broken my bonds in sunder, I will offer unto Thee the sacrifice of thanksgiving.* I will tell how it was that you broke my bonds, and all your worshipers who hear this will say: "Blessed be the Lord in heaven and in earth, great and wonderful is His name."

Your words had stuck in my heart and *I was hedged around about on all sides by Thee.* Of your eternal life I was now certain, although I had seen it in an enigma and *as through a glass.* But I had ceased to have any doubt that there was an incorruptible substance from which came every substance. I no longer desired to be more certain of you, only to stand more firmly in you.

In my own temporal life everything was unsettled and *my heart had to be purged from the old leaven.* The way—the Saviour Himself—pleased me; but I was still reluctant to enter its narrowness. It was you who put the idea into my mind (and the idea seemed good to me) to go to Simplicianus. He seemed to me a good servant of yours and your grace shone in him. I had heard too that from his youth he had lived a life devoted to you. He had now grown old, and it seemed to me that he must have experienced much and learned much as a result of having lived so long in so earnestly following your way, and so indeed he had. So, after telling him of my troubles, I wanted him to make use of his experience and learning in order to show me the best means by which someone feeling as I did could set his foot on your way.

For I saw the Church full, and one went this way, and another that way. But I was displeased with the worldly life which I was leading. It was a really great burden to me and to help me bear such a heavy form of slavery I no longer had the impulse and encouragement of my old hopes and desires for position and wealth. Compared with your sweetness and the beauty of your house, which I loved, these things no longer pleased me. But I was still closely bound by my need of woman. Not that the apostle forbade me to marry, although he might recommend something better, his great wish being that all men should be as he was. But I lacked the strength and was inclined to choose the softer place; and because of this one thing everything else with me was in confusion; I was tired out and wasted away with gnawing anxieties, because I was compelled to put up with all sorts of things which I did not want simply because they were inseparable from that state of living with a wife to which I was utterly and entirely bound. I had heard from the mouth of Truth that *there were some eunuchs, which had made themselves eunuchs for the Kingdom of heaven's sake; but,* he says, *let him who can receive it, receive it. Surely vain are all men who are ignorant of God, and could not out of the good things which are seen, find out Him who is good.* But I was no longer in that kind of vanity; I had gone beyond it, and, by the common witness of all creation, I had found you, our Creator, and your Word, God with you, and one God together with you, by whom you created all things. But there is also another kind of impiety, that of those *who knowing God, glorified Him not as God, neither were thankful.* I had fallen into this wickedness too, but your right hand upheld me, took me out of it, and placed me where I might recover. For you have said to man, *Behold, the fear of the Lord is wisdom,* and *Desire not to seem wise;* because they *who affirmed themselves to be wise, became fools.* And I had now found that pearl of great price, and I ought to have sold all that I had and bought it. But I hesitated.

2 So I WENT TO Simplicianus who, in the matter of receiving grace, had been the father of Ambrose, now bishop, and indeed Ambrose loved him as a father. I described to him the winding paths of my error. But when I told him that I had read some books of the Platonists which had been translated into Latin by Victorinus—once professor of rhetoric at Rome, who, so I had heard, had died a Christian—he congratulated me for not having fallen upon the writings of other philosophers full of *fallacies and deceits, after the rudiments of this world,* whereas in the Platonists God and His Word are everywhere implied. Then, in order to lead me toward the humility of Christ *(hidden from the wise, and revealed to little ones),* he went on to speak of Victorinus himself, with whom he had been on very friendly terms when he was in Rome. I shall make no secret of what he told me about him, for it is a story which ought to be confessed to you, containing, as it does, great praise of your grace. For Victorinus was an extremely learned old man, an expert scholar in all the liberal sciences, one who had read and weighed very many of the works of the philosophers; one who had been the teacher of numbers of distinguished senators and who, because of the exceptional brilliance of his teaching, had earned and accepted the honor of having his statue set up in the Roman forum, a thing which the citizens of this world regard as something quite remarkable, and up to old age he worshiped idols and took part in those sacrilegious ceremonies which were the craze with nearly all the Roman nobility, who had inspired the people with their enthusiasm for Osiris and

> The dog Anubis and that monstrous brood
> Of deity which once took arms and fought
> In arms against Minerva, Neptune, Venus

—gods which Rome had conquered and to which she now prayed, and for all these years old Victorinus, with his thundering eloquence, had been the champion of these gods; yet he did not blush to become the child of your Christ, an infant at your font, bending his neck to the yoke of humility and submitting his forehead to the ignominy of the Cross.

O Lord, Lord, *Which has bowed the heavens and come down, touched the mountains and they did smoke,* by what means did you find your way into that man's heart? According to Simplicianus, he read the Holy Scripture and examined all Christian literature with the most thorough and exact attention. He then said to Simplicianus—not in public, but in a private friendly conversation—"I should like you to know that I am now a Christian." Simplicianus replied: "That I will not believe, and I shall not count you as a Christian until I see you in the Church of Christ." Victorinus smiled and said: "Is it the walls, then, that make Christians?" And he often repeated that he was a Christian, and Simplicianus often made the same reply which was again countered by the joke about the walls. For Victorinus was afraid of offending his friends, who were important people and worshipers of these devils; he feared a great torrent of ill will falling upon him from the height of their Babylonian dignity, as from the tops of the cedars of Lebanon which the Lord had not yet brought down. But from his reading and deep meditation he drew strength. He feared that, if he was afraid to confess Christ before men, Christ might deny him in front of the holy angels, and it seemed to him that he was guilty of a great crime in being ashamed of the sacraments of the humility of your Word, while not being ashamed of the sacrilegious rites of those proud demons, in which he, imitating their pride, had taken part. So he turned his pride against what was vain, and kept his humility for the truth. Quite suddenly and unexpectedly he said to Simplicianus, as Simplicianus himself told me, "Let us go to the Church. I want to be made a Christian." And Simplicianus, who could not contain himself for joy, went along with him. Soon after he had received instruction in the first mysteries, he gave in his name as one who wished to be regenerated by baptism. Rome wondered and the Church rejoiced. The proud *saw and were wroth; they gnashed with their teeth and melted away.* But the Lord God was the hope of your servant, and *he regarded not vanities and lying* madness.

Finally the time came for him to make his profession of faith. At Rome this was usually done by those who were about to enter into your grace, and there was a fixed form of words which was learned by heart and spoken from a platform in the sight of the faithful. In the case of Victorinus, however, so Simplicianus told me, the priests gave him the opportunity to make his profession in a less public manner—as was often allowed to those who seemed likely to be frightened or embarrassed by the ceremony. But Victorinus preferred to declare openly his salvation in front of the holy congregation. In the past he had taught rhetoric and there had been no salvation in that; yet he had publicly professed it. He had shown no nervousness when using his own words in front of crowds of people who could scarcely be described as sane; why, then, in front of your meek flock, should he fear to pronounce your Word? So, when he mounted the platform to make his profession, all those who knew him (and who was there who did not?) began to whisper his name one to another in glad murmurs. From the lips of the whole rejoicing people came the soft sound: "Victorinus, Victorinus." Quickly the sound had arisen because of the exultation they felt when they saw him, and now quickly they became silent again so as to hear him speak. With a fine confidence he declared openly the true faith, and they all wished that they could draw him into their very hearts. And in their love and their rejoicing (for these were the hands they used) they did take him into their hearts.

3   O GOOD GOD, what is it in men that makes them rejoice more when a soul that has been de-spaired of and is in very great danger is saved than when

there has always been hope and the danger has not been so serious? For you too, merciful father, dost *more rejoice over one penitent than over ninety-nine just persons, that need no repentance.* We too are filled with joy whenever we hear the story of how the sheep which had strayed was brought back on the exultant shoulders of the shepherd and of how the coin was put back into your treasury with all the neighbors of the woman who found it rejoicing. And the joy we feel in the solemn service of your house brings tears to our eyes, when in your house we hear read the story of your *younger son, that he was dead and lived again; had been lost and is found.* Indeed you rejoice in us and you rejoice in your angels who are holy in holy charity. For you are always the same, and as to those things which do not always exist or do not always exist in the same way, you know all of them, always and in the same way.

What is it in the soul, then, which makes it take more pleasure in the finding or recovery of things it loves than in the continual possession of them? There are all sorts of other examples of this; indeed the evidence is everywhere, simply crying out: "It is so." The victorious general has his triumph; but he would not have been victorious if he had not fought a battle, and the more danger there was in the battle, the more joy there is in the triumph. Sailors are tossed by a storm and in danger of shipwreck; they all grow pale at the thought of approaching death; then sky and sea become calm and their joy is just as excessive as was their fear. A friend is ill and his pulse shows that he is in danger; all who want him to be well become sick in mind with him; then he recovers, though he cannot walk yet quite as easily as he used to do; but there is already more joy than there was before, when he was well and perfectly able to walk. Also with regard to the ordinary pleasures of life, men seek them by way of difficulty and discomfort which are voluntary and self-chosen and not the kind which comes upon them unexpectedly and against their wills. There is no pleasure in eating or drinking unless it

is preceded by the discomfort of being hungry or thirsty.
Drunkards eat various kinds of salty things in order to
produce an uncomfortable dryness, and, when this is al-
leviated by drink, they feel pleasure. It is also customary
for girls who are engaged not to be given over immediately to their bridegroom, the idea being that the husband may hold a woman cheap unless, while engaged,
he has sighed for the long time he has had to wait.

We notice this, then, in pleasures that are foul and
disgraceful and also in pleasures which are lawful and
permitted; we notice it in the pure sincerity of friendship,
and also in the case of him who was dead and became
alive again, who had been lost and was found. Everywhere we find that the more pain there is first, the more
joy there is after. Why is this, my Lord God? For you
are to yourself eternal joy, you yourself are joy, and
those beings who are around you find their joy forever
in you. Why is it that this part of the universe alternates
between deprivation and fulfillment, between discord
and harmony? Or is this its condition, the measure given
to it by you when, from the heights of heaven to the
depths of earth, from the beginning to the end of time,
from the angel to the worm, from the first movement to
the last, you settled all the varieties of good and all your
just works each in its proper place, each to be in its
appointed time? I am abashed when I think how high
you are in what is highest, how deep in what is deepest.
Nowhere do you depart from us, and hard it is for us to
return to you.

4   COME, LORD, act upon us and rouse us up and
call us back. Fire us, clutch us, let your sweet
fragrance grow upon us! Let us love, let us run! Certainly there are many who from a deeper hell of blindness than Victorinus come back to you and approach
you and are enlightened with that light which *those who
receive, receive power from Thee to become Thy sons.*
But if they are not so well known in the world there is

not so much rejoicing even among those who do know them; for when many people rejoice together, the joy of each individual is all the richer, since each one inflames the other and the warmth spreads throughout them all. Then too by the mere fact of being well known they have a great influence on others, leading them to salvation; they go first and many will follow in their steps. Thus even those who have gone before them on the same way feel great joy, and the joy is not only for them. Indeed we must certainly not think that in your tabernacle the persons of the rich should be more welcome than the poor, or the people of birth more welcome than the ordinary man. Since *Thou hast chosen the weak things of the world, to confound the strong, and the base things of this world, and the things despised hast Thou chosen, and those things which are not, that Thou mightest bring to nought things that are.* These words of yours were spoken by the tongue of *the least of your apostles.* Yet when, as the result of his good service, the pride of Paulus the proconsul was so beaten down that he came under the light yoke of your Christ and became a simple subject of the great king, the apostle, to mark the glory of such a victory, wished to be called Paul instead of Saul, as he was called previously. For the defeat of the enemy is all the more conspicuous when one wins over from him a man of whom he has a particular hold and through whom he can particularly influence others. And people of importance in the world satisfy both conditions; their nobility gives him a particular hold over them, and their authority enables him to use them as an influence over others. It was natural, therefore, for there to be a particular welcome for the heart of Victorinus, which the devil had held as an impregnable stronghold, and for the tongue of Victorinus, which the devil had made use of as a strong and keen weapon for the destruction of so many. And it was right for your sons to feel a particular joy because our King had bound the strong man, and they saw his *vessels taken from him and cleansed,* and *made meet for Thy honor, and become serviceable for the Lord, unto every good work.*

5   WHEN THIS MAN of yours, Simplicianus, told me all this about Victorinus, I was on fire to be like him, and this, of course, was why he had told me the story. He told me this too—that in the time of the Emperor Julian, when a law was passed forbidding Christians to teach literature and rhetoric, Victorinus had obeyed the law, preferring to give up his talking-shop rather than your Word, by which you make even the tongues of infants eloquent. In this I thought that he was not only brave but lucky; because he had got the chance of giving all his time to you. This was just what I longed for myself, but I was held back, and I was held back not by fetters put on me by someone else, but by the iron bondage of my own will. The enemy held my will and made a chain out of it and bound me with it. From a perverse will came lust, and slavery to lust became a habit, and the habit, being constantly yielded to, became a necessity. These were like links, hanging each to each (which is why I called it a chain), and they held me fast in a hard slavery. And the new will which I was beginning to have and which urged me to worship you in freedom and to enjoy you, God, the only certain joy, was not yet strong enough to overpower the old will which by its oldness had grown hard in me. So my two wills, one old, one new, one carnal, one spiritual, were in conflict, and they wasted my soul by their discord.

In this way my personal experience enabled me to understand what I had read—that *the flesh lusteth against the spirit and the spirit against the flesh.* I, no doubt, was on both sides, but I was more myself when I was on the side which I approved of for myself than when I was on the side of which I disapproved. For it was no longer really I myself who was on this second side, since there to a great extent I was rather suffering things against my will than doing them voluntarily. Yet it was my own fault that habit fought back so strongly against me; for I had come willingly where I now did not will to be. And who has any right to complain when just punishment overtakes the sinner? Nor did I have any longer the excuse which I used to think I had when I said that the reason why I had not yet forsaken the world and given myself up to your service was because I could not see the truth clearly. Now I could see it perfectly clearly. But I was still tied down to earth and refused to take my place in your army. And I was just as frightened of being freed from all my hampering baggage as I ought to have been frightened of being hampered. The pack of this world was a kind of pleasant weight upon me, as happens in sleep, and the thoughts in which I meditated on you were like the efforts of someone who tries to get up but is so overcome with drowsiness that he sinks back again into sleep. Of course no one wants to sleep forever, and everyone in his senses would agree that it is better to be awake; yet all the same, when we feel a sort of lethargy in our limbs, we often put off the moment of shaking off sleep, and, even though it is time to get up, we gladly take a little longer in bed, conscious though we may be that we should not be doing so. In just the same way I was quite certain that it was better to give myself up to your charity rather than to give in to my own desires; but, though the former course was a conviction to which I gave my assent, the latter was a pleasure to which I gave my consent. For I had no answer to make to you when you called me: *Awake, thou that sleepest, and arise from the dead, and Christ shall give thee light.* And, while you showed me wherever I looked that what you said was true, I, convinced by the truth, could still find nothing at all to say except lazy words spoken half asleep: "A minute," "just a minute," "just a little time longer." But there was no limit to the minutes, and the little time longer went a long way. It was in vain that *I delighted in Thy law according to the inner man, when another law in my members rebelled against the law of my mind, and led me captive under the*

law of sin which was in my members. For the law of sin
is the strong force of habit, which drags the mind along
and controls it even against its will—though deservedly,
since the habit was voluntarily adopted. *Who then should
deliver me thus wretched from the body of this death, but
Thy grace only, through Jesus Christ our Lord?*

6   Now, LORD, my helper and my redeemer, I
shall tell and confess to your name how it was
that you freed me from the bondage of my desire for
sex, in which I was so closely fettered, and from my
slavery to the affairs of this world. I was leading my
usual life; my anxiety was growing greater and greater,
and every day I sighed to you. I went often to your
Church, whenever I had time to spare from all that business under the weight of which I was groaning. Alypius
was with me. He was free from his official legal work
after a third term as assessor and was now waiting to
sell his legal advice to anyone who came along, just as
I was selling the ability to make speeches—if such an
ability can be imparted by teaching. Nebridius, as an
act of friendship to us, had consented to teach under
Verecundus, a great friend of us all, a citizen and elementary schoolmaster of Milan. He had been very eager
to have Nebridius on his staff and indeed had claimed
it as something due from our friendship that one of us
should come and give him the help and support which
he badly needed. Nebridius was not influenced by any
desire for profit; he could have done better for himself
by teaching literature, if he had wanted. But he was the
kindest and best of friends, and, being always ready to
help others, would not turn down our request. He conducted himself very carefully in his work, being unwilling
to become known in what are regarded by the world as
"distinguished circles," and avoiding everything which
could disturb his peace of mind; for he wanted to have
his mind free and at leisure for as many hours as possible

so as to pursue wisdom, to read about it, or to hear about it.

One day, when Alypius and I were at home (Nebridius, for some reason which I cannot remember, was away) we were visited by a man called Ponticianus who, coming from Africa, was a fellow countryman of ours and who held an important appointment at the emperor's court. He had something or other which he wanted to ask us, and we sat down to talk. In front of us was a table for playing games on, and he happened to notice a book lying on the table. He took it, opened it, and found that it was the apostle Paul. He was quite surprised at this, since he had imagined it would be one of the books over which I wearied myself out in the course of my profession. Next he began to smile and, looking closely at me, told me that he was not only surprised but pleased at his unexpected discovery that I had this book and only this book at my side. For he was a Christian, and baptized. He often knelt before you, our God, in Church, praying long and frequently to you. I told him that I gave the greatest attention to these works of Scripture, and then, on his initiative, a conversation began about the Egyptian monk Antony, whose name was very well known among your servants, although Alypius and I up to this time had never heard of him. When Ponticianus discovered this he talked all the more about him, since he wanted us in our ignorance, at which he was much surprised, to learn more about such a great man. And we were amazed as we heard of these wonderful works of yours which had been witnessed by so many people, had been done in the true faith and the Catholic Church, and all so recently—indeed practically in our own times. All of us were full of wonder, Alypius and I at the importance of what we were hearing, Ponticianus at the fact that we had never heard the story before.

He went on to speak of the communities living in monasteries, of their way of life which was full of the sweet fragrance of you, and of the fruitful deserts in the wilderness, about which we knew nothing. There was

actually a monastery in Milan outside the walls of the
city. It was full of good brothers and was under the care
of Ambrose, but we had not even heard of this. So Ponticianus went on speaking and we sat quiet, listening to
him eagerly. In the course of his talk he told us how
once, when the emperor was at Treves and busy with
holding the chariot races in the Circus, he himself with
three friends had gone for a walk in the afternoon
through the gardens near the city walls. It happened that
they walked in two groups, one of the three going one
way with him, and the others going another way by
themselves. These other two, as they strolled along, happened to come to a small house which was inhabited by
some of your servants, *poor in spirit, of whom is the
kingdom of heaven*, and there they found a book in
which was written an account of the life of Antony. One
of the two friends began to read it. He became full of
wonder and excitement and, as he read, he began to
think of how he himself could lead a life like this and,
abandoning his profession in this world, give his service
to you. For these two men were both officials in the
emperor's civil service. Suddenly, then, he was filled with
a holy love; he felt a sober shame, and, angry with himself, he looked toward his friend and said: "Tell me now;
in all this hard work which we do, what are we aiming
at? What is it that we want? Why is it that we are state
officials? Can we have any higher hope at court than to
become friends of the emperor? And is not that a position difficult to hold and full of danger? Indeed does
one not have to go through danger after danger simply
to reach a place that is more dangerous still? And how
long will it take to get there? But, if I want, I can be
the friend of God now, this moment." After saying this,
he turned back to the book, troubled and perplexed by
the new life to which he was giving birth. So he read
on, and his heart, where you saw it, was changed, and,
as soon appeared, his mind shook off the burden of the
world. While he was reading and the waves in his heart
rose and fell, there were times when he cried out against

himself, and then he distinguished the better course and chose it for his own. Now he was yours, and he said to his friend: "I have now broken away from all our hopes and ambitions and have decided to serve God, and I am entering on this service now, this moment, in this place. You may not like to imitate me in this, but you must not oppose me."

The other replied that he would stay with him and be his comrade in so great a service and for so great a reward. Both of them were now yours; they were building their own fortress at the right cost—namely, the forsaking of all that they had and the following of you.

At this point Ponticianus and his companion, who had been walking in a different part of the garden, looking for their friends, came and found them in this place. When they found them, they suggested that they should go back, as it was now nearly sunset. The others however told them of the decision which they had reached and what they proposed to do; they described how the whole thing had started and how their resolution was now fixed, and they begged their friends, if they would not join them, not to interfere with their purpose. Ponticianus and his friend, while not changing from their former ways, did (as Ponticianus told us) weep for themselves and, devoutly and sincerely congratulating the others, asked them to remember them in their prayers; then, with their own hearts still down on the earth, they went off to the palace. But the other two, with their hearts fixed on heaven, remained there in the cottage. Each of these two was engaged to be married, and when the girls to whom they were engaged heard what had happened, they also dedicated their virginity to you.

7   THIS WAS WHAT Ponticianus told us. But you, Lord, while he was speaking, were turning me around so that I could see myself; you took me from behind my own back, which was where I had put myself during the time when I did not want to be observed by

myself, and you set me in front of my own face so that
I could see how foul a sight I was—crooked, filthy, spot-
ted, and ulcerous. I saw and I was horrified, and I had
nowhere to go to escape from myself. If I tried to look
away from myself, Ponticianus still went on with his
story, and again you were setting me in front of myself,
forcing me to look into my own face, so that I might see
my sin and hate it. I did know it, but I pretended that
I did not. I had been pushing the whole idea away from
me and forgetting it.

But now the more ardent was the love I felt for those
two men of whom I was hearing and of how healthfully
they had been moved to give themselves up entirely to
you to be cured, the more bitter was the hatred I felt
for myself when I compared myself with them. Many
years (at least twelve) of my own life had gone by since
the time when I was nineteen and was reading Cicero's
Hortensius and had been fired with an enthusiasm for
wisdom. Yet I was still putting off the moment when,
despising this world's happiness, I should give all my
time to the search for that of which not only the finding
but merely the seeking must be preferred to the discovered treasures and kingdoms of men or to all the pleasures of the body easily and abundantly available. But
I, wretched young man that I was—even more wretched
at the beginning of my youth—had begged you for chastity and had said: "Make me chaste and continent, but
not yet." I was afraid that you might hear me too soon
and cure me too soon from the disease of a lust which
I preferred to be satisfied rather than extinguished. And
I had gone along evil ways, following a sacrilegious superstition—not because I was convinced by it, but simply
preferring it to the other doctrines into which I never
inquired in a religious spirit, but merely attacked them
in a spirit of spite.

I had thought that the reason why I was putting off
from day to day the time when I should despise all
worldly hopes and follow you alone was because I could
see no certainty toward which I could direct my course.

But now the day had come when in my own eyes I was
stripped naked and my conscience cried out against me:
"Can you not hear me? Was it not this that you used to
say, that you would not throw off the burden of vanity
for a truth that was uncertain? Well, look. Now the truth
is certain, and you are still weighed down by your burden. Yet these others, who have not been so worn out
in the search and not been meditating the matter for ten
years or more, have had the weight taken from their
backs and have been given wings to fly."

So I was being gnawed at inside, and as Ponticianus
went on with his story I was lost and overwhelmed in a
terrible kind of shame. When the story was over and the
business about which he had come had been settled he
went away, and I retired into myself. Nor did I leave
anything unsaid against myself. With every scourge of
condemnation I lashed my soul on to follow me now
that I was trying to follow you. And my soul hung back;
it refused to follow, and it could give no excuse for its
refusal. All the arguments had been used already and
had been shown to be false. There remained a mute
shrinking; for it feared like death to be restrained from
the flux of a habit by which it was melting away into
death.

8 AND NOW inside my house great indeed was the
quarrel which I had started with my soul in that
bedroom of my heart which we shared together. My
looks were as disordered as my mind as I turned on
Alypius and cried out to him: "What is wrong with us?
What is this which you have just heard? The unlearned
rise up and *take heaven by force,* while we (look at us!)
with all our learning are wallowing in flesh and blood.
Is it because they have gone ahead that we are ashamed
to follow? And do we feel no shame at not even following at all?" Some such words as these I spoke, and then
the disturbance in my mind tore me away from him,
while he stared at me in silence and amazed. For I

sounded strange to him. My forehead, cheeks, eyes, color of face, and inflection of voice expressed my mind better than the words I used.

There was a garden attached to our lodging, and we had the use of this as of the whole house; for our landlord, the owner of the house, did not live there. To this garden the tumult in my heart had driven me, as to a place where no one could intervene in this passionate suit which I had brought against myself until it could be settled—though how it would be settled you knew, not I. As to me I was mad and dying; but there was sanity in my madness, life in my death; I knew how evil I was; I did not know how well I would be soon.

So I withdrew to the garden and Alypius followed close after me. When he was there, I still felt myself in privacy, and how could he leave me when I was in such a state? We sat down as far as possible from the house. My spirit was in a turmoil; I was boiling with indignation against myself for not entering into your will and covenant, my God, where all my bones cried out that I should enter and praised it to the skies. And the way there is not by ship or chariot or on foot; the distance is not so great as that which I had come from the house to the place where we were sitting. All I had to do was to will to go there, and I would not only go but would immediately arrive; but it was necessary for the will to be resolute and sincere, not the turning and twisting this way and that of a will that was half maimed, struggling, with one part rising and another part falling.

Then in the middle of this storm of mental hesitation I made many movements with my body—the kind of movements which people sometimes want to make, but cannot make, either because they have not the limbs, or because their limbs are bound or weakened by illness or in some way or other prevented from action. But I, if I tore my hair, beat my forehead, locked my fingers together, clasped my knee, was performing these actions because I willed to do so. But I might have willed to do so and still not done so if the power of motion in my limbs had not followed the dictates of my will. So I was performing all sorts of actions where the will to do and the power to do are not the same thing, and I was not doing something the idea of which pleased me incomparably more and which soon after, when I should have the will, I should have the power to do, since when I willed, I should will it thoroughly. For in this matter the power was the same thing as the will, and merely to will was already to perform. And yet this was not done. It was easier for my body to obey the slightest intimation of the soul's will that the limbs should be put immediately in motion than it was for the soul to give obedience to itself so as to carry out by the mere act of willing what was its own great will.

9   WHAT CAN BE the explanation of such an absurdity? Enlighten me with your mercy, so that I may ask the question, if perhaps an answer may be found in the secret places of man's punishment and in those darkest agonies of the sons of Adam. What can be the explanation of such an absurdity? The mind gives an order to the body, and the order is obeyed immediately: the mind gives an order to itself, and there is resistance. The mind orders the hand to move, and such readiness is shown that you can hardly distinguish the command from its execution. Yet the mind is mind, and the hand is body. The mind orders the mind to will; it is the same mind, yet it does not obey. What can be the explanation of such an absurdity? The mind, I say, orders itself to will: it would not give the order, unless it willed it, yet it does not obey the order. The fact is that it does not will the thing entirely; consequently it does not give the order entirely. The force of the order is in the force of the will, and disobedience to the order results from insufficiency of the will. For the will orders that there should be a will—not a different will, but itself. But it is not entire in itself when it gives the order, and therefore its order is not obeyed. For if it were

entire in itself, it would not give the order to will; the will would be there already. So it is not an absurdity partly to will and partly not to will; it is rather a sickness of the soul which is weighed down with habit so that it cannot rise up in its entirety, lifted aloft by truth. So the reason why there are two wills in us is because one of them is not entire, and one has what the other lacks.

10 LET THEM PERISH from your presence, God, as perish empty talkers and seducers of the soul, who, having observed that there are two wills in the act of deliberating, conclude from this that we have in us two minds of two different natures, one good and one evil. They themselves are truly evil, when they hold these evil opinions, and they are just as capable of becoming good if they will realize the truth and agree with the truth, so that your apostle may say to them: *Ye were sometimes darkness, but now light in the Lord.* But these people, by imagining that the nature of the soul is what God is, want to be light, not in the Lord, but in themselves, and the result is that they have become an even deeper darkness, since in their appalling arrogance they have gone further away from you—from you, *the true Light that enlighteneth every man that cometh into the world.* Take heed what you say, and blush for shame: *draw near unto Him and be enlightened, and your faces shall not be ashamed.*

As to me, when I was deliberating about entering the service of the Lord my God, as I had long intended to do, it was I who willed it, and it was I who was unwilling. It was the same "I" throughout. But neither my will nor my unwillingness was whole and entire. So I fought with myself and was torn apart by myself. It was against my will that this tearing apart took place, but this was not an indication that I had another mind of a different nature; it was simply the punishment which I was suffering in my own mind. It was not I, therefore, who caused it, but *the sin dwells in me,* and, being a son of Adam, I was suffering for his sin which was more freely committed.

For if there are as many contrary natures as there are conflicting wills, we shall find that there are not two only, but many more. Suppose a man is wondering whether to go to one of the Manichaean conventicles or to the theater; the Manichees will say: "Here is an example of the two natures, one good, leading in one direction, one bad, leading in another. How else can you explain the hesitation caused by two wills in opposition to each other?" But I should say that both wills are bad—the one that takes a man to the Manichees and the one which takes him to the theater instead. But they of course believe that the will which takes a man to them must necessarily be good. Very well, then. Suppose now the case of one of us who, also with two wills struggling inside him, is wondering whether to go to the theater or to our Church. Will not the Manichees also be in a state of indecision about what to say on this point? They will either have to make an admission which they would be most reluctant to make—namely, that it is a good will which takes a man to our Church, just as the will is good which leads men who have received and are bound by their sacraments to their church; or else they will have to assume that in one man there are two evil natures and two evil wills in conflict, and then what they are always saying will not be true—that there is one evil and one good will. Otherwise they will have to be converted to the truth and not deny that when one is making up one's mind there is just one soul which is pulled in different directions by different wills.

Therefore, they can no longer say, when they observe two conflicting wills in one man, that the conflict is between two opposing minds, of two opposing substances, from two opposing principles—one good, one evil. Their arguments are checked, overthrown, and put out of court by you, God of truth. Take the case, for example, when both wills are bad, as when a man deliberates whether to commit a murder by poison or by a dagger; whether to seize this or that part of another man's property, since he

cannot seize both; whether to squander his money on pleasure or to hoard it up like a miser; whether to go to the
races or to the theater, if they happen both to be on the
same day; or, as a third possibility, this same man may be
wondering whether to commit a theft from someone else's
house, if he gets the chance; or, as a fourth possibility,
whether to commit adultery, supposing that the opportunity occurs at the same time. Now if all these four possibili-
ties become practicable at the same moment and all are
equally desired, though they cannot all be done simultaneously, the mind will be torn apart by four conflicting wills;
indeed, considering the multitude of things which can be
desired, there may be even more than four wills in conflict.
But the Manichees do not hold that there is a similar abundance of different substances.

The same principle holds with regard to wills that are
good. Let me ask them this question: Is it good to take pleasure in reading the Apostle, and also good to take pleasure
in a sober psalm, and also good to discuss the Gospel? In
each case they will reply: "It is good." If then all these
activities at one and the same time offer us equal pleasure, must it not be that different wills are pulling at a
man's heart while he makes up his mind which activity
in particular he should choose? All these wills are good,
yet they conflict with one another until one particular
choice has been made, toward which the whole will,
which was previously divided, now turns entirely. So too
when eternity offers us a higher pleasure and the delight
in some temporal good holds us down below, it is the
same soul which feels both impulses; only its will for
one or the other course is not total and complete, and
consequently it is torn apart and heavily distressed as
truth puts one way first and habit will not allow the
other way to be abandoned.

11 So I was sick and in torture. I reproached myself
much more bitterly than ever; and I turned and
twisted in my chain till I could break quite free. Only a
little of it still held me, but it did still hold me. And you,

Lord, in the secret places of my soul, stood above me in the severity of your mercy, redoubling the lashes of fear and shame, so that I should not give way once more and so that that small weak piece of chain which still remained should not instead of snapping grow strong again and tie me down more firmly than before. I was saying inside myself: "Now, now, let it be now!" and as I spoke the words I was already beginning to go in the direction I wanted to go. I nearly managed it, but I did not quite manage it. Yet I did not slip right back to the beginning; I was a stage above that, and I stood there to regain my breath. And I tried again and I was very nearly there; I was almost touching it and grasping it, and then I was not there, I was not touching it, I was not grasping it; I hesitated to die to death and to live to life; inveterate evil had more power over me than the novelty of good, and as that very moment of time in which I was to become something else drew nearer and nearer, it struck me with more and more horror. But I was not struck right back or turned aside; I was just held in suspense.

Toys and trifles, utter vanities had been my mistresses, and now they were holding me back, pulling me by the garment of my flesh and softly murmuring in my ear: "Are you getting rid of us?" and "From this moment shall we never be with you again for all eternity?" and "From this moment will you never for all eternity be allowed to do this or to do that?" My God, what was it, what was it that they suggested in those words "this" or "that" which I have just written? I pray you in your mercy to keep such things from the soul of your servant. How filthy, how shameful were these things they were suggesting! And now their voices were not half so loud in my ears; now they no longer came out boldly to contradict me face to face; it was more as though they were muttering behind my back, stealthily pulling at my sleeve as I was going away so that I should turn and look at them. Yet still they did hold me back as I hesitated to tear myself away and to shake them off and to take the great step in the direction where I was called. Violence of habit spoke the words: "Do you think that you can live without them?"

But by now it spoke very faintly. In the direction toward which I had turned my face and still trembled to take the last step, I could see the chaste dignity of Continence; she was calm and serene, cheerful without wantonness, and it was in truth and honor that she was enticing me to come to her without hesitation, stretching out to receive and to embrace me with those holy hands of hers, full of such multitudes of good examples. With her were so many boys and girls, so much of youth, so much of every age, grave widows and women grown old in virginity, and in them all was Continence herself, not barren, but *a fruitful mother of children,* her joys, by you, Lord, her husband. She smiled at me and there was encouragement in her smile, as though she were saying: "Can you not do what these men and these women have done? Or do you think that their ability is in themselves and not in the Lord their God? It was the Lord God who gave me to them. Why do you try and stand by yourself, and so not stand at all? Let him support you. Do not be afraid. He will not draw away and let you fall. Put yourself fearlessly in His hands. He will receive you and will make you well."

And I was blushing for shame, because I could still hear the dim voices of those vanities, and still I hung back in hesitation. And again she seemed to be speaking: "Stop your ears against those unclean members of yours, so that they may be mortified. They tell you of delights, but not of such delights as the law of the Lord your God tells."

So went the controversy in my heart—about self, and self against self. And Alypius stayed close by me, waiting silently to see how this strange agitation of mine would end.

12   AND NOW FROM my hidden depths my searching thought had dragged up and set before the sight of my heart the whole mass of my misery. Then a huge storm rose up within me bringing with it a huge downpour of tears. So that I might pour out all these tears and speak the words that came with them I rose up from Alypius (solitude seemed better for the business of weeping) and went further away so that I might not be embarrassed even by his presence. This was how I felt and he realized it. No doubt I had said something or other, and he could feel the weight of my tears in the sound of my voice. And so I rose to my feet, and he, in a state of utter amazement, remained in the place where we had been sitting. I flung myself down on the ground somehow under a fig tree and gave free rein to my tears; they streamed and flooded from my eyes, an *acceptable sacrifice to Thee*. And I kept saying to you, not perhaps in these words, but with this sense: *"And Thou, O Lord, how long? How long, Lord; wilt Thou be angry forever? Remember not our former iniquities."* For I felt that it was these which were holding me fast. And in my misery I would exclaim: "How long, how long this 'tomorrow and tomorrow'? Why not now? Why not finish this very hour with my uncleanness?"

So I spoke, weeping in the bitter contrition of my heart. Suddenly a voice reaches my ears from a nearby house. It is the voice of a boy or a girl (I don't know which) and in a kind of singsong the words are constantly repeated: "Take it and read it. Take it and read it." At once my face changed, and I began to think carefully of whether the singing of words like these came into any kind of game which children play, and I could not remember that I had ever heard anything like it before. I checked the force of my tears and rose to my feet, being quite certain that I must interpret this as a divine command to me to open the book and read the first passage which I should come upon. For I had heard this about Antony: he had happened to come in when the Gospel was being read, and as though the words read were spoken directly to himself, had received the admonition: *Go, sell all that thou hast, and give to the poor, and thou shalt have treasure in heaven, and come and follow me.* And by such an oracle he had been immediately converted to you.

So I went eagerly back to the place where Alypius was sitting, since it was there that I had left the book of the Apostle when I rose to my feet. I snatched up the book, opened it, and read in silence the passage upon which my eyes first fell: *Not in rioting and drunkenness, not in chambering and wantonness, not in strife and envying: but put ye on the Lord Jesus Christ, and make not provision for the flesh in concupiscence.* I had no wish to read further; there was no need to. For immediately I had reached the end of this sentence it was as though my heart was filled with a light of confidence and all the shadows of my doubt were swept away.

Before shutting the book I put my finger or some other marker in the place and told Alypius what had happened. By now my face was perfectly calm. And Alypius in his turn told me what had been going on in himself, and which I knew nothing about. He asked to see the passage which I had read. I showed him and he went on further than the part I had read, nor did I know the words which followed. They were these: *Him that is weak in the faith, receive.* He applied this to himself and told me so. He was strengthened by the admonition; calmly and unhesitatingly he joined me in a purpose and a resolution so good, and so right for his character, which had always been very much better than mine.

The next thing we do is to go inside and tell my mother. How happy she is! We describe to her how it all took place, and there is no limit to her joy and triumph. Now she was praising you, *Who art able to do above that which we ask or think;* for she saw that with regard to me you had given her so much more than she used to ask for when she wept so pitifully before you. For you converted me to you in such a way that I no longer sought a wife nor any other worldly hope. I was now standing on that rule of faith, just as you had shown me to her in a vision so many years before. And so you had changed her mourning into joy, a joy much richer than she had desired and much dearer and purer than that which she looked for by having grandchildren of my flesh.

Book IX

1 *O Lord, I am Thy servant; I am Thy servant and
the son of Thy handmaid: Thou hast broken my
bonds in sunder. I will offer to Thee the sacrifice of
praise.* Let my heart and my tongue praise you, and let
all my bones say, O Lord, who is like unto Thee? Let
them speak, and then, Lord, answer me and *say unto
my soul, I am thy salvation.*

Who am I and what am I? Is there any evil that I
have not done in my acts, or, if not in my acts, in my
words, or, if not in my words, in my will? But you, Lord,
are good and merciful; your right hand had regard for
the profundity of my death, and from the bottom of my
heart you dragged up that abysmal load of corruption.
And this was what you did: I was able totally to set my
face against what I willed and to will what you willed.
But where had this ability been for all those years? And
from what profound and secret depth was my free will
suddenly called forth in a moment so that I could bow
my neck to your *easy yoke* and my shoulders to your
*light burden, O Christ Jesus, my Helper and my Re-
deemer?* How sweet it suddenly became to me to be
without the sweetness of those empty toys! How glad I
was to give up the things I had been so afraid to lose!
For you cast them out from me, you true and supreme
sweetness; you cast them out and you entered in to me
to take their place, sweeter than all pleasure, but not to
flesh and blood; brighter than all light, but more inward
than all hidden depths; higher than all honor, but not to
those who are high in themselves. Now my mind was
free of those gnawing cares that came from ambition

175

and the desire for gain and wallowing in filth and
scratching the itching scab of lust. And now I was talking
to you easily and simply, my brightness and my riches
and my health, my Lord God.

2 AND I DECIDED in your sight that, without making any violent gesture, I would gently withdraw
from a position where I was making use of my tongue
in the talking-shop; no longer should my young students
(who were not so much interested in your law and your
peace as in absurd deceptions and legal battles) buy
from my mouth material for arming their own madness.
And luckily it happened that there were only a few days
more before the Vintage Vacation, and I decided to endure them so that I might retire from the profession in
a regular way. I had been bought by you and was not
going to return again to put myself up for sale. So our
plan was known to you, but not known to men—except
to our own friends. We had agreed among ourselves not
to let the news out at all, although, as we were making
our way up from *the valley of tears* and singing that *song
of degrees,* you had given us *sharp arrows* and *destroying
coals* against the subtle tongues of people who, under a
show of care for us, would try to thwart us and by loving
us would eat us up, as men do with their food.

You had shot through our hearts with your charity,
and we carried about with us your words like arrows
fixed deep in our flesh; stored up in the recesses of our
thought were the examples of your servants whose darkness you had turned to light and whose death to life,
and so that heavy sluggishness of ours that might have
dragged us down again to the depths was utterly burned
up and consumed. So much on fire were we that all the
blasts of *the subtle tongue* of contradiction, so far from
extinguishing the fire, only made it burn more fiercely.
However because of your name, which you have sanctified throughout the earth, there would no doubt also be
people who would praise the resolution and vows which

we had taken, and I thought it would look like ostentation if, instead of waiting for the vacation which was now so close, I should resign from a public position which everyone knew about. All eyes would be upon me and upon what I had done; it would be noticed that I had not wished to wait for the day of the Vintage, although it was so close, and there would be much talk of me to the effect that I wanted to make myself seem important. And what good would it do me to have people thinking and talking about my state of mind and to have *our good to be evil spoken of?*

There was also the fact that that summer my lungs had begun to give way as the result of overwork in teaching. I found it difficult to breathe deeply; pains in the chest were evidence of the injury and made it impossible for me to speak loudly or for long at a time. At first this had distressed me, since I was being almost forced and compelled to give up this burden of teaching—or, at any rate, if I were able to be cured and made well again, to give it up for the time being. But now my will in its entirety had arisen and was set on having leisure and on seeing *how that Thou art the Lord,* and from this moment I began actually to be pleased that in this illness also I had quite a genuine excuse to soften the injured feelings of those parents who, so that their children might be free to learn, wanted me never to be free at all. And so, filled with such joy as this, I put up with the interval of time—I think it was about twenty days—which still had to pass. But I needed some resolution to do this. What had helped me in the past to bear my hard labor had been the desire to make money. The desire had now gone, and, if its place had not been taken by patience, I should have been quite overwhelmed by staying on at my work. Some of your servants, my brothers, may say that I sinned in this, because, with my heart fully set on your service, I continued to hold even for one hour my professorship of lies. It may be so. But I know that you, most merciful Lord, have pardoned and remitted this sin too along with any other terrible and deadly sins in the holy water of Baptism.

3 VERECUNDUS WAS MAKING himself ill with worry because of the good which we had found. He saw that, because of his own chains in which he was so tightly bound, he was losing our companionship. He was not yet a Christian, though his wife was. However she was a fetter which clung to him more tightly than all the rest, preventing him from setting out on the journey on which we had started. For he said that he would not be a Christian in any other way except the way that was impossible to him. Nevertheless, he most kindly offered us the hospitality of his house so long as we should remain there. You, Lord, will reward him *in the resurrection of the just,* seeing that you have already given him the lot of the just. This happened when we were away; we were already at Rome when Verecundus became ill of a bodily sickness; in the course of his illness he became a baptized Christian and then departed from this life. So *hadst Thou mercy not on him only but on us also;* for otherwise we should have been tortured with intolerable pain whenever we thought of the wonderful kindness that our friend had shown to us and reflected that we could not count him as one of your flock. We thank you, our Lord. We are yours, as is shown by your exhortations and your consolations. You are true to your promises and you will repay Verecundus for that country estate of his at Cassiciacum where we rested in you far from the turmoil of the world, with the loveliness of your eternally green and fresh paradise; for you have forgiven him his sins on earth and have placed him in that mountain rich in milk, your own mountain, the mountain of abundance.

But at that time Verecundus was sad and worried. Nebridius however was full of joy. He too was not yet a Christian and in the past he had fallen into that pit of deadly error, believing that the flesh of your Son, of your truth, was a phantom. However, he had emerged from this error and his present state was that, though he had not yet received any of the sacraments of your Church, he was a most ardent searcher for truth. Not long after our conversion and regeneration by your baptism, you took him from this fleshly life; by then he too was a baptized Christian, serving you in perfect chastity and continence among his own people in Africa, and having converted his whole household to the Christian faith. And now he lives in the bosom of Abraham. Whatever is meant by that bosom, there my Nebridius lives, my sweet friend, your son by adoption and no longer merely a freedman. There he lives. For what other place could there be for such a soul? There he lives in a place about which he used often to ask questions of me, an ignorant weak man. Now he no longer turns his ear to my lips; he turns his own spiritual lips to your fountain and drinks his fill of all the wisdom that he can desire, happy without end. And I do not think that he is so inebriated with that wisdom as to forget me; since it is of you, Lord, that he drinks, and you are mindful of us.

This, then, was how it was with us. We comforted Verecundus in his sorrow (for our friendship was not impaired by our conversion) and we urged him to keep the faith of his own state, that of the married life. But we waited for Nebridius to follow us, and he was so close that he might well have done so; indeed he was just on the point of doing so when at last those days of waiting came to an end. Long and many they had seemed to me because I was longing for the peace and the liberty in which I could sing to you from the depths of my being: *My heart hath said unto Thee, I have sought Thy face: Thy face, Lord, will I seek.*

4   AND THE DAY CAME on which I was actually to be freed of this profession of rhetoric, from which in my mind I was already free. So it was done. You rescued my tongue as you had rescued my heart. I

rejoiced and blessed you and with all my friends went off to the country house. My writing was now done in your service, though still, in this kind of breathing space, the breath it drew was from the school of pride. The books I wrote then will show what I did in the way of writing—debates with my friends who were present, and debates held with myself in your presence—and my letters to Nebridius will show what I discussed with him while he was away. But I shall never have time to tell of all your great kindnesses to me, especially at this period, since I must hurry on to more important matters still. For my memory brings all this before me, and it is a pleasure to me, Lord, to confess to you by what inward goads and stings you utterly tamed me, and how you evened me down, *lowering the mountains and hills of my high imaginations, straightening my crookedness, and smoothing my rough ways,* and how you also subdued that brother of my heart, Alypius, to the name of your only-begotten Son, our Lord and Saviour Jesus Christ. At first he felt that this name was not grand enough to have a place in our writings since he wanted them to have the redolence of the cedars of the literary world (cedars which the Lord has now broken down) rather than of those health-giving herbs which your Church uses against serpents.

My God, how I poured out my heart to you as I read the Psalms of David, those faithful songs and sounding syllables of holiness, quite excluding the swelling boastfulness of the spirit! I, still untrained in your true love, a catechumen resting in that country house with Alypius, another catechumen, and having my mother constantly with us in her woman's clothing, but with her masculine faith, tranquil in her age, maternal in her love, Christian in her goodness. How I cried aloud to you in those psalms! How they fired me toward you! How I burned to utter them aloud, if I could, to the whole world against the pride of mankind! And yet they are sung through the whole world, nor can *any hide himself from Thy heat.* How strong and full of bitter grief was the

indignation I felt against the Manichees! Yet I pitied
them too for their ignorance of those medicinal sacraments and for raging in madness against the antidote
which might have made them sane. I would have liked
them to have been standing somewhere near me (without my knowing that they were there) and to have seen
my face and heard what I said when in this time of
quietness I read the fourth Psalm, and to have seen what
effect those words of the Psalm had on me: *When I
called, the God of my righteousness heard me; in tribula-
tion Thou enlargedst me. Have mercy upon me, O Lord,
and hear my prayer.* I should like them to have heard
me without my knowing whether they heard. Otherwise
they might think that what I was saying as I read these
verses was being said because of them. And in fact I
should neither say the same things nor speak in the same
way, if I realized that they were watching me and listening to me. And even if I did say the same things,
they would not have understood how I was speaking
with myself and to myself in front of you, out of the
natural feelings of my soul.

I trembled with fear, and then again I was on fire with
hope and with exultation in your mercy, Father. And all
these emotions were shown in my eyes and in my voice
when your good Spirit turned to us and said: *O ye sons
of men, how long, slow of heart? Why do ye love vanity
and seek after lying?* For I had loved vanity and had
sought after lying. *And Thou, O Lord,* hadst already
*magnified Thy Holy One, raising Him from the dead, and
setting Him at Thy right hand,* whence *from on high* He
should send His *promise, the Comforter, the Spirit of
Truth.* And He had sent Him already, though I did not
know it. He had sent Him because He was already magnified, risen from the dead and ascended into heaven.
For till then, *the Spirit was not yet given, because Jesus
was not yet glorified.* And the prophet cries out, *How
long, slow of heart? Why do ye love vanity and seek after
lying?* He cries out, *How long?* He cries out, *Know this.*
And I so long, not knowing, loved vanity and sought after

lying. And so I listened and trembled, because these words were spoken to such people as I remembered myself to have been. For there was both vanity and lying in those phantasms which I had accepted as the truth, and now in the grief I felt at the remembrance of it I loaded myself with bitter and sincere reproaches. I wish that those who still love vanity and seek after lying could have heard me. Then perhaps they would have been disturbed and would have vomited up their error. And you would have heard them when they cried to you. For it was by a true death in the flesh that He died for us who now *intercedeth unto Thee for us.*

I read too: *Be angry and sin not.* How deeply, my God, was I moved by this—I who had now learned to be angry with myself for the past so that I might not sin in the future! Yes, and to be justly angry with myself; for it was not the case of some other nature belonging to the race of darkness which committed the sin in me, as the Manichees believe, who are not angry with themselves and who *treasure up wrath against the day of wrath and of the revelation of Thy just judgment.*

And now my good things were not external and were not sought with the eyes of the flesh in this sun that we see. For those who find their joys in things outside easily become vain and waste themselves on things seen and temporal and, with their minds starving, go licking at shadows. Oh that they would grow tired of their lack of nourishment and would say: *Who will show us good things?* Then we should say and they would hear, *The light of Thy countenance is sealed upon us, Lord.* For we are not ourselves *that light which enlighteneth every man,* but we are enlightened by you, so that *having been sometimes darkness, we may be light in Thee.* If only they could see the eternal light inside themselves! I had tasted of it and I was in a rage because I could not show it to them so long as they brought me their hearts looking out of their eyes away from you, while saying: *Who will show us good things?* For it was there, there in the place where I had been angry with myself, inside, in my own room, there where I had been pierced, where I had made my sacrifice, offering up my old self, and starting on the purpose of a new life, with my hope set on you—there it was that you began to grow sweet to me and *hadst put gladness in my heart.* I cried out as I read this with my outward eye and inwardly recognized its truth. Nor did I wish for any multiplication of earthly goods; in these one wastes and is wasted by time. In the Eternal Simplicity I had other *corn and wine and oil.*

And in the next verse how my heart cried out from its depths! *O in peace, O for the Selfsame!* And then this, I *will lay me down and sleep,* for who shall stand against us when *cometh to pass that saying which is written, Death is swallowed up in Victory?* And you supremely are the Selfsame, you who do not change, and in you is the rest which is oblivious of all labors, since there is no other beside you, nor are we to seek for those many other things which are not what you are. But you, Lord, *alone,* have *made me dwell in hope.* As I read, my heart became on fire. What could be done, I wondered, with those deaf corpses, of whom I myself had been one? For I, like a disease, like a blind man, had raised my bitter barking voice against these writings which are so honey-sweet of heaven and brilliant with your own light. And now my heart boiled as I thought of the enemies of this Scripture.

I shall never be able to recall and write down the whole story of those days of quiet. But I have not forgotten, and I will not pass over in silence how bitter was the scourge with which you afflicted me, and how wonderfully quickly came your mercy. At that time you tortured me with toothache, and when the pain became so bad that I was unable to speak it came into my heart to ask all my friends who were present to pray for me to you, the God of all kinds of health. I wrote this down on wax and gave it to them to read. As soon as we had in our simple devotion gone down on our knees, the pain went away. But what pain was it? And how did it go? I was terrified, I admit, my Lord and my God; for

in all my life I had never felt anything like it. And so in
the depths of me I experienced the power of your nod
and, rejoicing in faith, I praised your name. But this faith
would not let me be at ease about my past sins, since
these had not yet been forgiven me by means of your
Baptism.

5   AT THE END OF the Vintage holiday I gave notice to the citizens of Milan that they must find
someone else to sell words to their students, both because I had chosen to enter your service and because I
was no longer able to continue in my profession because
of the pain in my lungs and my difficulty in breathing.
And in a letter which I wrote to your bishop, the holy
Ambrose, I explained my former errors and my present
resolution and asked him to advise me what parts of
your Scripture in particular I should read in order to
prepare myself and become better fitted to receive so
great a grace. He told me to read the prophet Isaiah,
his reason, I think, being that Isaiah foretells the Gospel
and the calling of the Gentiles more clearly than the
other writers. I, however, could not understand the first
part that I read and, thinking that all the rest would be
like this, laid it by with the intention of taking it up
again when I should be better trained in the Lord's style
of speech.

6   THEN, WHEN THE TIME CAME for me to give in
my name, we left the country and returned to
Milan. Alypius had decided to be born again in you at
the same time. He was already clothed in that humility
which so befits your sacraments, and he had so tamed
and mastered his own body that, showing the most extraordinary fortitude, he could go, barefooted over the
icy soil of Italy. We also had with us young Adeodatus,
the son of my flesh, begotten by me in my sin. You had
made him well. He was scarcely fifteen, but he showed

more intelligence than many serious and learned men.
Here it is your gifts that I acknowledge to you, Lord
God, Creator of all things, abundantly powerful to reform our deformities; for I myself had no part in that
boy except for the sin. As to the fact that we brought
him up in your discipline, it was you and no one else
who inspired us to do this. Yours are the gifts which I
acknowledge to you. There is a book of mine called *The
Master*; it is a dialogue between Adeodatus and me. You
know that all the ideas put into the mouth of the person
conversing with me were his own ideas, when he was
sixteen. And there were other things too, even more
remarkable, which I noticed in him. I found his intelligence really awe-inspiring. And who except you could
be the maker of such wonders? Soon you took away his
life from this earth and, as I think of him, I am perfectly
at ease, for there is nothing in his boyhood or youth or
indeed his whole personality to make one feel fear for
him. We took him with us as a companion, of the same
age as we in your grace, to be brought up in your discipline. And we were baptized and all anxiety for our past
life vanished away. In those days I could never have
enough of the wonderful sweetness of meditating upon
the depth of your counsel for the salvation of the human
race. What tears I shed in your hymns and canticles!
How deeply was I moved by the voices of your sweet
singing Church! Those voices flowed into my ears and
the truth was distilled into my heart, which overflowed
with my passionate devotion. Tears ran from my eyes
and happy I was in those tears.

7   THE CHURCH OF MILAN had only recently begun
to practice this kind of consolation and exhortation, and there was great enthusiasm among the brethren
as they joined together both with heart and voice in the
singing. In fact it was only a year or not much more,
than a year previously when Justina, the mother of the
boy emperor Valentinian, was persecuting your servant

Ambrose in the interests of her own heresy (she had been led astray by the Arians). Then the devout congregation stayed day and night in the church, ready to die with their bishop, your servant. In all this anxious watching, my mother, your handmaiden, took a leading part and lived in prayer. I myself had not yet been warmed by the heat of your Spirit, but I was nevertheless stirred up by the state of alarm and excitement in the city. It was then that the practice began of singing hymns and psalms in the manner of the Eastern Churches, so that the people should not grow faint and tired in this time of their sorrow. The custom has been kept from that day to this and has been imitated by many, indeed by almost all, of your congregations in other parts of the world.

At that time you revealed to your bishop Ambrose in a vision where the bodies of the martyrs Gervasius and Protasius lay hid. These you had kept stored up uncorrupted for so many years in your secret treasury until the right time should come for you to produce them in order to restrain the mad rage of a woman who was also an empress. For when the bodies had been found and dug up and brought with due honor to Ambrose's basilica people who were tormented by unclean spirits were cured and the devils who had been tormenting them openly admitted what they were and what they had done. Also, there was the case of a citizen of Milan, well known to everyone, who had been blind for many years. When this man inquired and was told what was the reason why the people were shouting with joy, he jumped up and asked his guide to lead him to the place. When he got there he begged to be allowed in so that he could touch with his handkerchief the bier on which were lying the *saints whose death is precious in Thy sight.* He did this, put the handkerchief to his eyes, and immediately his eyes were opened. Then the news spread abroad; then fervent and shining were your praises; then that enemy was at least checked in her fury of persecution, even though her mind was not brought back to the health of a true belief. Thanks be to you, my God! From

where and to what point have you led my memory that
I should confess to you these things also, which, though
they are great, I had passed over in forgetfulness? Yet
even then, when *the odor of Thy ointments was so fra-
grant,* I did not *run after Thee.* And so I wept all the
more at the singing of your hymns; once I had sighed
for you and now at last I was breathing you in, so far
as this house of grass allows the breath of your presence.

8 YOU, WHO MAKE MEN of one mind to dwell in
our house, led Euodius, a man from our own
town, to join company with us. He had been in the government service, had been converted to you and baptized before us, had resigned from his official post and
set himself to serve you. We stayed together with the
intention of finding a place to live together in the good
life which we planned. We asked ourselves what would
be the place where we could serve you most usefully,
and, as the result of our discussions, we went back again
to Africa. When we had got as far as Ostia on the Tiber,
my mother died.

I am passing over much because I am in much haste.
And I beg you, my God, to receive my confessions and
my thanksgivings for innumerable things about which I
am silent. But I shall not pass over whatever my soul
can bring forth about that servant of yours who brought
me forth, giving me birth in the flesh to this temporal
light, and in her heart to light eternal. It is not her gifts
that I shall tell of, but your gifts in her. For she did not
make herself or bring herself up. It was you who created
her, and neither her father nor her mother knew what
kind of child would be born of them. It was the scepter
of your Christ, the discipline of your only begotten Son,
that brought her up in your fear, in a faithful household
which was a worthy member of your Church. Yet she
used to talk not so much of her mother's care in training
her as of the care of an old womanservant, who had
carried my mother's father on her back when he was a

baby, as small children are often carried about on the backs of the bigger maidservants. Because of this and because of her age and her excellent character this servant was greatly respected by her master and mistress in that Christian household and was given the care of her mistress' daughters. She carried out her responsibilities most thoroughly; in checking the children, when it was necessary to do so, she acted sternly and with a holy severity, and in teaching them she showed prudence and good sense. For instance, except during those hours when they were receiving their very frugal meals at their parents' table, she would not allow them to drink water, however parched with thirst they might be. In this way, she was guarding against the formation of a bad habit; and she used to say very sensibly: "Now you are drinking water, because you are not allowed to have wine. But when you are married and become mistresses of your stores and cellars, water will not be good enough for you, but you will still have this strong desire to drink." By this kind of advice and by the authority which she was able to exercise she brought under control the greediness from which children suffer and succeeded in imposing a good and proper limit even on the little girls' thirst, so that they did not want to have more than they should.

And yet there did, there actually did (for so your servant told me, her son) steal over her an excessive fondness for wine. For when in the usual way she, as a good sober girl, was told by her parents to go and draw some wine from the barrel, she would hold the cup under the tap and then, before pouring the wine into the flagon, would take a little bit, just wetting her lips, since she did not like the taste and could not take more. Indeed she did not act in this way because of any desire for drunkenness; it was just an excess of high spirits which are natural at that age, which boil over on ridiculous impulses and which, when we are children, are usually kept under restraint by the sobering influence of our elders. And so to that daily drop of wine she added more and more drops day after day (*for whoso despiseth little things, shall fall by little and little*), and she fell into such a habit of drinking that she would greedily drink down cups which were nearly full of wine. Where then was that wise old woman with her stern prohibitions? Could there be anything strong enough to deal with a hidden disease, if it were not for the fact that your healing powers, Lord, were watching over us? Mother, father, and nurses may not be there, but you are there, you who made us, you who call us, you can also use those who are set over us to do something for the salvation of our souls. And what did you do then, my God? How did you cure her? How did you bring her to her right mind? Was it not as follows? Out of another soul you produced a bitter sharp taunt, as though from your secret store you were bringing out a surgeon's knife, and with one touch of this you cut out the putrefied matter in her. For there was a maid who often used to go with my mother to the cellar and once when there were just the two of them alone, this maid, as might easily happen, had a quarrel with her small mistress and in the course of it made the most bitter and insulting accusation possible. "You drunkard," she said. My mother was struck to the quick by this taunt. She saw the foulness of her conduct, at once condemned it and gave up the bad habit. Indeed just as the flattery of friends often leads us astray, so the insults of enemies often do us good. But you do not reward people for what you accomplish through them, but only in accordance with their intentions. That maid, for instance, was in a temper and wanted to hurt her small mistress, not to make her better; she said what she said privately, either as a result of the time and place where the quarrel started or perhaps because she was afraid that she might get into trouble herself for having kept silent about it for so long. But you, Lord, director of all things in heaven and on earth, who turn to your own purposes the very depths of running rivers, shaping to order the wild flow of time, brought health to one soul by means of the unhealthiness of another; thus showing us that if someone is improved by any word of ours, we must not attribute this to our own power, even if we meant this result to take place.

9 SHE WAS BROUGHT UP, then, in a modest, sober way. It was you who made her obedient to her parents rather than her parents who made her obedient to you. And when she reached marriageable age she was given to a husband whom she served as her master. She tried to win him to you, preaching you to him by the beauty of the character which you had given her and by which you made her able to provoke love and respect and the admiration of her husband. So she endured his infidelities and never had a single quarrel with him on this subject. She was waiting for your mercy to be shown upon him so that he might believe in you and be made chaste. He, in fact, though an extremely kind man, by nature, was also very hot-tempered. But my mother knew that an angry husband must not be contradicted, not in deed nor even in word. Only when he had calmed down and become quiet would she, when she saw her opportunity, explain to him the reasons for what she had done, if he had happened to fly into a rage for no good reason. Indeed there were many wives with husbands much milder than hers who went about with their faces disfigured by the marks of blows, and when they got together to talk they would often complain of the way their husbands behaved. But my mother, speaking lightly but giving serious advice, used to say that the fault was in their tongues. They had all heard, she said, the marriage contract read out to them and from that day they ought to regard it as a legal instrument by which they were made servants; so they should remember their station and not set themselves up against their masters. And they, knowing what a violent husband she had to put up with, were amazed that it had never been heard of nor had there been any evidence to show that Patric-

ius had ever beaten his wife or that there had been a
family quarrel that had lasted as much as a single day.
They asked her in confidence how she managed it, and
she told them her rule, which was as I have described.
Those who followed it found that they had every reason
to thank her for it; those who did not were still bullied
and kept under.

There was a time when her mother-in-law had been
angry with her. This had all started because of the whis-
pering of malicious servants. But my mother showed
such a respectful attitude to her and so won her over by
her constant patience and forbearance that she went herself to her son, told him the names of those whose in-
terfering tongues were disturbing the domestic peace
between her and her daughter-in-law and demanded that
those concerned should be punished. Then out of defer-
ence to his mother, care for good order in the household,
and consideration for peace in his own family he had
the servants whose names had been given to him beaten,
as his mother had asked, and she told them that this was
the reward that any of them else might expect from her
if they tried to please her by speaking ill of her daughter-
in-law. None of them ventured to do so after that, and
they lived together in future on the most remarkably
happy and kind terms.

And this was another great gift, my God and my
mercy, which you bestowed on that good servant of
yours in whose womb you created me: among people
who were quarreling or at discord she showed herself,
whenever she could, very much of a peacemaker. She
might hear many very bitter things said on both sides,
and this kind of outpouring of swelling and undigested
malice is very likely to take place when a woman talks
to a friend who is present about an enemy who is absent;
on these occasions hatred is expressed in its real crudity
and in the bitterest terms possible. But my mother would
never report to one woman what had been said about
her by another except insofar as what had been said
might help to bring the two together again. I might con-

sider this a small virtue if I had not had the sad experience of knowing countless numbers of people who, through some kind of horrible spreading infection of sin, not only tell others who are angry what their enemies said about them in anger, but actually add things which never were said. And yet ordinary humanity ought to make us feel that we have not done enough if we merely refrain from increasing and exacerbating ill feeling among men by our evil tongues; we ought to go further and try to use our tongues well so as to put an end to ill feeling. This was what my mother was like, and you were the master who, deep in the school of her heart, taught her this lesson.

Finally, toward the very end of his earthly life, she won her husband over to you, and now that he was a believer she no longer lamented in him the things which she had put up with in him before he was converted. She was also the servant of your servants. All of them who knew her found in her good reason to praise and honor and love you, because on the evidence of the fruit of her holy conversation they could feel your presence in her heart. For she had been *the wife of one man,* had *requited her parents, had governed her house* piously, *was well reported of for good works, had brought up children,* as often *travailing in birth of them* as she saw them straying away from you. Finally, Lord—since it is by your gift that we are allowed to speak—with regard to all of us your servants who, before she went to sleep in you, were living together after receiving the grace of baptism, she gave to each one of us the care that a mother gives to her son and to each one of us the service which a daughter gives to her father.

10 NOW THE DAY was approaching on which she was to leave this life (you knew when this day would be, but we did not), and it so happened (this, I believe, was by your secret ordering) that she and I were standing alone, leaning in a window which looked onto the garden inside the house where we were staying, at Ostia on the Tiber. There we were out of the crowds and after our long and weary journey by land were resting ourselves for the sea voyage. So we were alone and talking together and very sweet our talk was, and *forgetting those things which are behind, and reaching forth unto those things which are before,* we were discussing between ourselves and in the presence of Truth, which you are, what the eternal life of the saints could be like, *which eye hath not seen, nor ear heard, nor hath it entered into the heart of man.* Yet with the mouth of our heart we panted for the heavenly streams of your fountain, the fountain of life, which is with you, so that, if some drops from that fountain—all that we could take—were to be scattered over us, we might in some way or other be able to think of such high matters.

Our talk had reached this point: that the greatest possible delights of our bodily senses, radiant as they might be with the brightest of corporeal light, could not be compared with the joys of that eternal life, could not, indeed, even deserve a mention. Then, with our affections burning still more strongly toward the Selfsame, we raised ourselves higher and step by step passed over all material things, even the heaven itself from which sun and moon and stars shine down upon the earth. And still we went upward, meditating and speaking and looking with wonder at your works, and we came to our own souls, and we went beyond our souls to reach that region of never-failing plenty where *Thou feedest Israel* forever with the food of truth and where life is that Wisdom by whom all these things are made, both what is past and what is to come; but Wisdom herself is not made; she is as she has been and will be forever; or rather, there is no place in her for 'to have been' or 'to be going to be'; one can only say 'to be,' since she is eternal and 'have been' and 'going to be' are not eternal. And as we talked, yearning toward this Wisdom, we did, with the whole strength of our hearts' impulse, just lightly come into touch with her, and we sighed and we left bound

there *the first fruits of the Spirit,* and we returned to the
sounds made by our mouths, where a word has a beginning and an ending. And how unlike is this to your
Word, our Lord, you who abide in yourself forever,
without becoming old, making all things new!

So we said: if to any man the tumult of the flesh were
to grow silent, silent the images of earth and water and
air, and the poles of heaven silent also; if the soul herself
were to be silent and, by not thinking of self, were to
transcend self; if all dreams and imagined revelations
were silent, and every tongue, every sign; if there was
utter silence from everything which exists only to pass
away (for, if one can hear them, these all say: We did
not make ourselves. He made us that abideth forever)
but suppose that, having said this and directed our attention to Him that made them, they too were to become
hushed and He Himself alone were to speak; not by
their voice but in His own, and we were to hear His
word, not through any tongue of flesh or voice of an
angel or sound of thunder or difficult allegory, but that
we might hear Him whom in all these things we love,
might hear Him in Himself without them, just as a moment ago we two had, as it were, gone beyond ourselves
and in a flash of thought had made contact with that
eternal wisdom which abides above all things—supposing that this state were to continue, that all other visions,
visions of so different a kind, were to be withdrawn,
leaving only this one to ravish and absorb and wrap the
beholder in inward joys, so that his life might be forever
like that moment of understanding which we had had
and for which we now sighed—would not this be: *Enter
into Thy Master's joy?* And when shall that be? Shall it
be when *we shall all rise again,* though we *shall not all
be changed?*

Something like this I said, though not precisely in this
way and in these words. Yet, Lord, you know that on
that day when we were talking together as I have described and when, as we talked, this world with all its
delights seemed to us so worthless, my mother said: "My

son, as to me, I no longer find any pleasure in this life. What more I have to do here and why I am still here I do not know, since I have no longer anything to hope for in this world. There was only one reason why I wanted to stay a little longer in this life, and that was that I should see you a Catholic Christian before I died. Now God has granted me this beyond my hopes; for I see that you have despised the pleasures of this world and are become his servant. So what am I doing here?"

11 WHAT REPLY I MADE to these words of hers I cannot clearly remember. Within five days, or not much more, she fell into a fever. And one day while she was ill she had a fainting fit and temporarily lost consciousness of her surroundings. We hurried to her side, but she soon regained consciousness, and, seeing my brother and me standing by her, she said to us, as though she were trying to find the answer to some question, "Where am I?" Then, as we stood dumb with grief, she looked in our faces and said: "Here you will bury your mother." I remained quiet and kept back my tears; but my brother said something to her to the effect that he hoped that she would have the good fortune to die in her own country and not abroad. On hearing this an anxious expression came over her face, and she gave him a reproachful look for still savoring of such earthly things. Then she looked into my face and said: "See what he is saying!" Soon afterward she said to both of us, "You may lay this body of mine anywhere. Do not worry at all about that. All I ask you is this, that wherever you may be you will remember me at the altar of the Lord." This was what she said, speaking with difficulty, and then she became silent as the force of her illness grew heavier upon her.

But as I considered your gifts, invisible God, which you put into the hearts of your faithful ones to be the seeds of wonderful fruit, I rejoiced and gave you thanks. I knew well and I remembered how worried and anxious she had always been about the question of her burial. She had already provided for herself and prepared a tomb close to that of her husband. Since they had lived together in such harmony, she also wished (so little is the human mind capable of grasping things divine) to have this happiness of hers added to and to have it spoken of among men that after her pilgrimage across the seas it had been granted to her that the earthly part of both man and wife should lie covered under the same earth. Now when it was that, in the fullness of your goodness, this vain and empty notion of hers began to cease to be in her heart, I did not know, and I felt both joy and surprise now that I knew that it had ceased to be—although in that conversation we had had together in the window, when she said: "What am I still doing here?" she had shown no desire to die in her own country. Also I heard afterward how at this time when we were at Ostia she was talking one day with all the confidence and trust of a mother to some of my friends when I was not there. She was speaking about how one must despise this life and look forward to death, and they were amazed at finding such fortitude in a woman (it was you who gave it her) and asked whether she was not afraid to leave her body so far from her own city. "Nothing," she replied, "is far from God, and there is no reason to fear that, at the end of the world, He will not recognize the place from which to raise me up."

And so on the ninth day of her illness, in the fifty-sixth year of her age and the thirty-third of mine, that devout and holy soul was freed from the body.

12   I CLOSED HER EYES, and a great flood of sorrow swept into my heart and would have overflowed in tears. But my eyes obeyed the forcible dictate of my mind and seemed to drink that fountain dry. Terrible indeed was my state as I struggled so. And then, when she had breathed her last, the boy Adeodatus burst out into loud cries until all the rest of us checked him, and he

became silent. In the same way something childish in me which was bringing me to the brink of tears was, when I heard the young man's voice, the voice of the heart, brought under control and silenced. For we did not think it right that a funeral such as hers should be celebrated with tears and groans and lamentations. These are ways in which people grieve for an utter wretchedness in death or a kind of total extinction. But she did not die in misery, nor was she altogether dead. Of this we had good reason to be certain from the evidence of her character and from a faith that was not feigned.

Why, then, did I feel such pain within me? It was because the wound was still fresh, the wound caused by the sudden breaking off of our old way of living together in such sweet affection. I was glad indeed to have the testimony which she gave me in these very last days of her illness when, as I was doing what service I could for her, she spoke so affectionately to me, calling me her good and dutiful son, and, with such great love, she told me that she had never once heard me say a word to her that was hard or bitter. And yet, my God who made us, what comparison was there between the respect I paid to her and the slavery she offered to me? And so, now that I had lost that great comfort of her, my soul was wounded and my life was, as it were, torn apart, since it had been a life made up of hers and mine together.

So, when the boy had been quieted and had ceased to weep, Euodius took up the Psalter and began to sing—while the whole household joined in the responses—the Psalm: *I will sing of mercy and judgment to Thee, O Lord.* And when it became known what we were doing, many of the brethren and many religious women came to join us. Those whose duty it was began in the usual way to make preparations for the funeral, and I, with some of my friends who thought I ought not to be left alone, found another part of the house where we could decently be, and there I spoke to them on such subjects as I thought right for the occasion. So I was using truth as a kind of fomentation to dull my torture, a torture which was known to you, though the others, who listened intently to my words, did not know of it and thought that I had no feeling of pain. But in your ears, where none of them could hear me, I reproached myself for being so feeble, and I kept back the flood of my sorrow. And it did give way to me a little; then gathered strength and swept back on me again, though not to the point of making me break out into tears or change the expression of my face. But I knew well enough what I was crushing down in my heart. And I was deeply vexed that these human feelings should have such power over me—though in the proper order and lot of the human condition these things must be—and I grieved at my grief with a new grief and so was consumed with a double sorrow.

And now the body was carried to burial. I went and I returned and I did not weep at all. We poured forth our prayers to you when the sacrifice of our redemption was offered for her and when, as the custom is there, the body was laid down near the grave before being lowered down into it, and during all these prayers I did not shed a tear. But all that day my sorrow weighed heavily on me in secret, and in the disturbance of my mind I begged you, as well as I could, to heal my sorrow; but you did not, and I think this was because you were impressing on my memory, by this one instance, how strong is the bond of all habit, even upon a soul which is no longer nourished by deceiving words. It even seemed to me a good idea to go to the baths, because I had heard that the word for bath *(balneum)* was derived from the Greek βαλανεῖον, meaning something that drives sadness from the mind. And I confess this also to your mercy, Father of the fatherless: I went to the baths and I came back just the same as I was before. For the bitterness of my sorrow did not sweat itself out of my heart. Then I went to sleep and woke up again to find that my grief was much relieved. And as I was alone in my bed I remembered those true verses written by your servant Ambrose. For it is you who are

Creator Thou of everything,
Director of the circling poles,
Clothing the day in lovely light
And giving night the grace of sleep,

That peace may fall on loosened limbs
To make them strong for work again,
To raise and soothe the tired mind
And free the anxious from their care.

And then little by little my former thoughts of your handmaid returned. I remembered how devoutly and with what holiness she conducted herself in your sight, how kind and considerate she was to us. And now suddenly I had lost all this. With you seeing me I found solace in weeping for her and for myself, on her behalf and on my own. So I allowed the tears which I had been holding back to fall, and I let them flow as they would, making them a pillow for my heart, and my heart rested on them, for only your ears could hear my lament and not the ears of some man who might have given a wrong or contemptuous interpretation of it. And now, Lord, I am confessing this to you in writing and anyone who cares can read what I have written and interpret it as he likes, and if he finds that I did wrong in weeping during this small portion of an hour for my mother—a mother who for the time was dead to my eyes and who for so many years had wept for me, that I might live in your eyes—let him not despise me; let him rather, if he is a man of great charity, himself weep for my sins to you, the Father of all the brethren of your Christ.

13 BUT NOW THAT my heart is healed from that wound (in which later I blamed myself for a too carnal affection), I pour forth to you, our God, tears of a very different sort for your handmaid—tears that well up from a spirit shaken by the thoughts of the dangers that threaten every soul *that dieth in Adam*. Certainly she, after having been made alive in Christ and when still not freed from the flesh, lived such a life that in her faith and in her character your name was praised; yet even so I would not venture to say that from the time of her regeneration by you in baptism she never let fall a single word that was contrary to your commandment. Your son, the Truth, has said: *Whosoever shall say unto his brother, Thou fool, shall be in danger of hell-fire,* and it would go badly indeed with any man, however praiseworthy his life, if you were to lay aside your mercy before examining it. But because you do not look too rigorously into our sins, we confidently hope to find some place with you. But if a man recounts to you all the real merits he has, he is only telling you of your gifts to him. If only men would recognize that they are men, *and that he that glorieth, would glory in the Lord.*

And so, my praise and my life, God of my heart, I shall leave aside for the moment those good deeds of hers for which I joyfully thank you, and I shall now beg your mercy for my mother's sins. Hear me, I pray, in the name of that Medicine of our wounds, who hung upon the cross, and now *sitting at Thy right hand maketh intercession to Thee for us.* I know that she dealt mercifully and from her heart *forgave her debtors their debts; do thou also forgive her debts,* whatever she has contracted in all the years since the water of salvation. Forgive her, Lord, forgive her, I beg you; *enter not into judgment with her. Let Thy mercy be exalted above Thy justice,* because your words are true, and *Thou hast promised mercy unto the merciful.* And that they should be merciful was your gift, *who wilt have mercy on whom Thou wilt have mercy, and compassion on whom Thou hast had compassion.*

And I believe that you have already done what I am asking; but *accept, O Lord, the free-will offerings of my mouth.* For on that day when her death was so close, she gave no thought to having her body richly adorned for burial or embalmed in spices; she had no desire for any special monument, nor was she anxious about being buried in her own country. She gave us no instructions about any of these things. All she desired was that she should be remembered at your altar, which she had served without ever missing a single day, and from which she knew was dispensed that holy sacrifice by which *the handwriting that was against us is blotted out,* by which the enemy was triumphed over, who, reckoning up our sins and seeking what there was to lay to our charge, *found nothing in Him,* in whom we conquer. Who shall restore to Him His innocent blood? Who shall give Him back the price, for which He bought us, and so take us from Him? To the sacrament of this ransom of ours your handmaiden had bound her soul by the bond of faith. Let none wrest her from your protection; let neither *the lion nor the dragon* interpose himself by force or by fraud. For she will not reply that she has no debts, lest she should be convicted and seized by that cunning accuser. She will reply that her debts have been remitted to her by Him, to whom no one can repay the price which He, who owed nothing, paid for us.

So let her rest in peace with her husband, than whom she had no other husband either before or after; whom she obeyed, *with patience bringing forth fruit* for you, so that she might win him for you also. And inspire, my Lord and my God, inspire your servants my brethren, your sons my masters, whom I serve with heart and voice and pen, that as many as shall read this may remember at your altar Monica, your servant, with Patricius, her husband, through whose flesh you brought me into this life, though how I do not know. May they with holy affection remember those two who were my parents in this transitory light, who are my brethren under you, Our Father, in our Catholic mother, and my fellow citizens in the eternal Jerusalem for which your people in their pilgrimage sigh from the beginning of their journey until their return home. And so by means of these Confessions of mine I pray that my mother may have her last request of me still more richly answered in the prayers of many others besides myself.

Book X

1 LET ME KNOW YOU, my known; *let me know Thee even as I am known.* Power of my soul, enter into it and fit it for yourself, so that you may have and hold it *without spot or wrinkle.* This is my hope, *therefore do I speak,* and in this hope is my joy, when my joy is healthy. As to the other things of this life, the more we weep for them the less they ought to be wept for, and the less we weep for them the more we ought to weep. For, see, you love the truth, and he that *doth the truth, cometh to the light.* This is what I want to do in my heart, in front of you, in my confession, and in my writing before many witnesses.

2 INDEED, LORD, to your eyes the very depths of man's conscience are exposed, and there is nothing in me that I could keep secret from you, even if I did not want to confess it. I should not be hiding myself from you, but you from myself. But now when my groaning bears evidence that I am displeased with myself, you shine out on me and are pleasing and loved and longed for, so that I am ashamed of myself and renounce myself and choose you and, except in you, can please neither you nor myself. Whatever I am, then, Lord, is open and evident to you. And what profit I have from confessing to you, I have already said. And I do not make my confession by means of the words and sounds of the flesh, but with the words of the soul and the crying out of my thought which your ear knows. For

when I am wicked, confession to you is the same thing as being displeased with myself; when I am good, confession to you is the same thing as not attributing my goodness to myself. Since Thou, Lord, *blessest the godly,* but first *Thou justifieth him when ungodly.* So, my God, my confession in your sight is made to you both silently and not silently; there is no sound of words, but there is a clamor of feeling. For if I say anything good to men, you have heard it from me first, and if you hear any good from me, it was you who first told it to me.

3   WHY THEN DO I bother to let men hear my confessions? It is not as though men are likely *to heal all my infirmities.* Men are a race very inquisitive about other people's lives, very lazy in improving their own. Why should they want to hear from me what I am, when they do not want to hear from you what they are? And when they hear my own account of my own self, how do they know that I am telling the truth, seeing that *no man knows what is in man, but the spirit of man which is in him?* But if they hear from you something about their own selves they cannot say: "the Lord is lying." For to hear from you about themselves is simply to know themselves. And if one knows oneself and then says: "it is false," one must be lying oneself. But *charity believeth all things* (that is, among those whom it binds together and makes one), and so, Lord, I make my confession to you in such a way that men may hear it, though I cannot demonstrate to them that I am telling the truth; yet those whose ears are opened to me by charity believe what I say.

Yet still, my inmost Physician, I beg you to make clear to me what advantage I get from doing this. You have forgiven and covered up my past sins, blessing me in you and changing my soul by faith and by your sacrament; yet when the confessions of these past sins are read and heard, they rouse up the heart and prevent it from sinking into the sleep of despair and saying, "I can-

not." Instead they encourage it to be wakeful in the love
of your mercy and the sweetness of your grace, through
which the weak is made strong when, thanks to this grace
of yours, he becomes conscious of his own weakness. Also
good men are pleased when they hear of sins done in the
past by people who are now free from them; they are
pleased not because of the sins themselves, but because
what were sins have now ceased to exist.

But, my Lord, to whom every day my conscience
makes its confession, more secure in the hope of your
mercy than in its own innocence, tell me, I beg you, of
what advantage it is when, in front of you, I also by
means of this book confess to men not what I once was,
but what I now am. As to my confession of the past, I
have already seen and mentioned the advantages of that.
But as to what I now am, at the very moment of writing
these confessions, there are many people who want to
know about this—both those who know me personally
and those who do not, but have heard something about
me or from me; but their ear is not laid against my heart,
where I am whatever I am. And so they want, as I make
my confession, to hear what I am inside myself, beyond
the possible reach of their eyes and ears and minds. And
in wanting to hear, they are ready to believe; but will
they know? For that charity, by which they are good,
tells them that I am not lying about myself in my confessions, and it is the charity in them that believes me.

4   BUT WHAT ADVANTAGE do they wish to gain
from this? Do they desire to rejoice with me
when they hear how close I have come to you by your
grace? And to pray for me, when they hear how I am
kept back by my own weight? It is to people like this
that I shall show myself. For it is no small advantage,
my Lord God, that many people should give thanks to
you for me and that many people should pray to you
for me. I would wish that their brotherly minds should
love in me what you teach them is to be loved, and

should lament in me what you teach them is to be lamented. It is a brotherly mind that I would wish for, not the mind of strangers, not that of the *strange children, whose mouth talketh of vanity, and their right hand is a right hand of iniquity;* but that brotherly mind which is glad for me when it sees good in me and sorry for me when it sees bad in me, because, whether it sees good or bad, it loves me. It is to people like this that I shall show myself, hoping that in my good deeds they will be glad and in my evil deeds they will be sad. My good deeds are your work and your gift, my evil deeds are my faults and your punishments. So I would wish there to be gladness for the one, sadness for the other, and that hymns and lamentations should rise up into your sight from those censers which are the hearts of my brethren. And I pray that you, Lord, pleased with the sweet incense of your holy temple, may *have mercy upon me according to Thy great mercy for Thine own name's sake,* and, in no way forsaking what you have begun, perfect my imperfections.

So in confessing not only what I have been but what I am the advantage is this: I make my confession not only in front of you, in a secret *exultation with trembling,* with a secret sorrow and with hope, but also in the ears of the believing sons of men, companions in my joy and sharers in my mortality, my fellow citizens and fellow pilgrims—those who have gone before and those who follow after and those who are on the road with me. These are your servants and my brothers; those whom you have willed to be your sons, my masters whom I am to serve if I wish to live with you and of you. And this word of yours to me would be a little thing if it only gave me a spoken command and did not also go in front of me in action. And so I do it both in deed and in word; I do it under your wings, and the danger would be too great if under your wings my soul were not subdued to you and my weakness known to you. I am only a little child, but my Father lives forever and my Protector is sufficient for me. For he is the same who begot me and who watches over me, and you yourself are all my good, you Almighty, who are with me even before I am with you. So it is to people like this, those whom you command me to serve, that I shall show not what I was, but what I now am and continue to be. *But neither do I judge myself.* It is in this way that I should like to be heard.

5   FOR *Thou, Lord, dost judge me;* because, although *no man knoweth the things of a man, but the spirit of a man which is in him,* yet there is still something of man which even the spirit of man that is in him does not know. But you, Lord, know all of him, you who made him. And as to me, though in your sight I despise myself and consider myself dust and ashes, yet still I know something of you which I do not know of myself. *Certainly now we see through a glass darkly,* and not yet *face to face,* and so, as long as I am on pilgrimage away from you, I am more present to myself than to you; yet I know that you are not in any way subject to violence, whereas I do not know in my case what temptations I can and what I cannot resist. And there is hope, because *Thou art faithful, Who wilt not suffer us to be tempted above that we are able; but wilt with the temptation also make a way to escape, that we may be able to bear it.* So I will confess what I know of myself, and I will also confess what I do not know of myself; because what I know of myself I know by means of your light shining upon me and what I do not know remains unknown to me until *my darkness be made as the noonday* in your countenance.

6   THERE IS NO DOUBT in my mind, Lord, that I love you. I feel it with certainty. You struck my heart with your word, and I loved you. But, see, *heaven and earth and all that therein is* on every side are telling me to love you, and they never stop saying it to all men,

that they may be without excuse. But more deeply *wilt Thou have mercy on whom Thou wilt have mercy, and wilt have compassion on whom Thou hast had compassion;* otherwise heaven and earth are telling your praises to deaf ears.

But what do I love when I love you? Not the beauty of the body nor the glory of time, not the brightness of light shining so friendly to the eye, not the sweet and various melodies of singing, not the fragrance of flowers and unguents and spices, not manna and honey, not limbs welcome to the embraces of the flesh: it is not these that I love when I love my God. And yet I do love a kind of light, melody, fragrance, food, embracement when I love my God; for He is the light, the melody, the fragrance, the food, the embracement of my inner self—there where is a brilliance that space cannot contain, a sound that time cannot carry away, a perfume that no breeze disperses, a taste undiminished by eating, a clinging together that no satiety will sunder. This is what I love when I love my God.

And what is this God? I asked the earth and it answered: "I am not he," and all things that are on the earth confessed the same. I asked the sea and the deeps and the creeping things with living souls, and they replied: "We are not your God. Look above us." I asked the blowing breezes, and the universal air with all its inhabitants answered: "Anaximenes was wrong. I am not God." I asked the heaven, the sun, the moon, the stars, and "No," they said, "we are not the God for whom you are looking." And I said to all those things which stand about the gates of my senses: "Tell me about my God, you who are not He. Tell me something about Him." And they cried out in a loud voice: "He made us." My question was in my contemplation of them, and their answer was in their beauty. And I turned my attention on myself and said to myself: "And you, who are you?" And I replied: "A man." Now I find evidently in myself a body and a soul, the one exterior, the other interior. Which of these should I have employed in seeking for my God? I had already looked for Him by means of the body, searching from earth to heaven, as far as I could send the beams of my eyes as messengers. But the interior part of me is the better. It was to this part that all the messengers from my body gave in their reports and this part sat in judgment weighing the replies of heaven and earth and all things within them when they said: "We are not God," and when they said: "He made us." The inner man knew these things by means of the ministry of the outer man. I, the inner man, knew them, I, the soul, knew them through the senses of my body. I asked the whole mass and frame of the universe about my God, and it replied: "I am not he, but He made me."

Is not this appearance of the universe evident to all whose senses are not deranged? Then why does it not give the same answer to all? Animals, small and great, see it, but cannot ask the question. They are not gifted with reason to sit in judgment on the evidence brought in by the senses. But men can ask the question, so that *the invisible things of God are clearly seen, being understood by the things that are made;* but by loving these things, they become subject to them, and subjects cannot judge. And these things will only answer the questions of those who are prepared to judge. Not that they alter their speech—that is, their appearance. If one man merely looks at them and another not only looks but asks his question, they do not appear one thing to one man, and a different thing to the other. They look just the same to both, but to one man they say nothing and to the other they speak. O it would be truer to say that they speak to everyone, but are only understood by those who compare the voice which comes to them from outside with the truth that is within. For truth says to me: "Your God is not heaven or earth or any other body." Their very nature declared this. Obviously there is less bulk in a part than in the whole. And now, my soul, I say to you that you are my better part; you animate the whole bulk of the body, giving it life—a thing which no body can do for another body. But your God is for you too the life of your life.

7 WHAT, THEN, do I love when I love God? Who is He that is the summit of my soul? It is by my soul herself that I shall ascend to Him. I shall go past that force in me by which I cling to the body and fill its frame with life. It is not by that force that I can find my God; if it were so, the *horse and mule that have no understanding* might find Him, since their bodies too live by this same force. But there is another force—not the one by which I give life, but the one by which I give perception to my flesh. The Lord created this power in me, commanding the eye not to hear and the ear not to see, but giving me the eye to see by and the ear to hear by, and so allotting to each of the other senses its own particular duty and function, and through these senses, with all their diverse functions, I act, retaining my identity as one soul. But I shall go past this force too; for the horse and the mule have it too; they also perceive by means of the body.

8 I SHALL PASS ON, then, beyond this faculty in my nature as I ascend by degrees toward Him who made me. And I come to the fields and spacious palaces of memory, where lie the treasures of innumerable images of all kinds of things that have been brought in by the senses. There too are our thoughts stored up, if by thought we have increased or diminished or in any way altered those things with which our senses have been in contact, and there too is everything else that has been brought in and deposited and has not yet been swallowed up and buried in forgetfulness. When I am in this treasure house, I ask for whatever I like to be brought out to me, and then some things are produced at once, some things take longer and have, as it were, to be fetched from a more remote part of the store, and some things come pouring out all together and, when in fact we want and are looking for something quite different, they thrust themselves forward as though they were saying: "Surely you must be looking for me." With the hand of my heart I brush them away from the face of my memory, until the thing that I want is discovered and brought out from its hidden place into my sight. And some things are produced easily and in perfect order, just as they are required; what comes first gives place to what comes next, and, as it gives place, it is stored up ready to be brought out when I need it again. All this happens when I repeat anything by heart.

Here are kept distinct and in their proper classifications all sensations which come to us, each by its own route: for instance, light, color, and the shapes of bodies reach us through the eyes; all kinds of sound through the ears; all smells by the nostrils; all tastes by the mouth, and by the sensation of the whole body we derive our impression of what is hard or soft, hot or cold, rough or smooth, heavy or light, whether from outside or inside the body itself. And the great harbor of memory, with its secret, numberless, and indefinable recesses, takes in all these things so that they may be reproduced and brought back again when the need arises. They all enter the memory by their various ways and are all stored up in the memory. Or rather it is not the things themselves that enter; what happens is that the images of things perceived are there ready at hand for thought to recall.

Precisely how these images are formed who can tell? Though it is clear enough which sense was responsible for seizing hold of them and storing them up inside us. For even when I am surrounded by darkness and silence I can, if I wish, summon up colors in my memory and tell the difference between black and white and any other colors I like, and while I am considering the images drawn in by my eyes, sounds do not come running in to disturb it, though they too are in my memory, stored up, as it were, in a separate compartment. For I can call for sounds also, if I wish, and they are present immediately; with no movement of tongue or vocal cords I sing as much as I like, and those images of color, which are still there in the memory, do not break in and interrupt when I call for something from that other storehouse which contains impressions brought in by the ear. In the same way I call up at pleasure all those other things which have been brought in and stored up by means of the other senses. I can tell the difference between the smell of lilies and of violets though at the time I am smelling nothing; I prefer honey to sweet wine, something smooth to something rough, simply by memory and without using the sense either of taste or touch.

All this I do inside me, in the huge court of my memory. There I have by me the sky, the earth, the sea, and all things in them which I have been able to perceive—apart from what I have forgotten. There too I encounter myself; I recall myself—what I have done, when and where I did it, and in what state of mind I was at the time. There are all the things I remember to have experienced myself or to have heard from others. From the same store too I can take out pictures of things which have either happened to me or are believed on the basis of experience; I can myself weave them into the context of the past, and from them I can infer future actions, events, hopes, and then I can contemplate all these as though they were in the present. "I shall do this," or "I shall do that," I say to myself in this deep recess of my mind, full of the images of so many and of such great things, "and this or that follows." "Oh if only this or that could happen!" or "May God prevent this or that!" So I speak to myself, and, while I am speaking, the images of all the things that I am saying are present to my mind, all from this same treasury of my memory; indeed I would not be able to speak of these things at all if the images were not there.

How great, my God, is this force of memory, how exceedingly great! It is like a vast and boundless subterranean shrine. Who has ever reached the bottom of it? Yet this is a faculty of my mind and belongs to my nature; nor can I myself grasp all that I am. Therefore, the mind is not large enough to contain itself. But where can that uncontained part of it be? Is it outside itself and not inside? In that case, how can it fail to contain itself? At this thought great wonder comes over me; I am struck dumb with astonishment. And men go abroad to wonder at the heights of mountains, the huge waves of the sea, the broad streams of rivers, the vastness of the ocean, the turnings of the stars—and they do not notice themselves and they see nothing marvelous in the fact that when I was mentioning all these things I was not seeing them with my eyes, yet I would not have been able to speak of them unless these mountains and waves and rivers and stars (which I have seen) and the ocean (which I have heard about) had been visible to me inside, in my memory, and with just the same great spatial intervals and proportions as if I were really seeing them outside myself. Yet, when I saw them with my eyes, I did not by the act of seeing draw them into myself; it is not they but their images that are in me, and I know by what bodily sense each impression has come to me.

9   YET MORE STILL is contained in this immense capacity of my memory. Here too is everything that I have learned in the liberal sciences and not forgotten—removed somehow to an inner place, which is yet no place. And here I have with me not the images but the things themselves. What grammar is, or the art of disputation, or how many types of question there are—everything of this sort that I know is in my memory, in a different way. Here it is not the case that I retain the image and leave the thing itself outside me. It is not the case of the sound of words which has ceased to sound, like a void which has left a fixed impression on the ear by which it can be recalled as though it were sounding, when in fact it is not sounding; or like a smell which,

while it is passing and vanishing into air, affects the sense of smell and so carries into the memory an image of itself which we can recall by the act of recollection; or like food, which certainly has no taste when it is in the stomach, but still has a kind of taste in our memory; or like something which is perceived by the sense of bodily touch and can still be imagined in our memory when it is no longer in contact with us. In all these cases it is not the things themselves that are brought into our memory; it is only their images which are seized upon with such amazing speed and are then, as it were, stored up in wonderful secret hiding places, from which by the act of remembering they can wonderfully be brought out again.

10 But when I hear that there are three types of question—"Does the thing exist? What is it? Of what kind is it?"—I certainly hold in my mind the images of the sounds of which these words are composed, and know that they passed through the air, making a particular kind of noise, and have now ceased to be. But as to the things themselves that are signified by these sounds, I never approached them by any bodily sense; my only means of discerning them was through the mind, and in my memory I have stored up, not their images, but the things themselves. How they got into me, let them say if they can. For as I go over all the gateways of my body, I cannot find by which one they gained entrance. The eyes say: "If these images were colored, it was we who gave notice of them." The ears say: "If they made a sound, it was by us that they were reported." The nostrils say: "If they had a smell, they came in by way of us." And the sense of taste says: "Unless one could taste them, it is no use asking me." Touch says: "If the thing is not a body I did not handle it, and if I did not handle it, I gave no information about it." From where, then, and how did they enter into my memory? I do not know. For when I learned them, I

was not taking them on trust from some other mind; I
was recognizing them in my own mind; I accepted them
as true and committed them to my mind as though I
were depositing them in some place where I could find
them again whenever I wanted. So they were in my
mind, even before I learned them, but they were not in
my memory. Then where were they? Or how was it that,
when I heard them spoken, I recognized them and said:
"That is right. That is true," unless in fact they were in
my memory already, but so far back and so buried, as
it were, in the furthest recesses that, if they had not been
dragged out by the suggestion of someone else, I should
perhaps not have been able to conceive of them?

11   WE FIND, THEREFORE, that to learn those things
      which we do not draw into us as images by
means of our senses, but which we perceive inside ourselves as they actually are without the aid of images
means simply this: by the act of thought we are, as it
were, collecting together things which the memory did
contain, though in a disorganized and scattered way, and
by giving them our close attention we are arranging for
them to be as it were stored up ready to hand in that
same memory where previously they lay hidden, neglected, and dispersed, so that now they will readily
come forward to the mind that has become familiar with
them. My memory carries a very great number of things
of this sort, which have been discovered and, as I said,
placed as it were ready to hand. These are the things
which we are said to have learned and to know. Yet if
I cease, even for quite a short space of time, to bring
them up into my mind, down they sink again and slip
away into some sort of distant hidden place, so that I
have to think them out afresh from that same place (for
there is nowhere else where they can have gone) and
once again gather them together so that they may be
known. In fact what one is doing is collecting them from
their dispersal. Hence the derivation of the word "to

cogitate." For *cogo* (collect) and *cogito* (re-collect) are in the same relation to each other as *ago* and *agito, facio* and *factito*. But the mind has appropriated to itself this word ("cogitation"), so that it is only correct to say "cogitated" of things which are "re-collected" in the mind, not of things re-collected elsewhere.

12 THE MEMORY also contains the innumerable principles and laws of numbers and dimensions. None of these has been imprinted on it by any bodily sense, since none of these is colored or can be heard, smelled, tasted, or touched. I have heard the sounds of the words by which these principles are signified when we discuss them, but the sounds and the principle are different things. The sounds will be different if the words used are Greek or Latin, but the principles are neither Greek nor Latin nor any other language. I have seen the lines drawn by architects, lines barely visible, like spiders' webs. But the principles involved are something different; they are not images of those things which are reported to me by my bodily eye, and the man who knows these principles recognizes them inside him without having to think of any kind of material body. Again, with all my bodily senses I have perceived the numbers which we use in counting; but the numbers by which we are able to count at all are not the same as these, nor are they images of these; they have a real existence of their own. Anyone who cannot see them may laugh at me for talking of them, and, while he laughs, I shall be sorry for him.

13 ALL THESE THINGS I hold in my memory, and I also hold in my memory how I learned them. And there are many completely false arguments which I have heard advanced against these things; these also I hold in my memory. And though they are false, it is not false to say that I remember them. I also remember that

I have distinguished between the truths and the false
objections made to those truths. And I see that for me
to make the distinction between them now is a different
thing from remembering how I often did make the distinction in the past, when I was thinking on these subjects. Therefore I remember that I often did understand
them and also I store up in my memory what I see and
understand now, so that later I may remember what I
did understand at this moment. So I remember that I have
remembered, and if in the future I recall that I have
now been able to remember these things, it will be by
the force of my memory that I shall recall it.

14   THIS SAME MEMORY also contains the feelings of
my mind. It does not contain them in the same
way as the mind itself has them when it is experiencing
them, but in a very different way, appropriate to the
nature of memory. For I remember that I was happy
when I am not happy now, and I recall my past sadness
when I am not sad now; when I am not frightened, I
can remember that I once was frightened, and I can
recall a desire I had once, when I have it no longer.
Sometimes it works the other way: when I am happy I
remember my past sadness, and when I am sad I remember my past happiness. There is nothing surprising in
this, so far as the body is concerned; for the mind is one
thing and the body another. So if I remember with joy
some past pain of the body, there is nothing strange in
that. But memory itself is mind. For example, when we
tell someone to remember something we say: "Be sure
to keep it in mind," and when we forget something we
say: "It was not in my mind," or "It slipped out of my
mind." So we call memory itself mind. Now since this is
so, how is it that when I, being happy, remember my
past sadness—so that the mind contains happiness and
the memory contains sadness—the mind is happy because of the happiness in it, but the memory is not sad
because of the sadness in it? Is it that the memory has

no connection with the mind? Obviously one cannot say that. Therefore the memory must be, as it were, the stomach of the mind, and happiness and sadness like sweet and bitter food, and when they are committed to the memory it is as though they passed into the stomach where they can be stored up but cannot taste. A ridiculous comparison, perhaps, and yet there is some truth in it.

Observe too that it comes from my memory when I say that there are four types of disturbance in the mind—desire, joy, fear, sorrow—and in any statements that I may be able to make on these subjects by means of definition or classification under genus and species, it is in my memory that I find what to say and it is from my memory that I bring it out. Yet in calling back to mind by the act of recollection disturbances of this sort, I myself feel no disturbance, and they were there, in the memory, before I recalled them and brought them back; indeed it was only because they were there that I was able to recollect them. May one say, then, that just as food is brought up from the stomach by chewing the cud, so these things are brought up from the memory by recollection? But why then is the actual sweetness of joy or bitterness of sorrow not tasted in the cogitational mouth of the man who makes statements about, i.e., remembers, these things? Or is this the point where the comparison between rumination and recollection is incomplete? For we would be reluctant to talk about these subjects if, whenever we used the words "sorrow" or "fear," we had actually to feel sorrow or fear. Yet we could not talk about them at all, unless we could find within our memory not only the sounds of the words (according to images impressed upon it by the senses of the body) but also concepts of the things themselves, and we did not receive these concepts by the gateway of any bodily sense; it was the mind itself which, by the experience of its own passions, felt them and entrusted them to the memory; or else the memory retained them, even if they were not entrusted to it.

15 BUT IT IS NOT easy to say whether this takes place by means of images or not. I pronounce the word "stone" or "sun" when the things themselves are not present to my senses; images of them however are in front of my memory. I pronounce the word for some physical pain; this pain is not present to me, since I am not in pain; but unless the image of it was in my memory, I should not know how to speak of it and, in any discussion, I should be unable to draw a distinction between it and pleasure. I mention physical health, when I myself am in good health; the thing signified by the words is actually present in me, yet unless its image also was in my memory, it would be impossible for me to recall what is meant by the sound of the words denoting it; nor, when the word "health" was mentioned, would sick people recognize the meaning of what was said, unless, in spite of the fact that health itself was not in their bodies, they still retained through the force of memory an image of health. I name the numbers that we use in counting; it is the numbers themselves and not their images that are in my memory. I name the image of the sun, and this image is in my memory—not the image of its image, but the image itself; that is what is before me when I recall it. I say "memory" and I recognize what I mean by it; but where do I recognize it except in my memory itself? Can memory itself be present to itself by means of its image rather than by its reality?

16 NOW SUPPOSE I say "forgetfulness" and once again recognize what I mean by the word, how do I recognize the thing itself unless it were that I remembered it? I am not speaking of the sound of the word, but the thing which the word signifies; for if I had forgotten the thing, I should certainly not be able to recognize what the word meant. When I remember memory, memory itself is, through itself, present to itself; but when I remember forgetfulness, there are present both memory and forgetfulness—memory by which

I remember, forgetfulness which I remember. But what is forgetfulness except privation of memory? How then can it be present for me to remember it, when I am not able to remember it when it is present? But if we retain in our memory what we remember, and if, unless we remembered forgetfulness, we should be quite unable to recognize what was meant by the word when we heard it, then forgetfulness must be retained in the memory. Therefore, what, when present, we forget is present in order that we should not forget. Must we understand from this that forgetfulness, when we remember it, is not present to the memory in itself, but by its image, because if it were present in itself, it would cause us, not to remember, but to forget? Who can possibly find the answer to this or understand how it comes about?

For me, Lord, certainly this is hard labor, hard labor inside myself, and I have become to myself a piece of difficult ground, not to be worked over without much sweat. For we are not now examining the regions of the heaven or measuring the distances of the stars or inquiring into how the earth is balanced in space. It is I myself who remember, I, the mind. There is nothing remarkable in the fact that something other than myself is far away from me; but what can be nearer to me than my own self? Yet this force of my memory is incomprehensible to me, even though, without it, I should not be able to call myself myself. What am I to say, when I see so clearly that I remember forgetfulness? Shall I say that what I remember is not in my memory? Or that forgetfulness is in my memory in order that I should not forget? Both answers are absurd. Is the third possibility any better? Could I say that it is the image of forgetfulness, not forgetfulness itself, which is held by my memory when I remember it? No, I could not; since when the image of a thing is impressed on the memory, it is first of all necessary that the thing itself should be present from which the impression can be derived. In this way I remember Carthage, or any other place where I have been; in this way I remember the faces of people I have seen and all things reported to me by the other senses; so too I remember the health or sickness of the body. When these things were present, the memory received their images from them and these images remained present for me to contemplate and bring back to mind when I recollected the objects themselves, which were absent. If, therefore, forgetfulness is retained in the memory by means of an image, and not in itself, then undoubtedly forgetfulness must at some time have been present so that its image could be received. But how, when it was present, could it inscribe its image on the memory, when its presence means the destruction even of all records that are already there? Nevertheless, however it may be, however incomprehensible and inexplicable, I am quite sure that I do remember this forgetfulness by which what we remember is effaced.

17 GREAT INDEED is the power of memory! It is something terrifying, my God, a profound and infinite multiplicity; and this thing is the mind, and this thing is I myself. What then am I, my God? What is my nature? A life various, manifold, and quite immeasurable. Imagine the plains, caverns, and abysses of my memory; they are innumerable and are innumerably full of innumerable kinds of things, present either in their images, as in the case of all bodies, or in themselves, as with the arts, or in the form of some kind of notion or consciousness, as with the affections of the mind, which, even when the mind is not experiencing them, are still retained by the memory (though whatever is in the memory is also in the mind). Through all this I range; I fly here and I fly there; I dive down deep as I can, and I can find no end. So great is the force of memory, so great is the force of life in man who lives to die.

What shall I do, you true life of mine, my God? I will go past this force of mine called memory; I will go beyond it so that I may draw nearer to you, sweet light. What is it that you are saying to me? I mount up through my mind toward you who dwell above me, and now I shall go beyond this force of mine called memory, for I desire to reach you at the point from which you may be reached, to cling to you at the point from which it is possible for me to cling to you. For even beasts and birds have memory; otherwise they would not be able to find their way back to their dens and nests or do any of the other things they are used to doing; indeed without memory they could not become used to doing anything. So I will pass beyond memory also, so that I may reach him who separated me from the four-footed beasts and made me wiser than the birds of the air. I will pass beyond memory to find you—Oh where, where, shall I find you, my truly good, my certain loveliness? If I find you beyond my memory, I can have no memory of you. And how shall I find you if I do not remember you?

18 THE WOMAN who had lost her groat sought for it with a light; but unless she had remembered it, she would not have found it. For when it was discovered, how could she have known whether it was the right one or not, if she had not remembered it? I remember many occasions when I have looked for and found something which I had lost, and from these experiences I know that when I was looking for the thing and people asked me: "Is this it?" or "Is that it?" I would go on saying: "No, it is not," until the thing that I really was looking for was produced. But unless I had remembered it, whatever it was, I would not have found it even if it were produced in front of me, since I would not have recognized it. And this is always the case when we look for and find something that was lost. If something happens to disappear from the eyes and not from the memory (as any visible body), its image is retained within us and is looked for until it is restored to sight, and when found, it is recognized by the image that is within. We do not say that we have found what was lost unless we recognize it, and we cannot recognize it unless we remember it. It was certainly lost to the eyes, but it was still held in the memory.

19 BUT WHEN THE MEMORY itself loses something, as happens when we forget a thing and try to recollect it, where can we possibly look for it except in the memory? And there if something other than what we are looking for is presented to us, we reject it until the thing that we are looking for turns up. And when it does turn up we say: "This is it." We would not say this unless we recognized it, and we would not recognize it unless we remembered it. Yet certainly we had forgotten it.

Or could this be the solution: the whole thing had not slipped from our memory; part of it was retained and by means of this part the other part was sought for, because the memory realized that it was not carrying along with it the totality which it was used to and, going unevenly, as it were, through the loss of something to which it was accustomed, eagerly demanded the restoration of what was lacking. For instance if we see or think of some man who is known to us, but have forgotten his name and are trying to recall it, any name that occurs to us other than his will not fit in, because we are not in the habit of thinking of that name and that person together. Consequently we go on rejecting names until the name presents itself with which our knowledge can rest satisfied, since it is the name with which it was accustomed to make the appropriate connection. And that name cannot come from any other source except the memory. Even when we recognize it after being reminded of it by someone else, the recognition still comes from the memory. We do not accept it as though it were something new; instead we agree that this was what it was because we remember it to be so. If it were entirely blotted out of our mind, we should not remember it even when reminded of it. For if we can remember that we have forgotten something, this means that we have not entirely forgotten it. Whatever has been utterly forgotten cannot even be thought of as lost and cannot be sought for.

20 HOW, THEN, LORD, do I seek you? For when I seek you, my God, I am seeking the happy life. *I will seek Thee, that my soul may live.* For my body lives by my soul, and my soul lives by you. How, then, do I seek for the happy life? For I cannot find it until I can reach the place where I can truly say: "It is enough; it is there." How then, do I seek it? Is it by remembrance, as though I had forgotten it but can still remember that I have forgotten? Or is it through desire to learn something unknown, something which either I never knew or which I have so completely forgotten that I cannot even remember that I have forgotten it? Is not the happy life the thing that all men desire, literally every single man without exception? But where did they get the knowledge of it, that they should desire it so? Where did they see it, that they should love it so? We have it, certainly; but how we have it, I do not know. In one sense a person may reach a certain degree of happiness and be called happy; others are happy in the hope of happiness. These latter do not have it in the same full sense as those who actually possess it; but they are better off than those who are neither happy in fact nor in hope. Though even these last must have it in some sense or other; otherwise they would not (as they certainly do) have such a wish to be happy. In some way or other they know of it and, therefore, may be said to possess it in some form of knowledge. Is this form of knowledge, I inquire, in the memory? If it is, then we must have experienced happiness at some time previously. I am not now asking whether this is an experience which we have all had individually, or whether the experience was in that man who first sinned, in whom we all died and of whom we are all born in misery. I am only asking whether the happy life is in our memory. For we could not love it, if we did not know it. We have heard the name "happiness" and all of us would agree that we desire the thing signified by the name; for it is not simply the sound of the word that pleases us. If a Greek hears the word in Latin, he derives no pleasure from it, since he does not know what has been said; but we are pleased, just in the same way as he would have been if he had heard the word in Greek. For the thing itself is neither Greek nor Latin, but it is something which Greeks, Latins, and men of all other languages long to attain. It is therefore known to all of them, and if they could all be asked with one voice: "Do you wish to be happy?" they would without any doubt reply, "We do." And this would not be so unless the thing itself, signified by the word, was contained in their memory.

21   BUT IS THIS an example of the same kind of memory as when I, who have seen Carthage, remember Carthage? No, it is not; for the happy life, not being a body, is not visible to our eyes. Do we then remember it in the same way as we remember numbers? No, we do not; whoever has a knowledge of numbers is content with that and need seek no further; but we who have a knowledge of the happy life and therefore love it, do want to go further so that we may reach it and become happy. Is it, then, as we remember eloquence? No, it is not. Though it is true that on hearing the word "eloquence" many people, who have not yet become eloquent, call to mind the thing signified by the word and many people would like to be eloquent—all of which shows that the thing is in their knowledge; yet it is by means of the bodily senses that they have observed others who are eloquent, have been pleased by it, and have wanted to become eloquent themselves (though unless they had some interior notion, they would not be pleased, and, if they were not pleased, they would not want to possess this quality); however, there is no bodily sense which enables us to experience the happy life in

others. Do we, then, remember it as we remember joy? This is possible. For I remember my joy even when I am sad, just as I remember the happy life even when I am unhappy. And never by any bodily sense did I see my joy, or hear it or smell it or taste it or touch it. I experienced it in my mind at the time when I was joyful, and the knowledge of it stuck in my memory so that I can call it back to mind, sometimes with contempt, sometimes with longing, according to the diversity of the things which I remember enjoying. For even base and disgraceful things have filled me with a kind of joy—things which now I detest and execrate when I recall them—and at other times I have had joy in good and worthy things which I remember with longing, though they may not be with me any more, so that I am sad when I recall the joy of the past.

Where, then, was it, and when was it that I experienced my happy life, so that I should remember it and love it and long for it? And not I alone, or I and a few others, but all of us; we all want to be happy. And unless we knew it with certain knowledge, we could not wish for it with so certain a will. But here is another point. Suppose two men are asked whether they want to join the army: it might happen that one would say "Yes" and the other would say "No." But if they are asked whether they want to be happy, both, without any doubt, would immediately say "Yes," and the only reason why one of them wanted to join the army and the other did not, was that they both wanted to be happy. Is it perhaps the case that different things make different people joyful and that so all agree that they want to be happy, just as they would agree, if they were asked, that they wanted to feel joy? And they think that joy itself is the same thing as the happy life? One may attain joy in one way, another in another way, but the end at which they are all aiming is one and the same, namely, a state of joy. And joy is something which no one can say he has no experience of; therefore, he finds it in his memory and recognizes it when he hears the words: "the happy life."

22 FAR BE IT, Lord, far be it from the heart of your servant who is confessing to you, far be it that I should think that any joy that I may experience makes me happy! For there is a joy that is not given to the ungodly, but only to those who love you for your own sake, and you yourself are their joy. And this is the happy life—to rejoice in you and to you and because of you. This is the happy life; there is no other. And those who think there is another, are in pursuit of another joy which is not the true joy. Yet all the same their will is still involved with some kind of an image of joy.

23 SO IT IS NOT certain that all men want to be happy. Those who do not want to find their joy in you (which alone is the happy life) certainly do not want the happy life. Or do all men really desire it, but *because the flesh lusteth against the Spirit and the Spirit against the flesh, that they cannot do what they would,* they fall into that state which is within their powers and are content with it because their will for a state which is beyond them is not strong enough to bring it within their reach? For if I ask anyone: "Would you rather have your joy in truth or in falsehood?" he would say: "In truth," with just as little hesitation as he would say that he wants to be happy. And certainly the happy life is joy in truth, which means joy in you, who are truth, God, *my light, health of my countenance, my God.* This is the happy life which all desire; this life which alone is happy all desire; joy in truth is what all desire. I have met many people who wanted to deceive, but no one who wanted to be deceived. But where did they gain their knowledge of this happy life except in the place where they also gained their knowledge of truth? For they love truth also (because they do not want to be deceived) and in loving the happy life (which simply means joy in truth) they must certainly love truth too, and they would not be able to love it, unless there were some knowledge of it in their memory. Why, then, do they not find their joy in it? Why are they not happy? Because they are more strongly taken up by other things which have more power to make them unhappy than that, which they so dimly remember, has to make them happy. For there is still only a little light in men, and they must walk, yes, they must *walk, that the darkness overtake them not.*

But why is it that "truth gives birth to hatred"? Why does your servant who preaches the truth incur enmity in spite of the fact that people love the happy life which simply is joy in truth? It is because truth is loved in such a way that those who love something else would like to believe that what they love is the truth, and because they would not like to be deceived, they object to being shown that in fact they are deceived. And so they hate truth for the sake of whatever it is they love instead of truth. They love the light of truth, but hate it when it shows them up as wrong. Because they do not want to be deceived and do want to deceive, they love truth when truth is giving evidence, but hate it when the evidence given is against themselves. And the retribution which will come to them is this: those who do not want to stand in the light of truth, will have to stand in it, whether they like it or not, but truth will not reveal her light to them. So it is, yes, so, indeed it is: this human mind of ours, so blind and sick, so foul and ill-favored, wants to be hidden itself, but hates to have anything hidden from it. But what happens is just the contrary: it cannot hide from truth, but truth can be out of its sight. Yet even so, wretched as it is, it prefers to find joy in truth than in falsehoods. It will be happy, therefore, when, with no distractions to interpose themselves, it will find its joy in that only truth by which all things are true.

24 SEE WHAT A DISTANCE I have covered searching for you, Lord, in my memory! And I have not found you outside it. Nor have I found anything about you which I have not kept in my memory from the time I first learned you. For from the time I learned you, I have not forgotten you. For when I found truth, then I found my God, truth itself, and from the time I learned it I have not forgotten it. And so, since the time I learned you, you stay in my memory, and there I find you whenever I call you to mind and delight in you. There are my holy delights, which in your mercy you have given me, having regard to my poverty.

25 BUT WHERE IS IT, Lord, in my memory that you stay? In what part of it do you stay? What resting place have you framed for yourself? What sanctuary have you built? You have given my memory the honor of staying in it: but in what part of it do you stay? This is what I now consider.

While I was calling you to mind, I went beyond those parts of the memory which the beasts also have (because I did not find you there among the images of material things), and I came to those parts of it where I had stored up the affections of my mind, but did not find you there either. And I went into the seat of the mind itself (which the mind has in my memory, since the mind remembers itself), and you were not there. For, just as you are not a material image, nor an affection of any living man (such as we feel when we are in a state of joy, sorrow, desire, fear, memory, forgetfulness, or anything else of this kind), so you are not the mind itself, because you are the Lord God of the mind, and all these things change, but you remain changeless over all things, and you have deigned to dwell in my memory, from the time I first learned of you. And why do I inquire in what place of my memory you dwell, as though there were any places there? Certainly you do dwell in my memory, because I remember you from the time I first learned of you, and I find you there when I call you to mind.

26 WHERE THEN did I find you, so that I could learn of you? For you were not in my memory before I learned of you. Where then did I find you, so that I could learn of you? I could only have found you in yourself, above me. Place there is none; we go *backward and forward*, and there is no place. Truth, you are everywhere in session, ready to listen to all who ask counsel of you, and at one and the same moment you give your answer to every diversity of question. You answer clearly, though everyone does not hear clearly. All ask what they wish, but they do not always hear what they want to hear. He serves you best who is not so anxious to hear from you what he wills as to will what he hears from you.

27 Late it was that I loved you, beauty so ancient and so new, late I loved you! And, look, you were within me and I was outside, and there I sought for you and in my ugliness I plunged into the beauties that you have made. You were with me, and I was not with you. Those outer beauties kept me far from you, yet if they had not been in you, they would not have existed at all. You called, you cried out, you shattered my deafness: you flashed, you shone, you scattered my blindness: you breathed perfume, and I drew in my breath and I pant for you: I tasted, and I am hungry and thirsty: you touched me, and I burned for your peace.

28 When in my whole self I shall cling to you united, I shall find no sorrow anywhere, no labor; wholly alive will my life be all full of you. Those whom you fill, you raise up, and now, since I am not yet full of you, I am a burden to myself. Joys in which I should find sorrow conflict with sorrows in which I should find joy, and on which side stands the victory I do not know. I am sad for myself. Lord, have pity on me! My evil sorrows conflict with my good joys, and on which side stands the victory I do not know. I am sad for myself. Lord, have pity on me! I am sad for myself. Look, I am not hiding my wounds: you are the doctor and I am sick; you are merciful, I need mercy. *Is not the life*

of man upon earth all trial? Does anyone want to be in trouble and difficulties? These you order us to endure, not to love. No one loves what he endures, even though he loves to endure. For however much he may rejoice in the fact of his endurance, he would still prefer that there were nothing to endure. In adversity I long for prosperity, in prosperity I fear adversity. What middle place is there between these two when the life of man is not all trial? All the prosperities of this world are cursed once and again—by the fear of adversity and by the corruption of joy. And the adversities of this world are cursed once, twice, and three times—by the longing for prosperity, by the very bitterness of adversity itself, and by the fear that it may break down our endurance. Is it not true, then, that the life of man upon earth is all trial without intermission?

29   AND ALL MY HOPE is nowhere except in your great mercy. Grant us what you command, and command us what you will. You demand that we should be continent. And *when I knew,* as it is said, *that no man can be continent, unless God give it, this also was a part of wisdom to know whose gift she is.* Certainly it is by continence that we are brought together and brought back to the One, after having dissipated ourselves among the Many. For he loves you insufficiently who loves something else with you which he does not love for your sake. O love, ever burning, and never extinguished, charity, my God, set me on fire! You command continence. Grant what you command, and command what you will.

30   CERTAINLY you command me to restrain myself from the *lust of the flesh, the lust of the eyes, and the ambition of the world.* You commanded me to abstain from sleeping with a mistress, and with regard to marriage you advised me to take a better course than the one that was permitted me. And since you gave me the power, it was done, even before I became a dispenser of your Sacrament. But there still live in that memory of mine, of which I have spoken so much, images of the things which my habit has fixed there. These images come into my thoughts, and, though when I am awake they are strengthless, in sleep they not only cause pleasure but go so far as to obtain assent and something very like reality. These images, though real, have such an effect on my soul, in my flesh, that false visions in my sleep obtain from me what true visions cannot when I am awake. Surely, Lord my God, I am myself when I am asleep? And yet there is a very great difference between myself and myself in that moment of time when I pass from being awake to being asleep or come back again from sleep to wakefulness. Where then is my reason which, when I am awake, resists such suggestions and remains unshaken if the realities themselves were presented to it? Do reason's eyes close with the eyes of the body? Does reason go to sleep when the bodily senses sleep? If so, how does it happen that even in our sleep we do often resist and, remembering our purpose and most chastely abiding by it, give no assent to enticements of this kind? Nevertheless, there is a great difference, because, when it happens otherwise, we return on waking to a peace of conscience and, by the very remoteness of our state now and then, discover that it was not we who did something which was, to our regret, somehow or other done in us.

Almighty God, surely your hand is powerful enough to cure all the sicknesses of my soul and, with a more abundant measure of your grace, to quench even the lustful impulses of my sleep. Lord, you will increase your gifts in me more and more, so that my soul, disentangled from the birdlime of concupiscence, may follow me to you; so that it may not be in revolt against itself and may not, even in dreams, succumb to or even give the slightest assent to those degrading corruptions which by means of sensual images actually disturb and pollute the flesh. It is not a hard thing for you, Almighty, who are

able to do above all that we ask or think, to prevent anything of this sort, not even the very slightest inclination (so
small that a mere nod would check it), from affecting the
chaste mind of a sleeper—and to prevent it not only in
this life but at this age at which I am now. But now I have
explained to my good Lord what is still my state in this
kind of evil, *rejoicing with trembling* in your gifts and griev-
ing for my imperfection and hoping that you will perfect
your mercies in me till I reach that fullness of peace which
both my inward and my outer self will have with you when
death shall be swallowed up in victory.

31 THERE IS ANOTHER *evil of the day,* and I wish
that it were *sufficient for it.* It is by eating and
drinking that we repair the losses suffered by the body
every day until the time comes when you *destroy both
belly and meat,* when you kill all need with a wonderful
fullness, and *clothe this corruptible* with an eternal *incor-
ruption.* But now this necessity is sweet to me, and I
fight against this sweetness, so that I may not become
its prisoner; by fasting I carry on war every day, often
bringing my body into subjection, and the pain I suffer
in this way is driven out by pleasure. For hunger and
thirst are pains; they burn us up and kill us like a fever,
unless we are relieved by the medicine of nourishment.
And this nourishment is at hand by the consolation of
your gifts, in which earth and water and sky serve our
weakness, and so our calamity is called our delight.

This you have taught me, that I should have the same
attitude toward taking food as I have toward taking
medicine. But while I pass from the discomfort of hunger
to the satisfaction of sufficiency, in that very moment of
transition there is set for me a snare of concupiscence.
For the moment of transition is pleasurable, and we are
forced to go through that moment; there is no other way.
And while we eat and drink for the sake of health, there
is a dangerous kind of pleasure which follows in atten-
dance on health and very often tries to put itself first,

so that what I say that I am doing, and mean to do, for the sake of my health is actually done for the sake of pleasure. Nor is there the same measure for both; what is enough for health is not enough for pleasure, and it is often hard to tell whether it is the necessary care of my body asking for sustenance or whether it is a deceitful voluptuousness of greed trying to seduce me. And because of this uncertainty the unhappy soul is delighted; it uses it as a cover and excuse for itself, and is glad that it is not clearly evident what is sufficient for a healthy moderation, so that under the cloak of health it may hide the business of pleasure. Every day I try to resist these temptations; I call upon your right hand to help me, and I refer my perplexities to you, since I have not yet found a settled plan in this matter.

I hear the voice of my God commanding: *Let not your hearts be overcharged with surfeiting and drunkenness.* I have no inclination to drunkenness, and in your mercy you will keep me far from it; but overeating has sometimes crept up on your servant. You will have mercy, so that it may be far from me. For *no one can be continent unless you give it.* You give us many things that we pray for, and everything good that we receive before we pray we receive at your hands. I have never been a drunkard, but I have known drunkards who have been made sober by you. Therefore, it is your doing that some men have never been drunkards; it is your doing that others who have been drunkards should not always remain so, and it is also your doing that both sorts of men should know that it is your doing.

I heard another voice of yours: *Go not after thy lusts, and from thy pleasure turn away.* This too, by your gift, I heard and I have greatly loved it: *Neither if we eat, shall we abound; neither if we eat not, shall we lack,* that is to say, the one will not make me rich and the other will not make me miserable. And I heard too: *For I have learned in whatever state I am, therewith to be content; I know how to abound, and how to suffer need. I can do all things through Christ that strengtheneth me.* There indeed speaks one who is a soldier of the heavenly army, not dust, as we are. But *remember, Lord, that we are dust,* and that *of dust Thou hast made man,* and *he was lost and is found.* Nor did he do it by his own power (since he was the same dust)—he, I mean, whom I loved so much when he said such things, through the breath of your inspiration. *I can do all things,* he says, *through Him that strengtheneth me.* Strengthen me, so that I can. Give what you command, and command what you will. Paul confesses that he has received, and when he glories, it is in the Lord that he glories. I have heard another also begging that he might receive: *Take from me,* he says, *the desires of the belly.* From which, O holy God, it appears that it is your gift when what you command to be done is done.

Good Father, you have taught me that *to the pure all things are pure;* but that *it is evil unto the man that eateth with offense,* and, that *every creature of Thine is good, and nothing to be refused, which is received with thanksgiving,* and that *meat commendeth us not to God,* and, that *no man should judge as in meat or drink,* and that *he which eateth, let him not despise him that eateth not, and let not him that eateth not, judge him that eateth.* These things I have learned, thanks and praise to you, my God, my master, knocking at my ears, enlightening my heart; deliver me from all temptation. It is not any uncleanness in the meat that I fear; it is the uncleanness of gluttony. I know that Noah was allowed to eat all kinds of meat that are good for food; that Elijah was fed with meat; that John the Baptist, who was endowed with the most remarkable abstinence, was not polluted by the living creatures, locusts, which were given him for food. I know too that Esau was deceived because of his greediness for lentils; that David reproached himself for desiring some water, and that our King was tempted not with meat, but with bread. And the reason why the Israelites in the wilderness deserved to be blamed was not because they desired meat but because, in desiring food, they murmured against the Lord.

Placed as I am among these temptations, I strive every day against concupiscence in eating and drinking; for this is not the sort of thing that I can decide to give up once and for all and never touch again, as I was able to do with sex. Therefore, I must keep a hold which is neither too loose nor too tight on the bridle of my throat. And it is scarcely possible, Lord, not to be carried slightly beyond the bounds of necessity. Anyone who can keep exactly within them is a great man and greatly should he praise your name. But I am not he, since I am a sinful man. Yet I too magnify your name, and *He maketh intercession to Thee* for my sins who *hath overcome the world*; numbering me among the *weak members* of His *body;* because *Thine eyes have seen* that of Him which is *imperfect, and in Thy book shall all be written.*

32 As to the enticements which come to us from the sense of smell, I am not much concerned with them. I do not miss them when they are absent, or reject them when they are present, and I am quite prepared to be without them altogether. So it seems to me, though I may be deceiving myself. For here too there is a sad kind of darkness, the darkness in which the abilities that are in me are hidden from me, so that when my mind questions itself about its own powers, it cannot be certain that its replies are trustworthy, because what is inside the mind is mostly hidden and remains hidden until revealed by experience, and in this life, which is described as a continuous trial, no one ought to feel sure that, just as he has been worse and become better, he may not also, after having been better, become worse. Our one hope, our one confidence, our one firm promise is your mercy.

33 The delights of the sense of hearing had a stronger grip and a greater authority over me; but you loosed the bond and set me free. Yet now when I hear sung in a sweet and well-trained voice those melodies

into which your words breathe life, I do, I admit, feel some
pleasurable relaxation, though not of the kind which would
make it difficult for me to tear myself away, for I could
get up and leave when I like. Nevertheless they do demand
a place of some dignity in my heart so that they may be
received into me together with the words that give them
life, and it is not easy for me to give them exactly the right
place. For sometimes it seems to me that I am giving them
more honor than is right. I may feel that when these holy
words themselves are well sung, our minds are stirred up
more fervently and more religiously into a flame of devotion than if they are not so well sung, and I realize that the
emotions of the spirit are various, each, by some secret kind
of correspondence, capable of being excited by its own
proper mode of voice or song. But I am often deceived by
this pleasure of my flesh, to which the mind should not be
given over to be enervated. The bodily sense only deserves
to be admitted because of the reason; but often, instead of
being content to follow behind reason, it tries to go ahead of
reason and take the lead. So in these matters I sin without
realizing it, only realizing afterward that I have sinned.

But at other times, when I am overanxious to avoid
being deceived in this way, I fall into the error of being
too severe—so much so that I would like banished both
from my own ears and those of the Church as well the
whole melody of sweet music that is used with David's
Psalter—and the safer course seems to me that of Atha-
nasius, bishop of Alexandria, who, as I have often been
told, made the reader of the psalm employ so very small
a modulation of the voice that the effect was more like
speaking than singing. But then I remember the tears I
shed at the singing in church at the time when I was
beginning to recover my faith; I remember that now I am
moved not by the singing but by the things that are sung,
when they are sung with a clear voice and correct modulation, and once again I recognize the great utility of this
institution. So I fluctuate between the danger of pleasure
and my experience of the good that can be done. I am
inclined on the whole (though I do not regard this opin-

ion as irrevocable) to be in favor of the practice of singing in church, so that by means of the delight in hearing the weaker minds may be roused to a feeling of devotion. Nevertheless, whenever it happens to me that I am more moved by the singing than by what is sung, I confess that I am sinning grievously; and then I would prefer not to hear the music. See what a state I am in! I hope that you will weep with me and weep for me, all those of you who have inside you some of the good feeling from which good actions come. Those of you who have not, will not be moved by these things. And I pray that you, my Lord God, will hear me and look down upon me and see me and cure me. In your eyes I have become a problem to myself, and *that is my infirmity.*

34 THERE REMAINS the pleasure of these eyes of my flesh, and it is of this pleasure that I now make my confessions in the hearing of the ears of your temple—those brotherly and devout ears. With this I shall conclude the account of the temptations arising from *the lust of the flesh,* temptations which still beset me, *groaning earnestly, and desiring to be clothed with my house that is from heaven.*

The eyes love beautiful shapes of all kinds, glowing and delightful colors. These things must not take hold on my soul; that is for God to do. Certainly God made these things very good, but it is He Himself, not these things, who is my good. These things affect me during all the time every day that I am awake. I get no respite from them, as I get from the sounds of music and sometimes, in silence, from all sounds. For light is the queen of colors, and wherever I am in daytime she is suffused over everything visible; she glides up to me in shape after shape, cajoling me when I am doing something quite different and am paying no deliberate attention to her. But she makes her way so forcibly into my mind that, if light is suddenly withdrawn, I look for it again with longing, and if it is absent for long, my mind grows sad.

Let me think of that light which Tobias saw when, with these eyes shut, he showed his son the way of life and, with the feet of charity, went in front of him and never missed the path. Or the light which Isaac saw when, with his fleshly eyes heavy and dim with age, it was granted him to bless his sons without being able to see which was which, and yet in the act of blessing to gain the power of distinguishing between them. Or the light which Jacob saw when he also had become blind through great age; yet his heart was illumined and in the persons of his sons he shed light on the tribes of the future which were foreshadowed by them, and he laid his hands, mystically reversed, on his grandchildren, the sons of Joseph, not as their father, seeing from without, directed, but according to his own inner discernment. This is light itself; it is one, and all who see it and love it are one. As to that corporeal light, of which I was speaking, it is a tempting and dangerous sweetness, like a sauce spread over the life of this world for its blind lovers. Yet those who know how to praise you for this light, "Creator Thou of everything," carry it up to you in your hymn, and are not carried away by it into spiritual sleep. So I would like to be. I resist these seductions of the eyes, so that my feet with which I walk your way may not be ensnared, and to you I lift up my invisible eyes, so that you may *pluck my feet out of the snare.* Repeatedly you do pluck them out, for they are ensnared. You do not cease to pluck them out, while I so frequently entangle myself in the traps spread around me on all sides; because *Thou that keepest Israel shalt neither slumber nor sleep.*

And to the temptations of the eyes, men themselves in their various arts and manufactures have made innumerable additions: clothes, shoes, vases, products of craftsmanship; pictures too and all sorts of statues—far beyond what is necessary for use, moderate or with any religious meaning. So men go outside themselves to follow things of their own making, and inside themselves they are forsaking Him who made them and are destroying what they themselves were made to be. But I, my God and my glory, find here also something from which to make a hymn to you, and I offer my praise in sacrifice to Him who sanctifies me. Because all those beauties which pass through men's souls into their skillful hands come from that Beauty which is above souls and for which my soul is sighing day and night. From it artists and enthusiasts for external beauties derive the criterion by which to judge what is beautiful or not, but they do not find the rule for making the right use of these forms of beauty. Yet the rule is there, though they do not see it—a rule telling them not to go too far, and to keep their strength for you instead of dissipating it upon delights that end in lassitude. Yet I who am saying this and who see the truth of what I say still entangle my steps in these outer beauties. But you will pluck me out, Lord, you will pluck me out, *because Thy loving kindness is before my eyes.* For I am most pitifully caught up by them, but you will pity me and pluck me out, and sometimes, when I am only lightly caught in the trap, I scarcely realize what you are doing; sometimes, when I have become deeply implicated, I feel pain.

35 I MUST NOW mention another form of temptation which is in many ways more dangerous. Apart from the concupiscence of the flesh which is present in the delight we take in all the pleasures of the senses (and the slaves of it perish as they put themselves far from you), there is also present in the soul, by means of these same bodily senses, a kind of empty longing and curiosity which aims not at taking pleasure in the flesh but at acquiring experience through the flesh, and this empty curiosity is dignified by the names of learning and science. Since this is in the appetite for knowing, and since the eyes are the chief of our senses for acquiring knowledge, it is called in the divine language *the lust of the eyes.* For "to see" is used properly of the eyes; but we also use this word of the other senses when we are

employing them for the purpose of gaining knowledge. We do not say: "Hear how it flashes" or "Smell how bright it is" or "Taste how it shines" or "Feel how it gleams"; in all these cases we use the verb "to see." But we not only say: "See how it shines," a thing which can only be perceived by the eyes; we also say "See how it sounds," "See how it smells," "See how it tastes," "See how hard it is." Therefore, the general experience of the senses is, as was said before, called "the lust of the eyes," because seeing, which belongs properly to the eyes, is used by analogy of the other senses too when they are attempting to discover any kind of knowledge.

In this it is easy to see how pleasure and curiosity have different objects in their use of the senses. Pleasure goes after what is beautiful to us, sweet to hear, to smell, to taste, to touch; but curiosity, for the sake of experiment, may go after the exact opposites of these, not in order to suffer discomfort, but simply because of the lust to find out and to know. What pleasure can there be in looking at a mangled corpse, which must excite our horror? Yet if there is one near, people flock to see it, so as to grow sad and pale at the sight. They are actually frightened of seeing it in their sleep, as though anyone had forced them to see it when they were awake or as if they had been induced to look at it because it had the reputation of being a beautiful thing to see. The same is true of the other senses. There is no need to go to the length of producing examples. Because of this disease of curiosity monsters and anything out of the ordinary are put on show in our theaters. From the same motive men proceed to investigate the workings of nature which is beyond our ken—things which it does no good to know and which men only want to know for the sake of knowing. So too, and with this same end of perverted science, people make inquiries by means of magic. Even in religion we find the same thing: God is tempted when signs and portents are demanded and are not desired for any salutary purpose, but simply for the experience of seeing them.

In this enormous forest, so full of snares and dangers,

many are the temptations which I have cut off and thrust away from my heart, as you, God of my salvation, have granted me the power. Yet since so many things of this kind are buzzing around our daily life in all directions, how can I dare to say, how can I ever dare to say that nothing of this sort can make me give my attention to it or fill me with the empty desire to possess it? True that I am no longer carried away by the theater; I am not interested in knowing about the courses of the stars; my soul has never made inquiries from the ghosts of the dead; I detest all sacrilegious mysteries. Yet, my Lord God, to whom I owe my humble and pure service, there are all kinds of artifices of suggestion by which the enemy urges me to seek for some sign from you. But I beg you by our King and by our country Jerusalem, the chaste and pure, that just as up to now it has been far from me to give my assent to such suggestions, so the possibility of doing so may become more and more remote. But when I pray to you for the good of someone else my mind is directed to a quite different end; you do as you will, and you give and will give me the grace cheerfully to accept your will.

Nevertheless, there are very many occasions, small and contemptible enough, in which this curiosity of ours is tempted every day, and it is impossible to count the times when we slip. It often happens that people talk to us in some empty idle way, and we listen to them tolerantly at first, so as not to give offense to the weak; but then we gradually begin to take a serious interest in their gossip. I no longer go to the Games to see a dog coursing a hare; but if I happen to be going through the country and see this sport going on, it may attract my attention away from some serious meditation—not so much as to make me turn my horse's body out of the way, but enough to alter the inclination of my mind. And unless you showed me my infirmity and quickly admonished me either by some thought connected with the sight itself to rise up toward you, or else to pay no attention to the thing at all and to pass by, I should stand there empty-headed like a stock. And then there are all the occasions when I am sitting at home and my attention is attracted by a lizard catching flies or by a spider entangling them in his web. The animals may be small, but this does not make the thing any different. I go on from them to praise you, wonderful Creator and Director of all things; but it was not this that first drew my attention. It is one thing to get up quickly and another thing not to fall down. My life is full of such things and my only hope is in your great, great mercy. For when our heart is made the receptacle for things of this kind and becomes laden with pressing throngs of vanity, the result is that even our prayers are interrupted and disturbed, and when, in your presence, we are directing the voice of our heart to your ears, our great and serious purpose is broken off by an invasion of idle empty thoughts, coming from I know not where.

36 CERTAINLY WE CANNOT regard this as among things of little importance. And there is nothing to bring us back to hope except your known mercy, since you have begun to change us.

And you know how far you have already changed me, you who first cured me of my lust for asserting myself against others, so that you may be merciful also to the rest of my iniquities, *and heal all my infirmities, and redeem my life from corruption, and crown me with mercy and pity, and satisfy my desire with good things*: you who curbed my pride with your fear and tamed my neck to your yoke. And now I bear that yoke and I find it light. This was what you promised and this is what you have done. And indeed it always was light, though I did not know it in the time when I was afraid to take it upon me.

But tell me, Lord, you who alone are Lord without pride, because you are alone the true Lord, who has no other Lord, has this third kind of temptation disappeared from me, or can it ever entirely disappear in this life? I mean the wish to be feared and loved by men for no other reason but to get from it a joy, which is no true joy. It is a wretched way of life, a disgusting kind of ostentation. Here in particular we may find the reason why you are not purely loved or feared, and therefore *dost Thou resist the proud, and givest grace to the humble,* and you thunder down upon the ambitions of this world, and *the foundations of the mountains tremble.* And so, because there are certain positions in human society where the holder of office must be loved and feared by men, the enemy of our true happiness is always close upon us, setting his snares everywhere in the words "Well done, well done," and hoping that, while we greedily snatch at them, we shall be taken unawares, shall no longer plan our joy in your truth but shall entrust it to the deceitfulness of men, and shall want to be loved and feared not because of you but instead of you. In this way our enemy will make us become like him and will have us united to him not in the bonds of charity but in the bonds of punishment—he who decided to *set his throne in the north*, so that there, in cold and darkness, men might become his slaves as he attempts pervertedly and crookedly to imitate you. But as to us, Lord, see, we are your *little flock.* Keep us in your possession. Stretch out your wings so that we may take refuge beneath them. It is you who must be our glory; let us be loved for your sake, and let it be your word that is feared in us. The man who wishes to be praised by men regardless of your approval will not be defended by men when you judge him, nor delivered by men when you condemn him. It may not be the case of a *sinner being praised in the desires of his soul* or a man *blessed who doth ungodly;* it may be that a man is praised for some gift which you have given him and takes more pleasure in hearing himself praised than in having that gift for which he is praised; this man too is praised by men, but blamed by you, and those who praise him are better than he who is praised; for what gives them pleasure is the gift of God in a man, but he takes more pleasure in what men give than in what God has given.

37 WE ARE TEMPTED, Lord, by these temptations every day; without intermission we are tempted. The tongue of man is the furnace in which we are tried every day. Here too you command us to be continent. Give what you command, and command what you will. You know how on this matter my heart groans to you and my eyes stream tears. For I cannot easily discover how far I have become cleaner from this disease, and I much fear my hidden sins which are visible to your eyes, though not to mine. For in other kinds of temptation I have at least some means of finding out about myself; but in this kind it is almost impossible. With regard to the pleasures of the flesh and the unnecessary curiosity for knowledge I can see how far I have advanced in the ability to control my mind simply by observing myself when I am without these things, either from choice or when they are not available. For I can then ask myself how much or how little I mind not having them. So too with regard to riches, which are desired for the satisfaction of one or two or all of those three concupiscences; if one is not able to be quite sure in one's own mind whether or not one despises them when one has them, it is possible to get rid of them so as to put oneself to the test. But how can we arrange things so as to be without praise and make the same experiment with regard to it? Are we to live a bad life, to live in such a wicked and abandoned way that everyone who knows us will detest us? Nothing could be madder than such a suggestion as that. On the contrary, if praise both goes with and ought to go with a good life and good works, we should no more part with it than with the good life itself. Yet unless a thing is not there I cannot tell whether it is difficult or easy for me to be without it.

With regard to this kind of temptation then, what, Lord, shall I confess? This I can say, that I take pleasure in praise, but more pleasure in truth than in praise. For if I were given the choice of either being out of my wits and wrong on every subject, yet praised by everyone, or being firm and sure in the truth, yet abused by everyone,

I know which I should choose. Yet I wish it were not the case that when someone else praises me, my joy in whatever good quality I may have is increased. It is increased however, I admit; not only that, but it is diminished by dispraise. And when I am troubled at this wretched state of mine, an excuse occurs to me, whether it is a good one or not, you, God, know; for it leaves me uncertain. You demand from us not only continence—that is, to restrain our love from certain things—but also justice—that is, to direct our love upon certain things—and it is your will not only that we should love you but also that we should love our neighbor. So it often seems to me that when I am pleased by intelligent praise I am pleased because of the sound judgment or the promise shown by my neighbor, and in the same way it is his faults that make me sad when I hear him dispraise something which he does not understand or which is good. For there are also times when I feel sad to hear myself praised, either when people praise things in me which I dislike in myself or when some trifling and unimportant good qualities in me are rated at more than their proper value. But again I am in doubt: do I feel like this simply because I do not want a man who praises me to think about me differently from the way I think myself? And am I moved not so much by what is good for him as by the fact that those good qualities of mine which I approve of in myself are all the more pleasing to me when someone else approves of them too? For in a sense I am not being praised when my own opinion of myself is not praised, when, that is, qualities of mine are praised of which I myself do not approve, or when a high value is set on things in me which I regard as unimportant. It seems then that I am doubtful of myself in this matter.

Yes, Truth, in you I see that when I am praised the pleasure I feel should not be for my own sake but for the sake of the good of my neighbor. But whether this is really how I do feel I do not know. In this matter I know less of myself than of you. I beg you, my God, to show me myself, so that I may confess the fault that is in me to my brethren who will pray for me. Let me question myself again more carefully. If, when I hear myself praised, I am moved by thoughts of the good of my neighbor, why is it that I am less moved when someone else is unjustly blamed than when I myself am unjustly blamed? Why am I more wounded by a reproach leveled against me than by one which, with equal injustice, is, while I am present, leveled against someone else? Am I ignorant of this too? Or is not the fact simply this, that I deceive myself and in your presence fail to be truthful in heart and tongue? Put this madness far from me, Lord, lest my own mouth be to me the *sinner's oil to make fat my head.*

38   *I am poor and needy,* yet I am the better when, groaning secretly in my dissatisfaction with myself, I seek your mercy till the time comes when what is defective in me will be made good and brought to perfection in that peace which is unknown to the eye of the proud. Words which come from the mouth and actions which are known to men carry with them a most dangerous temptation from the love of praise which goes around as it were canvassing and collecting votes for the advancement of one's personal distinction. It still tempts me even when I condemn it in myself; indeed it tempts me even in the very act of condemning it; often in our contempt of vainglory we are merely being all the more vainglorious, and so one cannot really say that one glories in the contempt of glory; for one does not feel contempt for something in which one glories.

39   INSIDE US TOO is another evil belonging to the same class of temptation. It is the vanity of those who are pleased with themselves, however much they may not please others, or may displease them, or may not care whether they please them or not. But those who are pleased with themselves certainly do not please you. Here it is not so much a case of taking pleasure in things that are not good as though they were good; the fault is in taking pleasure in good things which come from you as though they came from oneself; or, even if they are acknowledged as coming from you, in assuming that one deserves to have them; or, even if it is admitted that they are due to your grace, in not rejoicing with their brethren but envying your grace to others. In all these and other similar dangers and difficulties you see the trembling of my heart, and often as you heal my wounds I feel new wounds being inflicted upon me.

40 WHEN HAVE YOU not walked with me, O Truth, teaching me what to beware of and what to seek after, when I referred to you what I have been able to see here below and asked your advice? With my outward senses I surveyed, to the best of my ability, the world, and I observed both the life which my body has from me and these senses themselves. From these I entered into the recesses of my memory, space folded upon huge space and all miraculously full of innumerable abundance, and I considered it and I was amazed; no one of all the things there could I discover without you, and I did not find any of them was you. Nor was I myself the discoverer, though I went through them all and tried to distinguish each from each, estimating them according to their proper worth, taking some things on the report of my senses, questioning others which I felt to be somehow parts of myself, and I counted and distinguished between these messengers, and now in the vast treasury of my memory I would meditate on something stored there, or put something away or take something out. But it was not I myself who did all this—that is to say, the power by which I did it was not myself—nor were you that power, because you are the permanent and abiding light which I consulted on all these things, asking whether they are, what they are, and what they are worth. And I heard you teaching me and commanding me. And I often do this. I find a delight in it, and whenever I can relax from my necessary duties I have recourse to this pleasure. And in all these things over which I range as I am consulting you I find no secure place for my soul except in you, and in you I pray that what is scattered in me may be brought together so that nothing of me may depart from you. And sometimes working within me you open for me a door into a state of feeling which is quite unlike anything to which I am used—a kind of sweet delight which, if I could only remain permanently in that state, would be something not of this world, not of this life. But my sad weight makes me fall back again; I am swallowed up by normality; I am held fast and heavily do I weep, but heavily I am held. So much are we weighed down by the burden of custom! Here I have the power but not the wish to stay; there I wish to be but cannot; both ways, miserable.

41 So, UNDER THE HEADINGS of the three forms of concupiscence I have considered the sicknesses of my sins, and I have called your right hand to my help. For I have seen your splendor, but my own heart has been wounded; I have been beaten back and have said: Who can reach there? *I am cast away from the sight of Thine eyes.* You are Truth presiding over everything. But I in my covetousness, while not wanting to lose you, wanted at the same time to possess a lie; just as no man wants to speak so falsely that he himself ceases to be conscious of the truth. And this was why I lost you, because you will not be possessed together with a lie.

42 WHOM COULD I FIND to reconcile me to you? Was I to seek the help of angels? By what prayer, what sacraments? Many people in their attempts to return to you and not being able to do so by their own strength have, so I hear, tried this way and have fallen into a desire for strange visions and have become, rightly, the victims of delusions. For in seeking you they have drawn themselves up in the arrogance of their learning; they have thrown out their chests instead of beating their breasts, and so through likeness of heart they drew to themselves the *princes of the air* as their fellow-conspirators in pride and were deceived by them through magical powers. They were seeking a mediator through whom to become clean, but this was not he. It was the devil, *transforming himself into an angel of light,* and for proud flesh it proved a strong attraction that he himself had not a body of flesh. For they were mortal and sinners; you, Lord, to whom they wished to be reconciled, are immortal and without sin. So a mediator between God and men should have something in common with God and something in common with men. If he were in both respects like men, he would be far from God, and if he were in both respects like God, he would be far from men, and so neither way could he be a mediator. But that deceitful mediator, by whom, according to your secret judgment, pride deserves to be mocked, has one thing in common with men—namely, sin—and appears to have another thing in common with God—that is that, not being clothed in the mortality of flesh, he can pretend to be immortal. But, since *the wages of sin is death,* he has this in common with men—that he, like them, is condemned to death.

43 BUT THE TRUE mediator whom in your secret mercy you have shown to men and have sent Him so that they, by His example, might learn humility, that *Mediator between God and man, the Man Christ Jesus,* appeared between mortal sinners and the immortal Just One: mortal with men, just with God; so that, because the wages of justice is life and peace, He might, by a justice conjoined with God, make void the death of those sinners who were justified by Him; for He was willing to let that death be common both to Him and to them. He was revealed to the holy men of old so that they might be saved through faith in His passion that was to come, just as we may be saved through faith in His passion now that it is in the past. For insofar as He is man, He is mediator; but insofar as He is the Word, He is not midway between God and man; for He is equal to God, both God with God, and together one God. How greatly have you loved us, good Father, who *sparedst not Thine only Son, but deliveredst Him up for us ungodly!* How you have loved us, for whom, *He that thought it no robbery to be equal with Thee, was made subject even to the death of the cross.* He alone *free among the dead, having power to lay down His life, and power to take it again:* for us He was to you both victor and victim, and victor because victim: for us He was to you both priest and sacrifice, and priest because sacrifice: and He made us sons to you instead of slaves by being born of you and by becoming your slave. With reason, then, my hope in Him is strong, that *Thou wilt heal all my infirmities* by Him who *sitteth at Thy right hand and maketh intercession for us;* otherwise I should despair. For many and great are my infirmities, many they are and great; but your medicine has more power still. We might have thought that your Word was far from any union with man, and we might have despaired, unless it had been *made flesh and dwelt among us.*

Terrified by my sins and the mass and weight of my misery, I had pondered in my heart a purpose of flight to the wilderness. But you forbade me and gave me strength by saying: *Therefore Christ died for all, that they which live may now no longer live unto themselves, but unto Him that died for them.* See, Lord, *I cast my care upon Thee,* that I may live and *consider wondrous things out of Thy law.* You know my unskillfulness and my weakness; teach me and heal me. He, your only Son, in *Whom are hid all the treasures of wisdom and knowledge,* has redeemed me with His blood. *Let not the proud speak evil of me,* for my thoughts are on the price of my redemption; I eat it and drink it and give it to others to eat and drink, and, being poor myself, I desire to be satisfied by it among those that *eat and are satisfied, and they shall praise the Lord who seek Him.*

Book XI

1 LORD, SINCE ETERNITY is yours, can you be ignorant of what I say to you? Or do you see what happens in time only at the moment when it is happening? Why then do I put before you in order the stories of so many things? Not, certainly, so that you may come to know them through me, but to stir up my own and my readers' devotion toward you, so that we may all say: *Great is the Lord, and greatly to be praised.* I have said this before and I shall say it again: I do this for the love of your love. For we pray also in spite of the fact that Truth has said: *Your Father knoweth what you have need of, before you ask.* What we do, therefore, is to lay open our feelings to you, confessing to you our own wretchedness and your acts of mercy to us, so that you may set us entirely free, as you have already begun to free us, and we may cease to be wretched in ourselves and may become happy in you; for you have called us to be *poor in spirit, and meek, and mourners, and hungering and athirst after righteousness, and merciful, and pure in heart, and peacemakers.*

See, I have told you many things, so far as I could and with the will that I had, because you, my Lord God, first willed that I should make my confession to you; for *Thou art good, for Thy mercy endureth forever.*

2 BUT MY PEN'S tongue will never have strength to declare all your exhortations and your terrors, the consolations and the guidance by which you brought me to become a preacher of your word to your

people and a dispenser of your sacrament. And suppose
I have the strength to declare all this in order, yet the
drops of my time are too precious, and for long I have
been full of a burning desire to *mediate in Thy law* and
to confess to you both my knowledge and my lack of
skill in it, the first beginnings of the light you shed on
me and the remnants of my darkness, until my weakness
be swallowed up in strength. And I am reluctant to
spend on anything else the hours that I can find free
from the necessities of refreshing my body, intellectual
labor, and the services which we owe to others or, even
if we do not owe them, which we give to others.

My Lord God, listen to my prayer and let your mercy
give ear to my desire; it does not burn for myself alone,
but wishes to be of use in the service of brotherly charity, and you see in my heart that this is so. I want to
sacrifice to you the service of my thought and of my
tongue, and I beg you to give me what I may offer to
you. For *I am poor and needy, Thou rich to all that call
upon Thee.* You are free from care, yet care for us. From
all rashness and all lying *circumcise my lips* both within
and without. Let your Scriptures be my chaste delight.
Let me neither be deceived in them nor deceive others
by them. Lord, listen and have pity, my Lord God, light
of the blind and strength of the weak, light too of the
seeing and strength of the strong, listen to my soul and
hear its cry from the depths. For unless your ears are
there to hear us even in the depths, whither shall we
go? To whom shall we cry?

The day is Thine, and the night is Thine; at your nod
the moments fly past. Grant me from them a space for
my meditations on *the hidden things of Thy law,* and do
not close your law against me when I knock. For it was
not for nothing that you willed that so many pages
should be filled with the writing of such dark secrets;
not are those forests without their stags which shelter
there and range and walk, feeding, lying down, and
chewing the cud. O Lord, perfect me and reveal those
pages to me! See, your voice is my joy; your voice sur-

passes all abundance of pleasures. Give me what I love, for I do love it, and that love too was your gift. Do not forsake your own gifts; do not despise your grass that is thirsty for you. Let me confess to you whatever I shall find in these books of yours, let me *hear the voice of praise,* let me drink of you and consider the *wonderful things out of Thy land,* from the *beginning* in which *Thou madest the heaven and the earth* until the coming of the time when we are with you in the everlasting kingdom of your holy city.

Lord, have pity on me and give ear to my desire. For it is not, I think, a desire for earthly things, not for gold and silver and precious stones, or beautiful clothes or honors or power or pleasures of the flesh, or for things necessary for the body and for this life of our pilgrimage, *all which shall be added unto those that seek Thy kingdom and Thy righteousness.* See, my God, from what my desire springs! *The wicked have told me of delights, but not such as Thy law, O Lord.* That is the reason for my desire. See, Father, look well at it, see and approve, and I pray that it may be pleasing in the sight of your mercy that I may find grace before you so that the inner secrets of your words may be laid open to me when I knock. This I beg by our Lord Jesus Christ, Thy Son, *the Man of Thy right hand, the Son of man, whom Thou hast established for Thyself* as the mediator between you and us, through whom you sought for us when we were not seeking you—indeed you sought us so that we might seek you—your *Word, through whom Thou madest all things*—and me among them—your only-begotten through whom you have called to adoption the people of believers and me among them—in His name I make my prayer to you, in His name who *sitteth at Thy right hand, and intercedeth with Thee for us, in Whom are hidden all the treasures of wisdom and knowledge.* These are the treasures I seek in your books. *Of Him did Moses write;* this he says and this Truth says.

3 I WANT TO HEAR and I want to understand how "in the beginning you made heaven and earth." This is what Moses wrote; he wrote and went his way, passing hence from you to you; he is not now here in front of me. If he were, I should hold on to him and ask him and beg him in your name to explain these things to me; I should lay the ears of my body open to the sounds that would burst from his mouth, and if he spoke in Hebrew he would merely beat upon my hearing in vain; nothing of what was said would reach my mind; but if he spoke in Latin, I should know what he was saying. But how should I know whether what he said was true? And if I did know it, would it be from him that I knew it? No it would not; it would be from inside me, from that inner house of my thought, that Truth, which is neither Hebrew nor Greek nor Latin nor Barbarian, and which speaks without the aid of mouth or tongue, without any sound of syllables, would say: "He is speaking the truth," and at once I would be sure and I would say with perfect confidence to that servant of yours: "You are speaking the truth." Since, then, I am not able to question Moses, it is you that I ask, you, Truth, full of whom Moses spoke truth, you, my God, you I ask to forgive my sins and, just as you gave Moses the power to speak these words, give me the power to understand them.

4 SEE, THERE ARE the heaven and the earth. They cry aloud that they were created; for they change and vary. Whereas anything which exists but was not created cannot have anything in it which was not there before, and this is just what is meant by change and variation. They cry aloud also that they did not create themselves: "We exist because we were created; therefore we did not exist before we were in existence, so as to be able to create ourselves." And the voice of the speakers is in the very fact that they are there to be seen.

It was you, Lord, who made them, you who are beautiful (for they are beautiful), you who are good (for they are good), you who are (for they are). But they have neither the beauty, nor the goodness, nor the existence which you, their creator, have; compared with you they are not beautiful, not good, not in existence. This, thanks to you, we know, and our knowledge compared with your knowledge is ignorance.

5   BUT HOW DID YOU make heaven and earth? What instrument did you use for this tremendous work of yours? You were not like a craftsman who forms one body from another as the result of an act of choice made in his mind, which has the power somehow to impress on material the form which it perceives inside itself with its inner eye. And how could it have this power except because you made it? And it imposes the form on something which already exists and has a body—clay, for instance, or stone or wood or gold or something of the sort. And how could these things have come into existence except because you made them to be? It was you who made for the craftsman his body, you who made the mind that directs his limbs, the material out of which he makes anything, the intelligence by which he grasps the principles of his art and sees inwardly what he is to make outwardly; you made his bodily sense by which he translates what he is doing from the mind to the material and then reports back again to the mind what has been done, so that the mind may within itself consult the truth presiding over it as to whether the work has been well done or not. All these things praise you, the Creator of all. But how do you make them? How, God, did you make heaven and earth? Certainly it was not in the heaven or in the earth that you made heaven and earth; nor was it in the air or in water, since these too belong to heaven and earth; nor was it in the universe that you made the universe, because there was no place for it to be made in until it

was made to exist. Nor did you hold anything in your
hand from which to make heaven and earth. For how
could you have got something which you had not made
to use for making things? For nothing exists except because you exist. Therefore *Thou spakest and they were
made,* and *in Thy Word Thou madest them.*

6   BUT HOW DID YOU SPEAK? Was it in the same
way as when the voice came from the cloud,
saying: *This is my beloved Son?* That voice came and
passed, had a beginning and an end. The syllables were
heard and then ceased to be heard, the second after the
first, the third after the second, and so on in order until
the last came after all the others, and after the last there
was silence. From this it is plain and evident that the
voice was uttered through the motion of something created, something itself temporal, though serving your
eternal will. And these words of yours, created in time,
were reported by the outer ear to the intelligent soul,
whose inner ear listened to your eternal word. But the
soul compared those words which were pronounced in
time with your eternal word which is in silence, and said:
"It is different, utterly different. These words are far
beneath me, indeed they are not at all, because they pass
away and disappear; but the word of my God is above
me and abides forever."

If, then, in words that are pronounced and pass away
you said: "Let heaven and earth be made" and so created heaven and earth, there must have been in existence before heaven and earth a corporeal creature by
whose motion in time that voice could sound and end
in time. But there was no bodily thing in existence before heaven and earth; or, if there was, certainly you
had not brought it into existence by means of an utterance made in time which would produce the conditions
for making, later, another utterance in time by which to
say: "Let the heaven and the earth be made." For whatever may have been the source of such a voice, it must

have been made by you; otherwise it would not have existed at all. What word, then, did you use in order to produce a bodily substance by means of which these words could be created?

7 AND SO YOU call us to understand the Word who is God and God with you, the Word which is spoken eternally and by which all things are spoken eternally. For here it is not a case of first one thing being said and finished, then another thing so that all can be said: no, all things are said together and eternally. Otherwise there would be already time and change, and not a true eternity nor a true immortality. I know this, my God, and I thank you. I know it, Lord God, and I confess it to you. And everyone else who is not ungrateful to assured truth knows it as I do and praises you. We know, Lord, we know it; for insofar as a thing either ceases to be what it was or begins to be what it was not, to that extent it is undergoing death or birth. Therefore nothing in your Word can pass away and then be replaced, because your Word is truly immortal and eternal. So it is by a word coeternal with you that you say, together and eternally, all that you say, and everything is made that you say is to be made. Yet all the things which you make by saying are not made together and eternally.

8 BUT WHY, I beseech you, my Lord God? I see it in a way, but I do not know how to express it, except that everything which begins to exist and ceases to exist begins at that moment and ceases at that moment when in the eternal reason it is known that it ought to begin and ought to cease, and in that Reason there is no beginning and no ending. This is your Word which is also *the Beginning because also It speaketh unto us*. He says this in the Gospel, speaking through the flesh, and this sound was heard outwardly by the ears of men so that it might be believed and sought for inwardly

and found in the eternal Truth, which is where the good
and only master teaches all his disciples. It is there,
Lord, that I hear your voice as you speak to me; for it
is our teacher who speaks to us, and he who is not our
teacher, even if he speaks, is not speaking to us. And
who is our teacher except the steadfast truth? For even
when we learn something by means of a changing creature it is to this steadfast truth that we are led, and then
we truly learn *while we stand and hear Him,* and *rejoice
greatly because of the Bridegroom's voice,* giving ourselves back to that from which we are. And that, therefore, is the Beginning, because if it did not remain there
would be nowhere to which, after going astray, we could
return. But when we return from error, we return by
realizing the Truth, and it is by His teaching that we do
realize the Truth, *because* He is *the Beginning and speaking unto us.*

9   IT WAS IN this beginning, God, that you made
heaven and earth—speaking wonderfully, creating wonderfully in your Word, your Son, your power,
your wisdom, your truth. Who shall understand this?
Who shall put it into words? What is that light that
shines through me and strikes my heart without hurting
it? And I am both terrified and set on fire. Terrified
insofar as I am unlike it, on fire insofar as I am akin to
it. It is Wisdom, Wisdom herself that shines through me,
splitting through the cloud in which I am wrapped and
which, as I faint away from it, again enfolds me in the
thick mist and weight of my punishment. For *my strength
is brought down in need,* so that I cannot support my
good, till you, Lord, who have been *gracious to all mine
iniquities* shall *heal all my infirmities.* For *Thou shalt also
redeem my life from corruption, and crown me with loving kindness and tender mercies, and shalt satisfy my desire with good things, because my youth shall be renewed
like an eagle's.* For *in hope we are saved,* therefore *we
through patience wait for* your promises. Let him that is

able hear your discourse deep within him. I, in the words of your oracle, will confidently cry out: *How wonderful are Thy works, O Lord, in Wisdom hast Thou made them all,* and that Wisdom is "the Beginning," and in that Beginning you made heaven and earth.

10 CERTAINLY IT IS a mark of being full of the old error when people say to us: "What was God doing before He made heaven and earth?" Their argument is as follows: If God was unoccupied with the making of anything, why did He not go on forever remaining in the same state as that in which He had always been? For if there came into existence in God a new motion and a new will to make something which he had never made before, how can one call it a true eternity, when a will arises which was not previously in existence? For the will of God is not a creature; it is prior to all creation, because nothing could be created unless the will of the creator had come first. Therefore, God's will belongs to the very substance of God. But if something which was previously not there arose in God's substance, then one could not truly call that substance eternal. If, on the other hand, God's will that there should be a creation had been in existence from eternity, why is creation also not from eternity?

11 THOSE WHO SAY this do not yet understand you, O Wisdom of God, light of minds. They do not yet understand how these things are made which are made by you and in you, and they are trying to taste eternity while their mind is still fluttering about in the past and future movements of things, and so is still unstable.

Can we not hold the mind and fix it firm so that it may stand still for a moment and for a moment lay hold upon the splendor of eternity which stands forever, and compare it with the times that never stand, and see that no comparison is possible? Then it would see that a long time is long only because of the numbers of movements passing by in succession, which cannot have a simultaneous extension; but that in eternity nothing passes by; everything is present, whereas time cannot be present all at once. It would be seen too that all time past is driven on by time future, and all the future follows from the past, and that both past and future are created by and proceed from that which is perpetually present. Who can so hold the mind of man that it may stand and see how eternity, which stands still and is neither past nor future, dictates the times that are past and the times that are to come? Could my hand have strength enough, or could the hand of my mouth by speech achieve so great a thing?

12 AND NOW I HAVE my answer to the man who says: "What was God doing before He made heaven and earth?" Someone once, evading the force of this question, is said to have made the jesting reply: "God was making hells for people who look too deeply into things." This is not my answer. To make a joke about something does not mean that one understands the subject. No, that is not my answer. Personally I would rather say: "I don't know," when I don't know, than make that kind of reply which brings ridicule on someone who has asked a deep question and wins praise for an inaccurate answer.

But I say that you, our God, are the creator of every creature, and if by "heaven and earth" we mean "every creature," I boldly declare that: "Before God made heaven and earth, He did not make anything." For if He did, it could have been nothing else except a creature. And I wish I knew all those good and useful things which I want to know as clearly as I know this, that before there was any creature in existence there was no creature in existence.

13 A MAN MAY LET his fluttering mind wander through images of times past and may feel surprise at the thought that you, God all-powerful, all-creating, and all-supporting, the maker of heaven and earth, abstained from so vast a work for all those countless ages before you brought it into existence. Anyone who thinks like this should wake up and reflect that his reasons for surprise are false ones. For how could countless ages pass by, when you, the author and creator of all ages, had not yet made them? What times could there have been which were not created by you? And how could they pass by, if they had never been in existence?

So, since it is by your work that all times are made, how can it be said, if there was a time before you made heaven and earth, that you were abstaining from your work? That time itself was of your creation, and no times could pass by before you made those times. If, on the other hand, there was no time before the creation of heaven and earth, the question "What were you doing then?" is meaningless. For when there was no time, there was no "then."

When we say that you are before times, we cannot mean that you are before them in time; otherwise you would not be before all times. You are before all the past in the sublimity of your ever-present eternity, and you are above all future things because they are still to come, and when they have come they will be past; *but Thou art the Same,* and *Thy years fail not.* Your years neither go nor come; but these years of ours go and come, so that they may all come. Your years stand still all together, because they do stand still; the going years are not thrust out by the coming years, since there is no passing from one state to the other; but these years of ours will not all be until all will have ceased to be. Your years are one day, and your day does not come daily, but is today, because your today is followed by no to-morrow and comes after no yesterday. Your today is eternity, and so it was that you begot one who is coeternal with you to whom you said: *This day have I begotten*

Thee. You made all times and before all times you are;
nor was there ever a time in which there was no time.

14 THEREFORE, since you made time itself, one
cannot say that there was any time in which you
had not made anything. And no times are coeternal with
you, because you are permanent, whereas, if they were
permanent, they would not be times. What then is time?
Who can find a quick and easy answer to that question?
Whoever in his mind can grasp the subject well enough to
be able to make a statement on it? Yet in our ordinary
conversation we use the word "time" more often and more
familiarly than any other. And certainly we understand
what we mean by it, just as we understand what others
mean by it when we hear the word from them.

What then is time? I know what it is if no one asks
me what it is; but if I want to explain it to someone who
has asked me, I find that I do not know. Nevertheless,
I can confidently assert that I know this: that if nothing
passed away there would be no past time, and if nothing
were coming there would be no future time, and if nothing were now there would be no present time.

But in what sense can we say that those two times,
the past and the future, exist, when the past no longer
is and the future is not yet? Yet if the present were
always present and did not go by into the past, it would
not be time at all, but eternity. If, therefore, the present
(if it is to be time at all) only comes into existence because it is in transition toward the past, how can we say
that even the present *is*? For the cause of its being is that
it shall cease to be. So that it appears that we cannot truly
say that time exists except in the sense that it is tending
toward nonexistence.

15 NEVERTHELESS, we say "a long time" and "a
short time," though we only use these expressions about the past and the future. A hundred years

ago, for instance, we say is a long time past, and a hundred years from now a long time ahead; ten days ago a short time past, ten days from now a short time ahead. But how can we say that something which does not exist at all is either long or short? For the past no longer is, and the future has not yet come to be. Should we then not say: "It is long"? Should we instead say of the past: "It was long" and of the future: "It will be long"?

My Lord, my light, is it not so that here also man is mocked by your truth? For as to this time in the past that was long, when was it long? When it was already past or when it was still present? It could be long only while it was in existence to be long. But once past, it had ceased to exist. So, not being in existence at all, it could not be long.

Therefore we must not say: "the time past was long"; for we shall not find anything in it which could be long, since from the moment when it becomes past, it ceases to exist. Let us say instead: "that particular present time was long," because while it was present, it was long. For it had not yet passed away so as not to exist, and consequently there was something which could be long; though once it had passed away, it ceased to be long by also ceasing to exist.

Let us see, therefore, soul of man, whether present time can be long. For to you, soul of man, it has been granted to feel spaces of time and to measure them. Now what answer will you give me?

Is a present time of a hundred years a long time? But first let us see whether a hundred years can be present. If we are in the first of these years, it is present, but the ninety-nine other years are still to come and therefore do not yet exist. And if we are in the second year, one year is already past, one is present, and the rest are to come. In the same way, whatever year we may care to choose in the hundred-year series as being present, all the years before it will be past and all the years after it will be future. Therefore a hundred years cannot be present.

But let us at least see whether this one year itself which we have selected is present. Here too, if we are in the first month, the other months are still to come, and if we are in the second month, the first is already in the past and the others do not yet exist. For a year is twelve months, of which just that one month in which we are is present, all the rest being either past or future. Yet even the month in which we are is not present; only one day of it is. If that day is the first, the other days are still to come; if the last, all the other days are in the past; if any intermediate day, it is between days past and days to come.

So now we see that this "present time," which we discovered to be the only time that could be called "long," has contracted to the space of scarcely one day. But let us look into this one day too, because not even a single day is wholly present. It (including the hours of day and night) is made up of twenty-four hours; the first of these has all the other hours still to come; the last has them all in the past; any intermediate hour has those before it in the past; those after it in the future. And that very hour itself is made of fleeting moments; whatever part of these has fled away is in the past, whatever remains is in the future. If anything can be meant by a point of time so small that it cannot be divided into even the most minute particles of moments, that is the only time that can be called "present." And such a time must fly so rapidly from future to past that it has no duration and no extension. For if it does have any extension, it can be divided into past and future; whereas the present does not take up any space.

Where, then, is the time that we can call "long"? Is it in the future? But we cannot say of the future: "It is long," because it is not yet in existence to be long. We have to say: "It will be long." But when will it be long? If we are still imagining it in the future, it will not be long, because there will still not be anything in existence to be long. If, on the other hand, we say that it will be long at the moment when out of the future (which does not yet exist) it will begin to take on being and become present; so that there can be something in existence to be long, then the present cries aloud in the words which we have just heard that it cannot be long.

16 AND YET, LORD, we do perceive definite periods of time and we compare them with each other and say that some are longer and others shorter. We even measure how much longer or shorter this time is than that, and we say that it is twice or three times as long, or equivalent—one time being of the same length as another. But when we measure time by our perception of it, it is time passing that we are measuring. For it is impossible to measure the past, which is no longer in existence, or the future which is not yet in existence, unless perhaps one is going to be rash enough to maintain that it is possible to measure something which does not exist. When, therefore, time is passing, it can be perceived and measured; but when it has passed, it cannot, because it does not exist.

17 I AM ASKING questions, Father, not making statements. My God, govern me and direct me. We learned at school and we teach at school that there are three times—past, present, and future. Am I now to be told that this is not so, that there is only the present, since the other two times do not exist? Or can we say that they do exist, but that there is some secret place from which time emerges when from the future the present comes into existence, and again some secret place into which it withdraws when the past comes out of the present? For where can those who have prophesied the future see the future, if the future is not yet in existence? For that which does not exist cannot be seen. And those who tell us about the past certainly could not tell us the truth unless they saw it in their mind's eye, and if the past were nonexistent, it would be quite impossible for it to be perceived. Therefore both the future and the past exist.

18 ALLOW ME, LORD, to push my questions further. My hope, let me maintain this line of inquiry without being distracted from it.

If the future and the past exist, I want to know where they are. And if I still lack the strength to know this, nevertheless one thing I do know, which is that, wherever they are, they are not there as future and as past, but as present. For if there too they are future, they are not yet there, and if there too they are past, they are no longer there. Thus, wherever they are, and whatever they are, they cannot be anything except present. Although with regard to the past, when this is reported correctly what is brought out from the memory is not the events themselves (these are already past) but words conceived from the images of those events, which, in passing through the senses, have left as it were their footprints stamped upon the mind. My boyhood, for instance, which no longer exists, exists in time past, which no longer exists. But when I recollect the image of my boyhood and tell others about it, I am looking at this image in time present, because it still exists in my memory. Whether a similar cause operates with regard to predictions of the future—namely, that images of things which do not yet exist are felt in advance as already existing— this, I confess, my God, I do not know. But I do know this, that we often premeditate our future actions, and this premeditation is present while the action which we are premeditating, being in the future, does not yet exist. But when we have embarked on it and begun to do what we were premeditating, then that action will exist, because then instead of being in the future, it will be in the present.

Whatever, then, may be the mode of this secret foreknowledge of the future, nothing can be seen which does not exist. And what is already in existence is not future, but present. Therefore, when we speak of seeing the future, what is seen is not the actual future itself (which, being future, does not yet exist), but the causes, or perhaps the signs of that future—causes and signs which are already in existence. And so to those who see them they are not future, but present, and from them future events are conceived in the mind and predicted. These concepts, again, are already in existence, and by those who make the predictions they are contemplated as being present in the mind.

Let me take one example out of the great number of possible examples. I am looking at the dawn sky and I foretell that the sun is going to rise. What I am looking at is present; what I foretell is future. What is future is not the sun, which is already in existence, but its rising, which has not yet taken place. Yet unless I could imagine in my mind this rising (as I do now in speaking of it), I should not be able to predict it. But the glow which I see in the sky is not the sunrise, although it comes before the sunrise; nor is the image in my mind the sunrise. Both those two are perceived in the present, so that the sunrise, which is in the future, can be foretold. The future, therefore, is not yet, and if it is not yet, it does not exist, and if it does not exist, it is quite impossible for it to be seen. But it can be predicted from the present which is already in existence and which can be seen.

19 RULER OF YOUR CREATION, tell me now how it is that you teach souls the things that are to come. For you have taught this to your prophets. To you nothing is future; how do you teach the future? Or rather, how do you give present indications of future events? For what does not exist cannot possibly be taught. Here your proceedings are beyond the reach of my sight; *it is too mighty for me, I cannot attain unto it.* But with your help I shall be able, when you grant it to me, sweet light of my hidden eyes.

20 IT IS NOW, HOWEVER, perfectly clear that neither the future nor the past are in existence, and that it is incorrect to say that there are three times—past, present, and future. Though one might perhaps say: "There are three times—a present of things past, a present of things present, and a present of things future." For these three do exist in the mind, and I do not see them anywhere else: the present time of things past is memory; the present time of things present is sight; the present time of things future is expectation. If we are allowed to use words in this way, then I see that there are three times and I admit that there are. Let us go further and say: "There are three times—past, present, and future." It is an incorrect use of language, but it is customary. Let us follow the custom. See, I do not mind, I do not object, I find no fault, provided that we understand what is said—namely, that neither what is to come nor what is past is now in existence. It is not often that we use language correctly; usually we use it incorrectly, though we understand each other's meaning.

21 I SAID JUST NOW that we measure time as it passes, and in such a way that we are able to say that one period of time is twice as great as another, or of the same length, and so on of any other parts of time which are measurable. For this reason, as I said, we measure time as it is passing, and if I am asked how I know this, I should reply that I know it because we do measure time, and we cannot measure what does not exist, and the past and the future do not exist. But how do we measure the present, since it has no extent? It is measured while it is passing; when it has passed by it is not measured, for then there will be nothing there to measure.

But where does time come from, by what way does it pass, and where is it going to when we are measuring it? It can only come from the future, it can only pass by way of the present, and it can only go into the past.

Therefore it comes from something which is not yet in existence, it passes through something which has no extension, and it goes in the direction of something which has ceased to exist.

But how can we measure time except in some sort of extension? When we say single and double and triple and all the other expressions of this sort which we use about time, we must be speaking of extensions or spaces of time. In what kind of extension, then, do we measure time as it is passing by? In the future, from which it comes? But we cannot measure something which is not yet in existence. In the present, through which it passes? But we cannot measure something which has no extension. In the past, toward which it is going? But we cannot measure something which no longer exists.

22 MY SOUL IS on fire to solve this very complicated enigma. Do not shut the door on these things, my Lord God, good Father, in the name of Christ I beg you, do not shut the door in the face of my longing to know these things which are so familiar and at the same time so obscure; but let my longing penetrate into them and let them shine out clearly in your enlightening mercy, Lord. Whom shall I ask about them? And to whom shall I confess my ignorance more profitably than to you, for you do not look with distaste at my violent burning enthusiasm for your Scriptures? Grant me what I love; for I do love and it was you who granted me to love. Give, Father, *who truly knowest to give good gifts unto Thy children.* Give, because I have *studied that I might know and it is a labor in my sight,* until you open the door to me. By Christ I beg you, in His name, the Holy of Holies, let no one disturb me. *I believed and therefore do I speak.* This is my hope and for this I live, that *I may contemplate the delights of the Lord. Behold Thou hast made my days old,* and they pass away, and how they do this I do not know. We are constantly using the word "time," both in the singular and the plural. We say. "How long did he speak?" "How long was he in doing that?" "For how long a time have I not seen that?" "This syllable is double the length of that short one." We use these expressions ourselves and we hear other people using them; we both understand and make ourselves understood; they are the commonest of expressions and the clearest, and yet on the other hand they are extraordinarily obscure and no one has yet discovered what they mean.

23 I ONCE HEARD a learned man say that what constitutes time is the motions of the sun and moon and stars. I did not agree. For one might equally well say that the motions of all bodies constitute time. Suppose that the lights of the heavenly bodies were to cease and a potter's wheel were to be turning around: would there be no time by which we could measure its rotations and say that these rotations were of equal duration, or, if it turned sometimes faster and sometimes slower, that in the one case the period taken by the turn was shorter and in the other case longer? And when we were saying these things, would not we too be speaking in time? In our words would there not be some syllables that are long and others that are short, simply because some take a longer and some a shorter time to pronounce? God, grant us men to see in a small thing principles which are common to things both small and great. There are stars and lights in the heavens to be for *signs, and for seasons, and for years and for days;* there certainly are; yet, just as I should not say that one turn of that little wooden wheel constituted a day, so that learned man should not say that it does not constitute any time at all.

What I want to know is the force and nature of time, by which we measure the motions of bodies and say, for example, that this motion is double the length of that one. And I put forward the following question: now what we mean by "a day" is not simply the time when the sun is above the earth (this merely distinguishes day from night), but the whole circuit of the sun from the east back to the east again (as, when we say "so many days have passed" we include the nights with the days and do not reckon up their spaces separately). Since, then, a day is constituted by the motion of the sun and its circuit from east to east, what I want to know is this: is it the motion itself which makes the day? Or is it the time taken by that motion? Or is it both?

If it were the movement of the sun that makes the day, then it would still be a day even if the sun completed its course in a time so small as to last only one hour. If it were the time now taken by the sun to complete its circuit that makes a day, then it would not be a day if there were only the space of one hour between one sunrise and the next; to make a day the sun would have to complete its circuit twenty-four times. If what makes a day is both the motion and the time taken, we could not call it "a day," if the sun stood still and a time passed which was equivalent to the time normally taken by the sun to go on its way from one dawn to the next.

So I shall not now inquire what it is which we call "a day." My question is: "what is time?" The time by which we measure the circuit of the sun and by which we should be able to say that the sun had gone around in half its normal time, if it went around in a time equal to twelve hours. The time by which we are able to compare the two periods and say that one is twice as long as the other, and this proportion of one to two would still hold good though the sun were, for its part, always doing its circuit from east to east; yet on some occasions it would be doing it in single, on others in double time.

Let no one tell me, then, that the motions of the heavenly bodies constitute time. When, at a man's prayer, the sun stood still so that he might fight and win a battle, the sun did indeed stand still but time went on; it went on for the space necessary for that battle to be fought and brought to its conclusion.

I see, therefore, that time is an extension of some sort.

But do I see this? Or do I only seem to see it? You, light, you, truth, will show me.

24 IS IT YOUR WILL that I should agree if someone tells me that time is the motion of a body? It is not your will. That no body can move except in time is something which I understand; it is what you say to me. But that the motion of a body actually *is* time is something which I do not understand; you do not say this to me. For when a body is in motion, I measure the length of the motion in time from the moment when it begins to move until the moment when it ceases to move. And if I did not observe the moment when the movement began and if the movement continues to go on so that I cannot observe the moment when it ends, then I am incapable of measuring it—except in the sense of measuring from the moment when I began to look until the moment when I stopped looking. If I look at it for a long time, all I can say is: "It was a long time." I cannot say how long a time; because we can only say "how long" by means of comparison—as, "this is as long as that," "this is twice as long," and so on. But when we can observe the points in space from which the body in motion comes and to which it goes (or the parts of a body, if it is revolving on its axis), then we can say exactly how much time has been taken to complete the movement of the body (or of its part) from one place to another place.

It is clear, then, that the motion of a body is one thing and the means by which we measure the duration of that motion is another thing. Is it not obvious which of the two deserves the name of "time"? A body may sometimes be in motion, at varying speeds, and may sometimes be standing still; but by means of time we measure not only its motion but its rest. We say: "It was at rest for the same time as it was in motion," or "It was at rest twice or three times as long as it was in motion," or any other proportion which we have either exactly measured or else guessed ("more or less" as we say).

Time, therefore, is not the motion of a body.

25 AND I CONFESS to you, Lord, that I still do not know what time is, and then again I confess to you, Lord, that I do know that I am saying these things in time, that I have been speaking of time for a long time and that this "long time" is only long because of the passage of time. But how do I know this, when I do not know what time is? Or by "not knowing" do I perhaps mean simply that I do not know how to express something which is in fact known to me? A bad state indeed to be in, not even to know what it is that I do not know! See, my God, I am in your presence and I do not lie. As I speak, so is my heart. *Thou shalt light my candle; Thou, O Lord my God, wilt enlighten my darkness.*

26 MY SOUL SPEAKS with truth when it confesses to you that I do measure time. Is it the case then, Lord my God, that I perform the act of measuring but do not know what I am measuring? I measure the motion of a body in time. Is it the case that I do not measure time itself? But could I measure the motion of a body—how long it lasts, how long it takes to go from one place to another—if I were not measuring the time in which the motion takes place? How, then, do I measure time itself? Do we measure a longer time by means of a shorter time, as, for instance, we measure a rood in terms of cubits? In this way, certainly, we seem to measure the quantity of syllables—the long by the short— and we say that a long syllable is double the length of a short. So we measure the length of poems by the lengths of the lines, and the lengths of the lines by the lengths of the feet, and the lengths of the feet by the lengths of the syllables, and the lengths of the long sylla-

bles by the lengths of the short ones. I do not mean
measuring poems by pages; that is a spatial and not a
temporal measurement. I mean the measurement of
words as they are pronounced and pass away, and we
say: "That is a long poem, for it is made up of so many
lines; the lines are long, for they are composed of so
many feet; the feet are long, for they extend into so
many syllables; that syllable is long, for it is the double
of a short one."

Yet all this still does not give us a fixed measure of
time. It may happen that a short line, if recited slowly,
may take up more time than a longer line, if spoken
hurriedly. The same holds good of a poem, or a foot or
a syllable. And so it seems to me that time can only be
a kind of extension; but I do not know what it is an
extension of. Could it not be, I wonder, an extension of
the mind itself? What is it, I beseech you my God, that
I measure when I say, either in an indefinite way: "This
time is longer than that" or, with precision: "This is double that"? That I am measuring time, I know. But I am
not measuring the future, because it is not yet in existence; I am not measuring the present, because the present has no extension in space; I am not measuring the
past, because it no longer exists. What then am I measuring? Is it time passing, but not past? That was what I
said previously.

27 PRESS ON, MY MIND! Go forward with all our
strength! *God is our helper. He made us and not
we ourselves.* Go forward toward the place where truth
begins to dawn.

Let us consider the case of a bodily voice. The voice
begins to sound, it sounds, it continues to sound, and
then it stops sounding. Now there is silence; the voice is
past and is no longer a voice. Before it began to sound,
it was in the future and could not be measured because
it did not yet exist, and now it cannot be measured because it no longer exists. Therefore, it could only be

measured while it was actually sounding, because only then was there something in existence which could be measured. But even then it was not static; it was going, and going away into the past. Was it this that made it the more measurable? For while it was in the process of going away it was extended through a certain space of time which made measurement possible; for the present occupies no space.

We grant, therefore, that then it was able to be measured. Now consider the case of another voice. This voice begins to sound; it still goes on sounding; it sounds at the same pitch continuously with no variation. Let us measure it while it is sounding; for when it has stopped sounding it will be in the past, and this will be nothing which can be measured. Obviously, then, we must measure it and say how long it is. But it is still sounding and measurement is only possible from the beginning, when it started to sound, to the end, when it ceased sounding. What we measure is the space between a beginning and an end. Therefore, a voice that has never ceased to sound cannot be measured; we cannot say how long or how short it is; it cannot be described as equal to another or single or double or anything of that sort. But when it has ceased to sound, it will no longer exist. How then shall we be able to measure it? And yet we do measure time. But the times we measure are not those which do not yet exist, not those which no longer exist, not those which are without duration, not those which are without beginning and end. Therefore, what we measure is neither the future nor the past nor the present nor what is passing. Yet nevertheless we do measure time.

"*Deus creator omnium*"—this line is composed of eight syllables, short and long alternately. Thus the four short syllables (the first, third, fifth, and seventh) are single in relation to the four long ones (the second, fourth, sixth, and eighth). Each long syllable has double the time of each short syllable—I pronounce them and I say that it is so, and, by the plain evidence of our senses, so it is. So far as sense can make things plain I measure a long syllable by a short, and I feel by means of my senses that it has twice the length. But when two syllables sound one after the other—the first short, the next long—how shall I keep hold of the short one? How, in my measurement, shall I apply it to the long one, so as to find that the long one has twice its length? The long one has not even begun to sound unless the short one has ceased to sound. And how can I measure the long syllable as something present? I cannot begin to measure it until it is finished. And when it is finished it has passed away.

What, then, is it that I measure? Where is that short syllable by which I measure? Where is that long syllable which I measure? Both have sounded, have fled away, have gone into the past, and no longer exist; and yet I do measure; I reply in all sincerity (my reply being based on the confidence one may have in a practiced sense) that one syllable is, so far as space of time is concerned, twice the length of the other. And I cannot make this judgment except when both the syllables have gone into the past and are finished. Therefore, what I am measuring is not the syllables themselves (they no longer exist) but something in my memory which remains there fixed.

It is in you, my mind, that I measure time. Do not interrupt me, or rather, do not allow yourself to be interrupted by the thronging of your impressions. It is in you, I say, that I measure time. As things pass by they leave an impression in you; this impression remains after the things have gone into the past, and it is this impression which I measure in the present, not the things which, in their passage, caused the impression. It is this impression which I measure when I measure time. Therefore, either this itself is time or else I do not measure time at all.

Now what happens when we measure periods of silence and say that this period of silence occupied the same amount of time as that period of speech? Is it not the case that we extend our thoughts up to what would have been the length of a speech if that speech were audible, and in this way are able to reach a conclusion about the intervals of silence in a given space of time? Without making any use of voice or tongue, we can go over in our mind poems, verses, speeches, and we can form our conclusions about the measurements of their movements and about the spaces of time taken up by one in relation to another just as well as if we were actually reading these passages aloud. If a man decides to utter a rather long sound and makes up his mind how long it is going to be, he has passed through that space of time in silence; then, committing it to memory, he begins to utter the sound and it goes on sounding until it reaches the limit which he set for it. Or it would be truer to say "it did sound" and "it will sound"; for the part of it which at any moment is completed *has* sounded, and the part of it which remains to be uttered *will* sound, and so it goes on, as the act of will, which is in the present, transfers the future into the past, the past growing as the future diminishes, until the future is consumed and it is all past.

28   BUT HOW CAN the future, which does not yet exist, be diminished or consumed? How can the past, which no longer exists, grow? Only because, in the mind, which performs all this, there are three things done. The mind looks forward to things, it looks at things, and it looks back on things. What it looks forward to passes on through what it looks at into what it looks back on. No one, of course, can deny that the future does not yet exist. But nevertheless there is in the mind already the expectation of the future. No one can deny that the past no longer exists. But nevertheless there is still in the mind the memory of the past. No one can deny that the present time has no extension, since it passes in a flash. But nevertheless our attention (our "looking at") is something constant and enduring, and through it what is to be proceeds into what has been. Thus it is not the future that is long, for the future does not exist; a long future is a long expectation of the future. Nor is the past long, since it does not exist; a long past is a long memory of the past.

Suppose I am about to recite a psalm which I know. Before I begin, my expectation (or "looking forward") is extended over the whole psalm. But once I have began, whatever I pluck off from it and let fall into the past enters the province of my memory (or "looking back at"). So the life of this action of mine is extended in two directions—toward my memory, as regards what I have recited, and toward my expectation, as regards what I am about to recite. But all the time my attention (my "looking at") is present and through it what was future passes on its way to become past. And as I proceed further and further with my recitation, so the expectation grows shorter and the memory grows longer, until all the expectation is finished at the point when the whole of this action is over and has passed into the memory. And what is true of the whole psalm is also true of every part of the psalm and of every syllable in it. The same holds good for any longer action, of which the psalm may be only a part. It is true also of the whole of a man's life, of which all of his actions are parts. And it is true of the whole history of humanity, of which the lives of all men are parts.

29 BUT BECAUSE *Thy loving kindness is better than all lives,* see, my life is a kind of distraction and dispersal. And *Thy right hand upheld me* in my Lord, the *Son of Man, the Mediator betwixt Thee,* the One, and us, the many (many also in our many distractions over so many things), so that *through Him I may apprehend in Whom I have been apprehended* and that I may be gathered up from my former days to follow the One, *forgetting what is behind,* not wasted and scattered on things which are to come and things which will pass away, but intent and *stretching forth to those things which are before*—no longer distracted, but concentrated as *I follow on for the prize of my heavenly calling,* where *I may hear the voice of Thy praise,* and contemplate Thy delight which is neither coming nor passing. But now *are my years spent in mourning,* and you, my comfort, my Lord, my Father, are eternal. But I have been spilled and scattered among times whose order I do not know; my thoughts, the innermost bowels of my soul, are torn apart with the crowding tumults of variety, and so it will be until all together I can flow into you, purified and molten by the fire of your love.

30 AND I SHALL STAND and become set in you, in my mold, in your truth. And I shall not endure the questions of men who, victims of a disease which is its own punishment, want to drink more than their stomachs can hold and who ask: "What was God doing before he made heaven and earth?" or: "Why did the idea of making something occur to Him, when previously He had never made anything?" Grant them, Lord, to think carefully what they are saying and to realize that when there is no time, one cannot use the word "never." To say, therefore, that God "never" made anything can only mean that God did not make anything "in any time." Let them see, then, that without created being, time cannot exist and let them cease to *speak* that *vanity.* I pray that they too may be *stretched out to those things which are before*, so that they may understand that before all times you are the eternal creator of all times, that no times are coeternal with you, nor is any other creature, even if there were a creature before all times.

31 LORD MY GOD, how deep are the inner recesses of your secrets, and how far from them have I been thrown by the consequences of my sins! Heal my eyes and let me share the joy of your light! Certainly if there were a mind gifted with such vast knowledge and foreknowledge as to know all the past and all the future as well as I know one well-known psalm, that mind is wonderful beyond belief, stupendous, and awe-inspiring. To that mind everything that is past and done, everything that is to come in future ages, is as clear as, when I was singing that psalm, it was clear to me how much and what I had sung from the beginning of it, how much and what remained to be sung before I reached the end. But far be it from me to say that it is in this way that you, the creator of the universe, creator of souls and bodies, know all the future and the past. No; your knowledge is far more wonderful, far more mysterious than this. When a man is singing or hearing a song that he knows, his feelings vary and his sense is distracted as the result of his expectation of the words to come and his memory of the words that are past. But nothing of this kind happens to you, the immutably eternal—that is, the truly eternal creator of minds. Therefore, just as *in the Beginning* you knew *the heaven and the earth* without any variation in your knowledge, so *in the Beginning* you created *the heaven and the earth* without any alteration of your action. Let him who understands confess to you, and let him who does not understand confess to you. How high you are! And the humble in heart are the house in which you dwell. For *Thou raisest up those that are bowed down;* you are their height and from that height they do not fall.

Book XII

1   LORD, IN THIS neediness of my life, my heart, at which the words of your Holy Scripture are knocking, is busily enough employed. And it is chiefly for this reason that the poverty of human understanding shows an exuberance of words, since inquiry has more to say than discovery, asking takes longer than obtaining, and the hand that knocks does more work than the hand that receives. We have the promise; no one can alter or distort it: *If God be for us, who can be against us? Ask, and ye shall have; seek, and ye shall find; knock, and it shall be opened unto you. For every one that asketh, receiveth, and he that seeketh, findeth, and to him that knocketh, it shall be opened.* These promises are yours, and when truth makes the promise, who can fear deception.

2   IN THE LOWLINESS of my language I confess to your highness that you made heaven and earth—this heaven, which I see; this earth, on which I tread and from which comes the earthly body which I wear. You made them. But where is that heaven of heavens, Lord, of which we hear in the words of the psalm, *The heaven of heavens is the Lord's; but the earth hath He given to the children of men?* Where is that heaven which we do not see, the heaven compared with which all that we do see is mere earth? For the entire corporeal universe, which is not present everywhere in its entirety, has received its beauty right down to its lowest parts of which this earth of ours is the lowest; but compared to that heaven of heaven even the heaven above our earth is only earth, and so it is reasonable to call both these great bodies "earth" in comparison with that unknown heaven which is for the Lord and not for the children of men.

3   NOW THIS EARTH WAS *invisible and without form,* a kind of depth of abyss over which there was no light, because it had no shape or form. Therefore you commanded it to be written that *darkness was upon the face of the deep.* What else can that mean but absence of light? For if there had been light, it could only have been from above, an illumination from on high. But since there was no light, the presence of darkness simply means the absence of light. *Darkness was upon it,* therefore, because light was not upon it—in the same way as when there is no sound there is silence. For the presence of silence simply means the absence of sound.

Was it not you, Lord, who taught this soul of mine which now makes its confession to you? Was it not you, Lord, who taught me that, before you gave shape and variety to this formless matter, there was nothing—no color, no outline, no body, no spirit? And yet not absolutely nothing; there was a kind of formlessness, lacking all definition.

4   WHAT NAME, THEN, can we give to this formlessness? How can we convey an idea of it to minds that are not very quick, unless we employ some word which is already familiar? And in the whole of the world what seems to come closest to utter formlessness are "earth" and "deep." They occupy the lowest position and are correspondingly less beautiful than the other higher things which are all transparent and shining. I may, therefore, accept that under the name of *earth invisible and without form* a sufficiently accurate intimation is given to men of that formless matter which you

had created without beauty and from which you were to make this beautiful world.

5 HERE OUR THOUGHTS may lead us to inquire what there is in this concept that can be grasped by sense. We may say: "It is not an intellectual form—as life, or justice—because it is the matter of which bodies are made; nor is it a sensible form, because there is nothing to be seen or apprehended by the senses in what is invisible and formless." When the mind of man questions itself in this way, it must aim either at knowledge through ignorance or at ignorance through knowledge.

6 AS TO ME, LORD—if by tongue and pen I may confess to you everything you have taught me about this formless matter—the fact is that previously I heard the name without understanding it, being told of it by others who did not understand it either. I thought of it as having an enormous variety of different forms, and consequently I was not thinking of it at all. I turned over in my mind the notions of forms which were hideous and horrible and disjointed from all order; but they were forms all the same, and this I called "the formless." By this I meant not something which was without form, but something which had a form of such a kind that, if it were to appear, my senses would recoil from it as from something utterly strange and incongruous and upsetting to the weakness of one's human nature. So what I was thinking of was "formless" not in the sense of being without form, but only in the sense of being less well formed in comparison with forms that were more beautiful. Right reason certainly led me to believe that I should strip away entirely every kind of remnant of form, if I wanted truly to conceive of "the formless"; but this I could not do. I found it easier to think that what was deprived of all form was nonexistent, than to conceive of something which was between form and

nothingness, something which lacked form yet was not nothing, something formless and almost nothing.

And my mind ceased to question my spirit on this, my spirit being full of images of formed bodies which it changed and varied at its will. Instead I turned my attention to the bodies themselves; I looked more deeply into their mutability, considering how they cease to be what they have been and begin to be what they were not. And I suspected that this transition from one form to another happened through something that was formless but was not absolutely nothing. But I wanted to know, not merely to suspect. And if my tongue and pen were to confess to you the whole story, all the knots that you untied for me on this question, which of my readers could hold out to take it all in? Nevertheless, my heart shall not cease to give you honor and to sing your praises for those things which it lacks power to express.

For it is just this mutability of changeable things which is itself capable of receiving all those forms into which mutable things are changed. And what is this mutability? Is it soul? Is it body? Is it any species of soul or of body? If one could speak of a nothing that was something or an existence which is nonexistent, that would be the expression I would use for it. Yet even then it must certainly have had some kind of existence in order to receive those visible and composite forms.

7   AND IN ANY CASE, whence could it have been except from you, from whom all things insofar as they exist, derive their existence? But the more a thing is unlike you, the further it is from you (though not, of course, in any spatial sense). So, Lord, you, who do not change with time or circumstance, you who are the Selfsame and the Selfsame and the Selfsame, *Holy, Holy, Holy, Lord God Almighty*—you, *in the Beginning,* which is from you, in your Wisdom, which is born of your substance, made something and made it out of nothing.

You *created heaven and earth;* but you did not create

them out of yourself. If you had, they would be equal to your only-begotten Son and therefore to yourself too, and it could not possibly be right that something not proceeding from you should be equal to you. And there was nothing else in existence besides you from which you might create them, God, Three in One and One in Three, and therefore you created heaven and earth out of nothing. You created a great thing and a little thing (for you are almighty and good, to make all things good)—a great heaven and a little earth. You were and nothing else was and of nothing you made heaven (i.e., the heaven of heaven) and earth, two things, one close to you, the other close to nothing, one which has only you superior to it, the other which is of all things the most low.

8   BUT THAT *heaven of heavens was for Thyself, O Lord;* but the earth which *Thou gavest to the sons of men to be* seen and felt was not like the earth which we now see and feel. It was *invisible, without form,* and there was a deep, over which there was no light; or, *darkness was* above *the deep,* that is, there was more darkness above than in the deep. This abyss of waters, which are now visible, does have even in its depths a kind of light of its own which is perceptible to the fish and living creatures which crawl on the bottom of the sea. But then all was close to nothingness, because it was still entirely formless; yet there was already something capable of receiving form. For you, Lord, made the world out of a matter which was without form, and it was from nothing that you made this formless matter, this next-to-nothing, out of which you were to create those great works which we sons of men look upon in wonder. Wonderful indeed is this corporeal heaven, this firmament set between water and water of which you said on the second day (after the creation of light on the first): *Let it be made, and it was made.* This *firmament Thou calledst heaven*—the heaven, that is, belonging to this earth and sea which you made on the third

day by giving visible shape to the formless matter which you had made before any day. You had indeed also made a heaven before any day, but that was the heaven of this heaven; because *In the Beginning Thou hadst made heaven and earth.* But that earth which you made then was formless matter, because *it was invisible and without form, and darkness was upon the deep.* And of this *invisible and formless earth,* of this formlessness, of this next-to-nothing you would make all those things of which our mutable world stands in its state of flux and where its mutability appears in the fact that the passage of time can be felt and measured. For time is made by the changes of things, as their forms vary and turn from one stage to the other. And the matter of all this is that invisible earth of which we are speaking.

9 FOR THIS REASON the Spirit, the teacher of your servant, when relating that you *In the Beginning created heaven and earth,* makes no mention of times and says nothing about days. Obviously because the heaven of heaven which you made *in the Beginning* is in some way an intellectual creature, and, though it is in no way coeternal with you, the Trinity, nevertheless it partakes of your eternity; in the sweet happiness of contemplating you it finds strength to restrain its own mutability; clinging to you without any lapse from the moment of its creation, it is outside and beyond the rolling vicissitudes of time. That formlessness also of the *earth invisible and without form* is not included in the number of the days of creation. For when there is no shape and no order, there is nothing to come into existence and pass away, and without that condition there are certainly no days nor any vicissitudes in the spaces of times.

10 LET TRUTH, the light of my heart, speak to me and not my own darkness! I fell away and I was in the dark, but even from there, even from there I loved you. I went astray and I remembered you. I heard your

voice behind me, calling me back, and I could scarcely
hear it for all the noise made by those without your
peace. And now, look, I return thirsty and panting to
your fountain. Let no one hold me back! I shall drink
of it, and I shall live of it. Let me not be my own life!
I lived evilly of myself; I have been death to myself; I
come back to life in you. Speak to me! Teach and instruct me! I have believed your books, and their words
are secret and mysterious indeed.

11   ALREADY, LORD, in my inner ear I have heard
      your voice loud and strong telling me that you
are eternal, *Who only hast immortality,* since you suffer
no change in form or by motion, and your will is not
altered in the course of time (for a will which is now
one thing and now another is not immortal). This is clear
to me in your sight, and I pray that it may become
clearer and clearer and that with this truth evident to
me I may continue calmly to dwell beneath the shadow
of your wings.

Also, Lord, in my inner ear I have heard your voice
loud and strong telling me that all natures and all substances, which are not what you are but which nevertheless
exist, are created by you. Only what does not exist is not
from you. Such is the movement of the will away from
you, who are, toward something which has less reality; the
movement is a fault and a sin and no man's sin can either
harm you or disturb the order of your government in any
way, great or small. This is clear to me in your sight, and
I pray that it may become clearer and clearer and with
this truth evident to me I may continue calmly to dwell
beneath the shadow of your wings.

Also in my inner ear I have heard your voice loud
and clear telling me that that creation of yours (the
heaven of heavens) is not coeternal with you: you alone
are its happiness and in unfailing chastity it drinks you
in and never and nowhere does it exhibit its natural mutability; you are always present to it and to you with

total and complete affection it holds; it has no future to expect; it has nothing to transfer from memory into the past; it is neither altered by changing circumstances nor distracted into time.

O happy creature, if such a creature there is! Happy in clinging to your blessed happiness, happy in you, its eternal inhabitant and enlightener! I can find no better name for this *heaven of heavens which is the Lord's* than your house—a house full of the contemplation of delight in you, from which there is no falling away to the contemplation of anything else, a pure mind, single in perfect concord, settled in the peace of holy spirits, the citizens of your city *in the heavenly places*—far above the heaven which we see.

From this a soul whose pilgrimage has been into a far country may understand if she now *thirsts for Thee*, if *her tears are now become her bread, while they say daily unto her, Where is thy God?* if she now *seeks of Thee one thing*, and *desireth it, that she may dwell in Thy house all the days of her life* (and what is her life, except you? And what are your days except your eternity—just as *Thy years which fail not, because Thou art ever the same);* from this, therefore, the soul that has the power may understand how far, beyond all times, you are eternal; for your house, which never went into a far country, although it is not coeternal with you, nevertheless, because it clings to you without lapse and without cessation, suffers no vicissitude of time. This is clear to me in your sight, and I pray that it may become clearer and clearer and, with this truth evident to me, I may continue calmly to dwell beneath the shadow of your wings.

Now in the changes that take place in the last and lowest creatures there is evidently a kind of formlessness. No one, I think, except a man whose empty mind is filled and disturbed with confused fantasies of his own, would maintain that, if all form were taken away so as to vanish entirely and if nothing were left but the formlessness (the medium in which things change and turn from one form to another), that this formlessness in itself could exhibit temporal variations. Obviously it could not possibly. For where there is no variety of motion, there is no time, and there can be no variety where there is no definition of form.

12 WHEN I CONSIDER these things, my God—insofar as you grant me the power, insofar as you incite me to knock, and insofar as you open to me when I do knock—I find that there are two things which you have created outside the realm of time, though neither of the two is coeternal with you. One of these is so formed that, though changeable, it is, nevertheless, unchanged and is able without any intermission of contemplation, without any interval of change, perfectly to enjoy eternity and changelessness. And the other was so formless that it could not change from one form to another, whether of motion or rest, and consequently was not subject to time. But you did not allow this to remain formless because you *in the Beginning didst create heaven and earth,* these two things of which I am speaking. But *the earth was invisible and without form, and darkness was upon the deep.* In these words the idea of formlessness is suggested to us, an idea which will gradually win over and convince those who are incapable of conceiving of an utter privation of all form which still does not amount to a reduction to nothingness. For out of that formlessness was to be made a second heaven and a visible and well-formed earth, the beautiful waters and everything else which we are told was made in the constitution of the world on the successive days of creation, and all these things are of such a kind that, because of the ordered alterations of motion and of form, they are subject to the vicissitudes of time.

13 THIS, MY GOD, is what I feel when I hear your Scripture saying: *In the Beginning God made heaven and earth; and the earth was invisible and without* *form, and darkness was upon the deep.* And when Scripture makes no mention of the day on which you made these, I conclude that this is because what is meant by "heaven" is the *heaven of heavens,* that intellectual heaven, where it is the property of the intellect to know all things in one act, not *in part,* not *darkly,* not *through a glass,* but as a whole, *in manifestation, face to face;* not to know one thing at one time and one at another, but, as has been said, to know everything together without any vicissitude of time. And I assume that by "earth" is meant that *earth invisible and without form,* not subject to the vicissitude of time in which there occurs now "this" and now "that," because where there is no form, there is no "this" and no "that."

So I consider that when the Scripture says, without making any mention of days, *In the Beginning God created heaven and earth*, it is referring to these two, the one formed from the beginning, the other entirely without form; the one heaven (meaning the *heaven of heaven*), the other earth (meaning the earth *invisible and without form*). For immediately afterward comes the reference to what earth is meant, and then it is recorded that on the second day the Firmament was created and *called heaven.* We can gather from this what "heaven" it was of which the Scripture first spoke without mentioning any days.

14 How amazing is the profundity of your utterances! See they lie before us with a surface that can charm little children. But their profundity is amazing, my God, their profundity is amazing. One cannot look into them without awe and trembling—awe of greatness, trembling of love. *The enemies thereof I hate* with all my strength. I wish that you would slay them *with a two-edged sword*, so that they might cease to be its enemies. So I love to have them slain to themselves that they may live to you.

But there are others too, not critics but admirers of

the Book of Genesis, who say: "The spirit of God, writing these words by means of his servant Moses, did not mean them to be understood as you say, but in another way, the way that we say." God of all of us, You are the judge. . . . To this objection of theirs my answer is as follows.

15 "YOU WILL NOT, I imagine, assert that what truth, with upraised voice, has told me in my inner ear about the true eternity of the creator is false—namely, that His substance suffers no change in time and that His will is not something separate from His substance. And, therefore, He does not will one thing at one moment and one at another; but once and at once and always He wills all things which He does will. He does not will one thing and then the same thing again; He does not will one thing and then another thing; He does not will later something which He had not willed previously, nor does He cease to will something which previously He had willed. Such a will is mutable, and nothing mutable is eternal; but our God is eternal.

"Again, would you deny this that he has told me in my inner ear—that the expectation of things to come turns into a "looking-at" them when they have come, and that this "looking-at" (or attention) turns to memory when they have passed? Now any mental experience which varies in this way is mutable; nothing mutable is eternal, but our God is eternal. I grasp these facts, I put them together, and I find that my God, the eternal God, did not in His creation exercise any new act of will and that His knowledge does not admit of anything that is transitory.

"What, then, are you going to say, you who contradict me? Are you going to maintain that these things are false?"

"No," they say.

"Well then, is this false—that every nature which has a form and all matter that is capable of receiving a form only exists from Him who is supremely good, because He supremely *is*?"

"No," they say, "we do not deny this either."

"Well then, do you deny that there is a kind of sublime creature which cleaves to the true and truly eternal God with so chaste a love that, although it is not coeternal with Him, yet it is never detached from Him nor does it flow away from Him into any variety and vicissitude of time, but rests in the true and perfect contemplation of Him alone?"

And this is because you, God, show yourself to him who loves you as much as you command, and you are sufficient to him, so that he never falls away from you nor declines toward self. This is the house of God, not of earthly mold nor of any heavenly stuff that is material; it is a spiritual house, partaking of your eternity, because it is for eternity without stain. *For Thou hast made it fast forever and ever, Thou hast given it a law which it shall not pass.* But it is not coeternal with you, for it is not without a beginning. It was created.

It is true that we do not find any time before it, for *wisdom was created before all things.* By this I do not mean the Wisdom who is altogether equal and coeternal with you, Our God, His Father—that Wisdom by Whom all things were created and in Whom, as *the Beginning, Thou createdst heaven and earth.* I mean the wisdom which was created, the intellectual nature which by contemplating the light is itself light; for this too, though created, is called wisdom. And between the wisdom that creates and the wisdom that is created there is just the same difference as between the light that enlightens and the light which comes from receiving enlightenment. So with the righteousness which justifies and the righteousness which comes from being justified. For we too are called "your righteousness." Does not a servant of yours say, *That we might be made the righteousness of God in Him?*

There was, therefore, a certain created wisdom which was created before all things; the rational and intellectual mind of that chaste city of yours, our mother which is above, and is free and eternal in the heavens. And what is meant by "heavens" must be those that *praise Thee, the heaven of heavens,* the *heaven of heavens for the Lord.* Before this wisdom we find no time because, being created before all things, it precedes the creation of time; yet before it is the eternity of the creator himself; it was created by him and from him it took its beginning—not a temporal beginning (for there was no time) but the beginning of its condition of existence.

Therefore, it is of you, our God, but of you in such a way that it is clearly other than you and not the selfsame. We find not only no time before it, but also no time in it, since it is fit always to see your face and is never drawn away from it and, therefore, suffers no change or variation. Nevertheless, there is in it the possibility of change, so that it could become dark and cold, if it were not that it clings to you with such great love that from you it receives heat and light in a perpetual noon. O home of light, house of beauty! *I have loved thy beauty, and the place of the habitation of the glory of my Lord,* your builder and your owner. Let me sigh toward you as I journey on my pilgrimage! And I ask Him who made you to take possession of me too in you, for me too He made. *I have gone astray like a lost sheep*, but I hope that on the shoulders of my shepherd, your builder, I may be brought back to you.

"Now what are you going to say to me, you contradictors whom I was addressing? You believe that Moses was the holy servant of God and that his books are oracles of the holy spirit. Is not this house of God, though not coeternal with God, yet nevertheless in its own way *eternal in the heavens?* For it is no use looking there for changes of time, since you will not find them. For that which finds its happiness in always cleaving to God surpasses all extension and all the rolling space of time."

"It is true," they say.

"Then in all those things which my heart cried out to my God when inwardly it *heard the voice of His praise,* what thing in particular, I ask you, do you maintain to be false? That the matter was *without form* when, because there was no form, there was no order? But when there was no order, there could be no succession of times; yet this next-to-nothing, insofar as it was not absolutely nothing, must have been from Him from Whom everything, insofar as it has any existence at all, is."

"This too," they say, "we do not deny."

16 I WISH TO SAY a few words in your presence, my God, to those who admit the truth of all those things which your truth utters to me in my soul within. As to those who deny their truth, they may bark as much as they like and deafen themselves. I shall attempt to persuade them to be quiet and to allow your word entry into them. But if they refuse and reject my advice, I beg you, my God, *be not Thou silent to me.* Speak to me truly in my heart, for it is you alone who speak so. And I will leave the others outside, blowing onto the dust and obscuring their vision with earth, and *I will enter my chamber* and sing to you songs of love, groaning *with groanings unutterable* in my far pilgrimage, remembering Jerusalem with heart stretching out in longing for it, Jerusalem my country, Jerusalem my mother, and you the ruler of it, enlightener, father, guardian, husband, the chaste and strong delight, the solid joy and all good things unspeakable, all, all together at once, because you are the one supreme and true good. And I shall not turn aside until from this dispersed and deformed state of mine you gather all that I am into the peace of that city, our dear mother, where are *the first fruits of my spirit* and from which my certain Knowledge is derived, and so you will conform and confirm me forever, my God, my mercy.

But with regard to those who do not maintain that all these truths are false, who honor your Holy Scripture as set forth by that holy man Moses, who, as I do, place it at the summit of authority deserving to be followed, and yet who disagree with me on certain points, my answer is as follows. And I would wish you, our God, to judge between what I confess to you and what they object to me.

17 THIS IS WHAT they say: "Though all this may be true, yet Moses was not thinking of these two creatures when, by the revelation of the spirit, he said *In the Beginning God made heaven and earth.* By 'heaven' he did not mean that spiritual or intellectual creature always contemplating the face of God, and by 'earth' he did not mean that formless matter."

I ask: "What then did he mean?" and they reply: "That great man meant what we say he meant, and it was this that he declared in those words."

"And what is that?" I ask. Then they reply as follows: "By the words 'heaven' and 'earth' he meant first to signify, in brief and comprehensive terms, the whole visible world, so that after this he could, by enumerating the days of creation, arrange in order and, as it were, piece by piece the whole of creation which it had pleased the holy spirit to express in those general terms. For the people to whom he was speaking were uncultured and carnally minded, and he naturally considered that he could only entrust them with the knowledge of those works of God which are visible."

They agree with me however that the words *earth invisible and without form and the dark deep* (from which it is subsequently shown that all these visible things which we all know were created and set in order during those "days") may quite naturally be taken to mean that formless matter of which I have been speaking.

But someone else may put forward another view and say: "The words 'heaven' and 'earth' were used first to convey the idea of this very formlessness and confusedness of matter, because out of this matter was created and perfected the visible world with all those natures which are clearly evident to us, and which we often call by the name of 'heaven and earth.' "

Or again someone else may say: "The words 'heaven'

and 'earth' are quite properly used to mean nature both visible and invisible, and so the universal creation which God made in His Wisdom—that is, *In the Beginning*—is comprehended under these two words. Nevertheless, all things were made, not out of the very substance of God, but out of nothing (because they are not the same as God and in all of them there is a principle of mutability, whether they stand fast, like the eternal house of God, or whether they change, like the soul and body of man). Therefore, the common matter of all things, visible and invisible—a matter still formless, though capable of receiving form, out of which was to be made both heaven and earth (i.e., the invisible and visible creation when finally given a form)—this common matter is what is meant by the expressions *earth invisible and without form* and *darkness upon the deep.* But there is a distinction between the two. *Earth invisible and without form* refers to corporeal matter at the stage before it was differentiated by any form: *darkness upon the deep* refers to spiritual matter at the stage before any restraint was put upon its unlimited fluidity and before it received the illumination of Wisdom."

There is still another view which a man may, if he likes, put forward. It may be said: "When we read *In the Beginning God made heaven and earth,* the words 'heaven' and 'earth' do not mean the visible and invisible natures already formed and perfected; they mean the first formless starting ground of things, a matter capable of receiving form, a matter out of which something could be made, because in it there did exist—though confused and with no distinction of quality or form—all these things which now, after being separated out, set in order, are called heaven and earth, the one a spiritual, the other a corporeal creation."

18   NOW AFTER I have heard all this and thought it over, I have no wish to *strive about words.* That is *profitable to nothing, but the subversion of the hearers.*

But the law is good to edify, if a man uses it lawfully, because *the end of it is charity, out of a pure heart and good conscience, and faith unfeigned*. And our Master knows on which *two commandments He hung all the Law and the Prophets*.

Now, as with burning heart I confess these things to you, my God, light of my eyes in secret, what harm does it do me if different meanings, which are nevertheless all true, can be gathered from these words? What harm can it do me if my view of what Moses meant is different from someone else's view? Certainly all of us who read are endeavoring to find out and to grasp what the man whom we are reading meant to say, and when we believe that he is a man who tells the truth we dare not imagine that he said anything which we ourselves know or believe to be false. So while we are all trying in our reading of the Holy Scriptures to grasp what it was that the author of them meant to say, what harm can it do if a man grasps hold of something which you, who are the light of all truthful minds, show him is true, even if the author whom he is reading did not grasp this truth — though of course the author did express a truth, but a different one?

19 FOR, LORD, it is certainly true that *Thou madest heaven and earth*. It is true that the Beginning is your Wisdom, in which you made all things. It is also true that this visible world is made up of two great parts, the heaven and the earth, which briefly comprise all natures which are made and established. And it is true that everything changeable must suggest to our intelligence a kind of formlessness, something by which form may be received or by which a change or mutation may take place. It is true that what clings so close to the immutable form that, though capable of change in itself, it does not change, is not subject to time. It is true that that formlessness which is next-to-nothing cannot be subject to the alterations of time. It is true that the material out

of which a thing is made can, in a certain sense, already
bear the name of the thing that is made from it; thus
any kind of formless matter out of which heaven and
earth were made can be called heaven and earth. It is
true that of all things which have form, nothing is nearer
to the formless than *earth* and *the deep*. It is true that
not only whatever has been created and given form, but
also whatever is capable of being created and given
form, is made by you, of *whom are all things*. It is true
that whatever is formed out of the formless, was itself
first formless, then given a form.

20 NOW OF ALL these truths—which are accepted
unhesitatingly by those to whom you have given
the power to perceive them with the inner eye, and who
believe unshakably that your servant Moses spoke in the
spirit of truth—out of all these truths a man chooses just
one who says: *In the Beginning God made heaven and
earth* means this: "In His Word, which is coeternal with
Himself, God made the intelligible and the sensible, or
the spiritual and the corporeal, creation."

Another truth is chosen by the man who says: *In the
Beginning God made heaven and earth* means this: "In
His Word, which is coeternal with Himself, God made
the formless matter of both the spiritual and corporeal
creation."

Another truth is chosen by the man who says: *In the
Beginning God made heaven and earth* means this: "In
His Word, which is coeternal with Himself, God made
the formless matter of the corporeal creation in which;
still in a confused state, were the heaven and the earth
which, now that they have been separated apart and
given form, we see at present in the mass of the world."

Another truth is chosen by the man who says: *In the
Beginning God made heaven and earth* means this: "At
the very start of His work of creation God made that
formless matter, which contained (though in a confused
state) heaven and earth, and out of which they were

formed so that now they stand out evident to the sight with all that is in them."

21 SO WITH REGARD to the understanding of the words that follow. Out of all the truths already mentioned, one is chosen by the man who says: *But the earth was invisible and without form, and darkness was upon the deep* means this: "The corporeal thing which God made was as yet the formless matter of corporeal things, without order and without light."

Another truth is chosen by the man who says: *The earth was invisible and without form, and darkness was upon the deep* means this: "All that which is now called heaven and earth was still only formless and lightless matter, from which the corporeal heaven and the corporeal earth was to be made, with all things in them which are known to our corporeal senses."

Another truth is chosen by the man who says: *The earth was invisible and without form, and darkness was upon the deep* means this: "All that which is now called heaven and earth was still formless and lightless matter, from which were to be made the intelligible heaven— elsewhere called *the heaven of heaven*—and the earth— that is to say, the whole corporeal nature. Under the name of 'earth' is to be understood also this corporeal heaven. From this matter, then, was to be made the whole of creation, visible and invisible."

Another truth is chosen by the man who says: *The earth was invisible and without form, and darkness was upon the deep* means this: "Scripture did not call that formlessness by the name of 'heaven and earth.' No; that formlessness was already in existence and was called *the earth invisible and without form and darkness upon the deep.* And Moses had previously said that it was out of this that God made heaven and earth, that is the spiritual and corporeal creation."

Another truth is chosen by the man who says: *The earth was invisible and without form, and darkness was upon the deep* means this: "There was already a kind of formlessness, the material out of which, as previously stated by Scripture, God made heaven and earth—that is to say, the corporeal mass of the world, divided into two great parts, the upper and the lower, with all the known and familiar creatures in them."

22 TO THESE LAST two opinions someone might make the following objection: "If you will not admit that what is meant by this formlessness of matter is, in fact, heaven and earth, then there must be something, not created by God, out of which God was able to make heaven and earth. For Scripture does not say that God made this formless matter unless we understand that it is this that is meant by the words 'heaven and earth' or only by the word 'earth,' when it is said: *In the Beginning God made heaven and earth.* Thus in the following passage, *and the earth was invisible and without form,* though Moses chose to use these words to describe the formless matter, we can only understand it to mean that which God made as written in the previous verse: *God made heaven and earth.*"

Those who hold the last two opinions, as stated above, or one or the other of them, will, when they hear this objection, reply as follows: "We do not deny that this formless matter was made by God, God from whom are all things very good; because, just as we say that what has been created and given a form is a greater good, so we admit that what has been made capable of being created and given a form is, though a lesser good, nevertheless a good. But we do say that Scripture has not recorded the fact that God made this formless matter, just as Scripture has not recorded God's creation of many other things, the Cherubim and Seraphim, for instance, and those things of which the Apostle distinctly speaks: *Thrones, Dominions, Principalities, Powers;* yet clearly all these were made by God. If all things are to be understood as comprehended in the expression *He made heaven and earth,* what are we to say about the waters upon which *the Spirit of God moved?* For if they are comprised in the word 'earth,' how can this formless matter also be described by the word 'earth,' when we see that the waters are so beautiful? Or, if we do take it in this way, why is it written that out of this same formlessness the firmament was created and called heaven, but it is not written that the waters were created? For the waters are not still formless and invisible; we see them flowing in all their beauty. If you say that they received their beauty when God said: *Let the water that is under the firmament be gathered together,* thus assuming that the gathering together was in itself the forming of them, then what will you say about the *waters which be above the firmament?* They would not have deserved so honorable a position if they had been without form, yet Scripture does not record by what word they were created. We may find, then, that in Genesis there is no mention of God's having created some particular thing, though sound faith and accurate intelligence have no doubt at all that He did make it. Obviously no reasonable doctrine would go on to suggest that those waters are coeternal with God because, though we find them mentioned in the Book of Genesis, we do not find any mention of when they were created. Why, then (with truth to teach us), should we not hold that this formless matter, described by Scripture as *earth invisible and without form and the dark deep,* was created by God out of nothing, and therefore is not coeternal with Him— though the Bible story has omitted to mention when it was made?"

23 WHEN I HEAR these views and examine them so far as the weakness of my capacities (and I confess this weakness to you, God, who know it) will allow, I see that two kinds of disagreement can arise when things are reported to us in words by truthful reporters: one concerns the actual truth of the things reported; the

other concerns the meaning of the reporter. To try to
find out the truth about the making of creation is one
thing; it is a different thing to try to find out what Moses,
that excellent minister of your faith, meant his reader or
his hearer to understand by his words. As to the first
inquiry, I wish to have nothing to do with those who
think they know things that are really false, and in the
second inquiry I will have nothing to do with those who
think that Moses said things which are false. I would be
with those in you, Lord, and I would take delight with
those in you who feed on your truth in the largeness of
charity. Together with them I would approach the words
of your book and in these words try to find out your
meaning through the meaning of your servant by whose
pen you gave them to us.

24   BUT IN FINDING the meaning there are so many
truths which occur to us from these words, according to whether we understand them in one way or
another. Is there any one of us who can say: "This is
what Moses thought," "This is what he meant us to understand in that passage," with the same confidence as
he would say: "This is true" or "That is true," whether
Moses meant it or not? Consider me, my God, me, your
servant, who have vowed to you the sacrifice of my confession in these words of mine and who pray to you that
in your mercy I may *pay my vows unto Thee;* see how
confidently I affirm that in your immutable Word you
created all things, visible and invisible; could I affirm
with the same confidence that Moses had just one particular meaning and no other when he wrote: *In the Beginning God made heaven and earth?* No. I can see in your
truth that this is a certainty; but I cannot see equally
clearly that this was in his mind as he wrote those words.

When he said *In the Beginning* he might have been
thinking of the very start of creation, and when he said
heaven and earth he might have wished us to understand
by the words no already formed and perfected nature,

spiritual or corporeal, but both of these inchoate and still formless. Certainly I see that whichever was his meaning, it would be true; but I do not see so clearly which he had in mind when he was writing those words. Although, whether this great man, while writing these words, saw in his mind one or other of these meanings, or some other meaning which I have not mentioned, I have no doubt that he saw what was true and that he expressed it correctly.

25 I HOPE, THEREFORE, to avoid being pestered by the person who says: "Moses did not think as you say; he thought as I say." If he said: "How do you know that your interpretation of Moses' words represents what Moses thought?" that would be a question which I should take in good part, and I should probably answer it as I have written above or at rather more length, if he needed more persuading. But when he says: "Moses did not think as you say; he thought as I say," and at the same time does not deny that what each of us says is true, then, O life of the poor, my God, in whose bosom is no contradiction, I beg you to pour down into my heart some balm of mitigation to help me put up patiently with such people as this. For they are not speaking because they are divinely inspired and have seen what they say in the heart of your servant; they are speaking out of pride; they do not know what Moses thought, but they love what they think themselves, and they love their own opinion not because it is true, but because it is their own. Otherwise they would love another true opinion just as much—as I love what they say, when what they say is true—not because it is theirs but because it is true. In fact it ceases to be theirs just because it is true. If, therefore, they love it because it is true, then it is both theirs and mine; it is the common property of all lovers of truth.

But this I will not have, this I do not love, when they assert that Moses did not think as I say but did think as

they say. Even if they happened to be right, nevertheless, their temerity in making the assertion comes from
arrogance, not from knowledge; it is born not of vision
but of swelling pride. And therefore, Lord, your judgments are terrible, because your truth is not my property
nor the property of this man or that man; it belongs to
all of us whom you publicly call into communion with
it, warning us in most terrible terms that we must not
hold it as private to ourselves lest we be deprived of it
altogether. For whoever claims as his personal possession what you have given for the enjoyment of all, and
wants to have as his own what belongs to everyone, is
driven out from what is in common to what really is his
own, that is, from a truth to a lie. For he *that speaketh
a lie, speaketh it of his own.*

Listen, best of judges, God, Truth itself, listen to what
I shall say to an opponent like this. Listen; for I am
speaking in your presence and in the presence of my
brethren who employ *the law lawfully, to the end of charity.* Listen, if you please, and see what I shall say to him.
The words I address to him are fraternal and designed
to make peace. I say: "If we both see that what you say
is true, and we both see that what I say is true, then
where, I ask, do we see this? I do not see it in you; you
do not see it in me, but both of us see it in that immutable truth which is above our minds. Since, therefore, we
do not disagree about the true light of our Lord God,
why should we disagree about the thought that was in
the head of a neighbor? For we cannot see this thought
as clearly as the immutable truth is to be seen. If Moses
himself appeared to us and said: 'This was what I was
thinking,' we should believe what he said, but still would
not actually see what was in his mind. Let us *not*, then,
be puffed up for *one against the other, above that which
is written: let us love the Lord our God with all our heart,
with all our soul and with all our mind: and our neighbor
as ourself.* Now we must believe that whatever Moses
thought when he was writing those books, his thoughts

were in accordance with those two precepts of charity; if we do not believe this, we shall be making the Lord a liar, for we shall be thinking of our fellow servant's soul in a way that is different from the way that God has taught us to think. Can you not see now how foolish it is out of all that abundance of perfectly true meanings which can be extracted from those words rashly to assert that one particular meaning was the one which Moses had chiefly in mind, and thereby in one's pernicious quarrelsomeness to offend charity herself, for whose sake he, whose words we are trying to explain, said everything that he did say?"

26   AND YET I—MY GOD, you who give height to my humility, my labor's rest, you who hear my confessions and forgive me my sins—since you tell me to love my neighbor as myself, I cannot believe that you gave less gift to your most faithful servant Moses than I would have wished and desired from you myself, if I had been born at the same time as he and had been put by you in the same position—namely, that by the service of my heart and tongue those books were to be produced which for so long after were to do good to all nations and which throughout the whole world, from such a height of authority, were to overtop the words of all the doctrines of falsehood and of pride.

Now if I had been Moses then (for we all come from the same lump and *what is man, saving that Thou art mindful of him?*), if, I say, I had been then what he was and had been given by you the task of writing the Book of Genesis, I should have wished to be granted to me such a power of expression and such stylistic abilities that those who cannot yet understand how God creates would still not reject my words as being beyond their capacity, and that those who already have understanding would find in the few words of your servant every true opinion which they had reached themselves in their own thinking, and I should wish too that if another man were to see some other true opinion by the light of truth, that that opinion also should be discoverable in these same Words of mine.

27   A SPRING SHUT in a small place has a more plentiful supply of water and distributes its flow to more streams over a greater area of ground than does any single stream, however far it goes, which is derived from that spring. It is the same with the writing of him who dispenses your word. This writing will do good to many who will preach and comment upon it, and from a narrow measure of speech it will spread and overflow into streams of liquid truth, and from these, as they wind away in lengthier stretches of language, each man may on these subjects draw what truth he can—one man one truth, one another.

Some people, for example, when they read or hear the words which we are discussing think of God as though He were a kind of man or else like some great force associated with an enormous mass, and they imagine that by some new and sudden decision He made heaven and earth outside Himself and, as it were, in some place spatially separated from Himself—heaven and earth being two great bodies, one above and one below, in which all things are contained. And when they hear *God said, Let it be made, and it was made,* they think of words with a beginning and an ending, audible in time and passing away, and they imagine that as soon as the words had passed away then what was commanded to come into existence came into existence. And there are other such notions too, all due to the fact that some people are used to thinking in material terms.

Such people are still feeble little creatures, but by this humble kind of language their weakness is protected and nourished as by a mother's breast, and so there is built up in them a healthy faith in which they have a hold for a certainty that God made all the natures which, all around them in wonderful variety, their senses look upon. And if any one of these, in a kind of proud debility, despises what may seem to him the commonness of your words and stretches out beyond the limits of the nest where you are nourishing him, then I fear that this poor creature will have a bad fall, and I pray, Lord God, that you will have pity and will not allow the passers-by to tread upon that unfledged nestling, but will send your angel to put him back in the nest so that he may live till he is able to fly.

28 BUT OTHERS NEED no longer think of your words as a nest. To them they are shady gardens of fruit, and they see the fruit hidden under the trees, and they flutter around it in joy, and, cheerfully chirping, they peer for it and pluck it.

When such people read or hear the words which we are discussing, they see that all times past and future are swallowed up in your eternal stable permanence, and yet that there is no creature of time which is not made by you. And because your will is identical with yourself, your will suffered no change when you made all things, nor did a new will arise which was not there before. And in making all things you did not make them out of yourself in your own likeness (which is the form of all things); you created from nothing something unlike yourself and without form, yet something which was capable of receiving form in your likeness by having recourse to your unity according to the capacity ordained by you and in the measure given by you to each being in its own kind. And all things are very good, whether they stay close around you or whether, further removed in degrees of time and space, they cause or undergo their beautiful variations.

These things they see, and, so far as they are able to do so here, they rejoice in the light of your truth.

And another one of these, after pondering on the words *In the Beginning God made heaven and earth,* takes "the beginning" to mean Wisdom, *because it also speaketh unto us.* Another, pondering on the same words, understands by "beginning" the actual start of the process of creation and so takes "in the beginning He made" as being equivalent to "He made first."

And of those who take *In the Beginning* to mean "In Wisdom He made heaven and earth," one believes that here the words "heaven and earth" mean the matter out of which heaven and earth were to be created; another believes that the words refer to natures already formed and distinct; another thinks that by "heaven" is meant a formed and spiritual nature, while "earth" means the formless nature of corporeal matter.

And those who understand by the words "heaven and earth" the still formless matter out of which heaven and earth were to be made, even so do not all understand the words in the same way. Some take it as meaning the matter out of which both the sensible and the intelligible creation were to proceed; others mean only the matter from which this sensible corporeal world was to come which contains in its vast embrace all natures that are visible and evident to our senses.

Nor is there agreement between those who believe that in this passage "heaven and earth" means created things already formed and set in order. Some take this to refer to both the invisible and the visible worlds, others only to the visible, in which we see the shining heaven and the dark earth and all things contained in them.

29   BUT IF ONE ADOPTS the view that *In the Beginning He made* must be equivalent to "He made first," then the only possible interpretation of "heaven and earth" is "the material of heaven and earth," that is, of the whole intelligible and corporeal creation. Any attempt to make the words mean "the universe already formed" will rightly provoke the question: "If God made this first, what did He make afterward?" One will not find anything coming after everything, and, whether one likes it or not, one will be faced with the question: "How could this be 'first,' if there was nothing afterward?"

But to say that God made matter first formless and then formed is not absurd so long as one is capable of distinguishing between priority in eternity, priority in time, priority in choice, priority in origin (in eternity, as God is before all things; in time, as the flower is before the fruit; in choice, as the fruit is before the flower; in origin, as the sound is before the tune).

Of these four which I have mentioned, the first and last are extremely difficult, the middle two very easy to understand. For rarely, Lord, do we have the insight, and hard it is for us to see your eternity creating in its changelessness things that change, and thus prior to them. Again not many people are acute enough in understanding as to be able to see without difficulty how it is that the sound is prior to the tune: the reason being that a tune is a sound that has been given form, and, though a thing that has not been formed can at least exist, a thing that does not exist cannot be given a form. Thus the matter is prior to the thing which is made from it—not prior because it makes the thing (it is rather the case that it is made than that it makes), and not prior in any temporal sense; for we do not first of all utter formless sounds without a tune and then later on shape them and fit them together into the form of a song, as we do in the case of the wood or silver out of which we are making a box or vessel. Such materials, certainly, are prior in time to the forms of the things which are made out of them. But it is not so in the case of a tune. When the tune is sung, the sound of it is heard; we do not first have an unformed sound and later a sound that is shaped into a song. Each sound, just as it is made, passes away; and you can find nothing that you can call back again and shape by art, and thus the tune has its being in the sound and the sound of the tune is the matter of the tune. And this matter receives a form so that it may become a tune. And therefore, as I said, the matter of the sound is prior to the form of the tune—not prior in the sense of

having the power to make it, for sound is not the composer
of tunes, it is merely supplied by the body to the mind of
the singer for him to use in making a song; nor is it prior
in time, for it is uttered simultaneously with the tune; nor
is it prior in choice, for a sound is not better than a tune,
since a tune is not only a sound, but a beautiful sound.
But it is prior in origin, because a tune is not given form
in order to become a sound, whereas a sound is given form
in order to become a tune.

From this example those who have the ability may
understand that the matter of things was first made and
called "heaven and earth," because heaven and earth
were made out of it. But this matter was not made first
in time, because the forms of things give rise to time,
but this matter was without form; only when time itself
was in existence could it be observed in time. Yet in
speaking of this formless matter we have to speak of it
as though it were first in time, while it is inferior in
value (since what is formed is clearly better than what
is formless) and it is preceded by the eternity of the
creator, so that from nothing there might be the material
out of which something was to be made.

30 IN THIS DIVERSITY of true opinions, let Truth
herself bring forth concord. And our God have
mercy upon us, that we may use *the law lawfully, the
end of the commandment, pure charity.*

So if anyone asks me which of these meanings was in
the mind of your servant Moses, I should not be speaking in the language of my Confessions, if I did not confess to you: "I do not know." But I do know that all
these opinions are true, except for those carnal ones,
about which I said what I thought. Yet those little ones
of high promise who understand the Scripture in this
carnal sense are kept safe from fear by the words of your
book, words so lofty in humility, so copious in brevity.

And let all of us who, as I confess, see the truth and
speak the truth that is in these words, love one another,

and let us all together love you, our God, the fountain of truth, if what we thirst for is truth itself and not vanity, and let us so honor that servant of yours, the dispenser of this Scripture, a man full of your spirit, as to believe that when, by your revelation, he wrote these things, his mind was bent toward that meaning in them which is the best meaning, both for the light of truth which it sheds, and for the practical good which it does.

31 So WHEN SOMEONE SAYS: "Moses meant what I think," and someone else says: "No, he meant what I think," would it not be more reverent to say: "Why not as you both think, if what each of you thinks is true?" And if in these words someone should see a third or a fourth truth, or indeed any other truth at all, why should we not believe that all these truths were seen by Moses, through whom the one God tempered the Holy Scriptures to the minds of many, so that their minds should see different things, though all true things. Certainly for my own part (and I say this fearlessly from my heart), if I were to write anything that could have this height of authority, I should prefer to write in such a way that my words could convey any truth that anyone could grasp on such matters, rather than to set down one true meaning so clearly as to exclude all other meanings which, not being false, could not offend me. And so, my God, I will not be so rash as to believe that Moses did not deserve as much at your hands. When he was writing these words he was entirely aware in his thought of all the truth that we have been able to find there, and also of all the truth which we have not been able to find, or not yet, though it still remains there to be found.

32 FINALLY, LORD, you who are God and not flesh and blood, even if one who was a mere man did not see everything, it is certain that everything which you yourself in those words intended to reveal to future readers must have been evident to *Thy good Spirit,* who shall *lead me into the land of uprightness*. This is so, even if Moses, through whom the words were said, perhaps was thinking of only one out of the many true meanings which are to be found in them. And if this was the case, then let us grant that the meaning which was in his mind was the highest and loftiest of all. And Lord, we ask you to show us either that meaning or any other true meaning that you please; so that, whether you make clear to us the same thing as that which you made clear to your servant, or whether you show us something else arising from the same words, we may still be fed by you, not mocked by error.

See, Lord my God, how much I have written on these few words! Really, how much! What strength of ours, what length of time would be enough to comment in this way on all your Scriptures!

Allow me, then, to speak more briefly to you in my confessions on these words, and to choose one meaning which, by your inspiration, I shall see to be true, certain, and good, even though many other meanings may occur to me, since many others are possible. For I wish my confession to be made in this faith—that, if I have said what your own minister meant himself, that is right and that is best and for that I ought to try; but if I have failed to achieve this, I shall nevertheless say what your Truth has been pleased to say to me by his words, that Truth which also said what it willed to Moses.

Book XIII

1 I CALL UPON YOU, my God, my mercy, who made me and did not forget me when I had forgotten you. I call you into my soul which you are making ready to receive you by the longing which you yourself inspire. Do not forsake me now that I call upon you; for before I could call upon you at all, you were ahead of me; by all sorts of voices and in all kinds of ways over and over again you pressed yourself on my attention, so that I might hear you from far away and be converted and might call upon you who were calling me.

For you, Lord, have wiped away all those acts of mine which deserved punishment; from my hands which sinned against you you did not exact the price due, and in everything I did that deserved well, you were ahead of me, so that you might give the due reward to the work of your own hands, the hands that made me. Because before I could be, you were; nor was I such as to deserve the gift of being. Yet, see, I am and I am because of your goodness which went before—before all that you have made me and before all out of which you made it. For you had no need of me, nor am I anything so good as to be of help to you, my Lord and my God. It is not that I should serve you in case you grew tired in your work, nor that without my service your power would be less. You are not like land which requires cultivation if it is not to be barren; it is not in that way that you need my worship. No, I worship you and I serve you so that it may be well with me in relation to you, from whom it comes that I exist as someone capable of well-being.

2 FROM THE FULLNESS of your goodness every created thing has its being, so that a good—which cannot benefit you in any way, which, not being of your substance, cannot be equal to you—might still be, because it could come into existence from you. For what did *heaven and earth which Thou madest in the Beginning* deserve of you? Let the two natures, spiritual and corporeal, which you made in your Wisdom say how they deserved it of you that they should depend on that Wisdom even in their inchoate and unformed state, whether in the spiritual or in the corporeal order (the spiritual, though *without form,* being superior to the corporeal, even if formed, and the corporeal in its formlessness being superior to absolute nothingness), a state which tended toward the chaotic in an increasing distance from your likeness. How did they deserve so to depend upon your Word, still formless and remaining so unless they were recalled by the same Word to your unity, and given form and made by you, the supreme good, altogether very good? How did they deserve it of you that they should even be *without form,* since they could not even have been this without you?

How had corporeal matter deserved it of you that it should exist even in that invisible and formless state, since even in that state it could not have existed unless you made it? Since it did not exist, it could not have deserved to exist.

And how had that original beginning of your spiritual creation deserved to have even that dark, watery existence, like the deep, and unlike you? An existence that by the same Word was to be turned toward the Word by which it was created and, receiving light from it, should become light, not in equality with you, but nevertheless conformed to a form that is equal to you. For as in a body to be is not the same thing as to be beautiful (otherwise there would be no ugliness), so in a created spirit to live is not the same thing as to live wisely; otherwise such a spirit would be changelessly wise forever. But *good it is* for it always to *hold fast to Thee,* lest it should lose by turning away from you the light which it gained by turning toward you, and should fall back again into the life that is like the dark deep. For we too who in our souls are a spiritual creation, when turned away from you, our light, have been in this life *sometimes darkness,* and we still labor among the remains of our obscurity, until in your only Son we become *Thy righteousness, like the mountains of God.* For we have been *Thy judgments, which are like the great deep.*

3 AT THE BEGINNING of the creation you said: *Let there be light, and there was light.* I think I have good reason to take these words as referring to the spiritual creation, for there was already a life of a sort for you to illuminate. But just as it had no claim upon you to be of a kind capable of illumination, so, when it did exist, it had no claim actually to be illuminated. Its formless state could not please you unless it became light, and became light not simply by existing but by beholding the light shining upon it and by cleaving to it; so that it owed entirely to your grace both its life and the happiness of that life, being turned, by a change for the better, toward that which can suffer no change either for the better or the worse—toward you, who alone exist in simplicity, to whom it is not one thing to live and another to live happily, because you are your own happiness.

4 YOU ARE YOURSELF your own good; what, then, could have been lacking to that good even if these created things had never existed at all, or if they had remained without form? These things you made not because of any want, but out of the fullness of your goodness, setting bounds to them, giving them form, though it was not as if your joy was increased by them. To your perfection their imperfection is displeasing; perfected by you they will please you, but not in the sense that you were imperfect and needed for your own per-

fection that they should be made perfect. For your good
spirit was *borne over the waters,* not borne up by them,
as though He rested on them. When one says that your
spirit rests on people, it means that He causes them to
rest in Him. But your incorruptible and immutable will,
itself sufficient to itself, was *borne upon* the life which
you had created, a life to which living is not the same
thing as living happily, because there was still life even
in its wavering watery darkness. But it remains for it to
turn to Him by whom it was made and more and more
to live by the fountain of life, and in His light to see the
light, and to be perfected and illuminated and blessed.

5   SEE NOW, there appears to me *in a glass darkly*
the Trinity, which is you, my God, since you,
Father, *in the Beginning created heaven and earth*—in
the beginning of our Wisdom, which is your Wisdom,
born of you, equal to you and coeternal that is, in your
Son. I have said much of the *heaven of heavens* and of
the *earth invisible and without form* and of the dark
deep, dark in respect to the flux and the disorder of its
spiritual formlessness, until it became converted to Him
from whom it received its humble degree of life and by
His illumination became a life of beauty, and was the
heaven of that other heaven which was later created *between water and water.* And now under the name of God
I understood the Father, who made these things, and
under the name of the Beginning I understood the Son,
in whom He made these things, and believing, as I did,
my God to be a Trinity, I searched in His holy writings
and, see, I found your Spirit *moving over the waters.*
There it is, the Trinity, my God, Father, Son, and Holy
Ghost, Creator of all creation.

6   BUT WHAT WAS the reason, O Light that speaks
the truth, I lift my heart to you; let it not teach
me vanities; dispel its darkness and tell me, I beg you

by our mother Charity, I beg you, tell me what was the reason why it was only after the mention of heaven and of *the earth invisible and without form and darkness upon the deep* that finally your Scripture made mention of your Spirit. Was it because it was right that your Spirit should be introduced in the phrase "borne above," and this phrase could not have been used unless there had previously been a mention of that above which your Spirit was to be understood as being borne? For the Spirit was not "borne above" the Father or the Son, nor could He rightly be said to be "borne above" nothing. It was necessary, therefore, that that over which He was borne should first be mentioned and that only then should come the mention of the Spirit who could not be described otherwise than as being "borne above." But why was it necessary that He could only be introduced to us in the phrase "borne above"?

7   I SHOULD LIKE everyone who can to follow in his understanding your Apostle when he says: *Because Thy love is shed abroad in our hearts by the Holy Ghost, which is given unto us,* and when *concerning spiritual gifts* he teaches and *showeth unto us a more excellent way* of charity, and when *he bows his knee, unto Thee for us,* that we may *know the supereminent knowledge of the love of Christ.* So from the beginning was the Spirit *borne* supereminent *above the waters.*

To whom can I tell it, and how can I tell of the weight of concupiscence dragging us toward that steep abyss, and of how charity raises us up by your Spirit which was *borne above the waters?* To whom shall I tell it? How shall I tell it. For it is not in space that we sink down and are raised up again. The experience is very like this, but at the same time quite unlike. There are affections, there are loves, there is the uncleanness of our spirit flowing away downward in love of care and distraction, and there is your sanctity raising us upward in the love of freedom from care, so that to you we may lift up our hearts, where your Spirit *is borne above the waters,* and come to that supereminent peace, when our soul shall have passed through *the waters that are without substance.*

8 THE ANGEL FELL, the soul of man fell, and they showed us the abyss in that deep darkness, the abyss for the whole spiritual creation, if from the beginning you had not said *Let there be light* and light was made and every obedient intelligence of your Heavenly City cleaved to you and rested in your Spirit which is borne unchangeably over all things mutable. Otherwise even the *heaven of heaven* would have been in itself a dark deep; but *now it is light in the Lord.*

For even in that miserable restlessness of spirits who fall away from you and discover their own darkness, bared of the garment of your light, you show us clearly enough how noble a thing is the rational creature which you have made, which, for its peace and happiness, can be contented with nothing less than you, and so cannot be contented with itself. For you, our God, will *lighten our darkness;* from you arises our *garment of light,* and then *shall our darkness be as the noonday.*

Give yourself to me, my God, and give yourself back to me. See, I love, and if my love is too little, I would love more. I cannot measure it so as to know how much my love falls short of what is enough for my life to run to your embraces and never be turned away until it is *hidden in the hidden place of Thy presence.* This is all I know, that apart from you it is ill with me, not only without, but within myself, and all my abundance, which is not my God, is poverty.

9 BUT WAS NOT either the Father or the Son also *borne above the waters?* If one is thinking in terms of a body in space, then it would not be true to say this even of the Holy Spirit. But if our meaning is the unchangeable supereminence of divinity over all things mutable, then both Father and Son and Holy Spirit were *borne above the waters*.

Why then are these words used only of your Spirit? Why only in His case is there mention of a place where He was (though it is not a place), in His case only of whom it was said that He is your gift? In your gift we rest; there we enjoy you. Our rest is our place. Love lifts us up to it, and your good spirit raises our lowness from *the gates of death*. In your *good pleasure is our peace*. A body tends to go of its own weight to its own place, not necessarily downward toward the bottom, but to its own place. Fire tends to rise upward; a stone falls downward. Things are moved by their own weights and go toward their proper places. If you put oil underneath water it will rise above the level of the water; if you pour water on top of oil, it will sink below the oil; things are moved by their own weights and go to their proper places. When at all out of their place, they become restless; put them back in order and they will be at rest. My weight is my love; wherever I am carried, it is my love that carries me there. By your gift we are set on fire and are carried upward, we are red hot and we go. We *ascend Thy ways that be in our heart* and sing a *song of degrees*. We are red hot with your fire, your good fire, and we go; for we are going upward toward *the peace of Jerusalem*; for *gladdened was I in those who said unto me, We will go up to the house of the Lord*. It is there that your good pleasure will have us settled, so that we may desire nothing else but to remain there forever.

10 HAPPY THE CREATURE which knows no other state! Yet even this creature would have been different, had it not been that by your gift, *borne above* all things mutable, it was raised up as soon as it was created and became light immediately by that summons of yours, *Let there be light*. With regard to us there is a distinction of time when it is said: *We were darkness and*

shall be made light; but with regard to that creation it is
only said what it would have been if it had not received
light, and the reason why the passage is so phrased as
to suggest that it was previously in a state of flux and
darkness is to make clear the cause why it was made to
be something different, that is the cause by which it was
turned toward the light that is unfailing and itself became light. Let him, who can, understand this. Let him
ask guidance from you and not trouble me. It is not I
who *enlighten every man that cometh into this world.*

11 WHO CAN UNDERSTAND the almighty Trinity?
Yet we all speak of it, if it really is the Trinity
of which we speak. Rare is the soul which in what it
says of the Trinity knows what it is saying. And men
struggle and contend, and no one without peace sees
that vision.

I should like men to consider three aspects of their
own selves. These three are something very different
from the Trinity; I only make the suggestion as a mental
exercise which will allow people to find out and to feel
how far distant they are from it. The three things I mean
are existence, knowledge, and will. For I am, and I know,
and I will. I am a being that knows and wills. I know that I
am, and I know that I will. I will to be and I will to
know. Now he who is capable of doing so will see how
there is in these three an inseparable life—one life, one
mind, one essence—and how, finally, how inseparable a
distinction there is between them, yet nevertheless there
is a distinction. Every man has this fact in front of him.
Let him look into his own self and see and tell me what
he sees. But when he has discovered something in these
and has stated it, he must not go on to suppose that he
has discovered that immutable which is above all these
things, that which exists immutably, knows immutably,
and wills immutably. But whether because of these three
there is in God also a Trinity, or whether all three are
in each Person so that each Person has three aspects, or

whether both views are correct and in some unimaginable way, in simplicity and in multiplicity, It itself, though unbounded, is within Itself and bound to Itself, by which it exists and is known to itself and is sufficient to itself, unchangeably the Selfsame in the plentiful magnitude of its unity—who can easily grasp this in his mind? Who can in any way tell of it? Who could in any way venture to make a pronouncement upon it?

12 GO ON WITH your confession, my faith. Say to your Lord: *Holy, Holy, Holy, O Lord my God,* in your name we have been baptized, *Father, Son, and Holy Ghost;* in your name we baptize, *Father, Son, and Holy Ghost,* because among us too God made in His Christ *a heaven and an earth,* namely the spiritual and the carnal members of His Church. And our "earth" before it received the form of doctrine was *invisible and without form,* and we were clothed in the darkness of ignorance. For *Thou chastenedst man for iniquity,* and *Thy judgments were like the great deep unto him.* But because *your Spirit was borne above the waters,* your mercy did not forsake our misery and you said: *Let there be light, Repent ye for the kingdom of heaven is at hand. Repent ye; let there be light.* And because our soul was *troubled within us, we remembered Thee, O Lord, from the land of Jordan, and that mountain,* equal to you, but *little for our sakes,* and our darkness was displeasing to us and we turned to you *and there was light.* And, see, we were sometimes darkness, but now light in the Lord.

13 BUT UP TO NOW it is still by *faith and not by sight, for by hope we are saved; but hope that is seen is not hope.* Still *deep calls to deep,* but now *in the voice of Thy waterspouts.* Still even he who says: *I could not speak unto you as unto spiritual, but as unto carnal,* does not yet *think himself to have apprehended,* and *forgetteth those things which are behind* and *reacheth forth* *to those which are before,* and *groaneth being burdened,* and *his soul thirsteth after the living God, as the hart after the waterbrooks,* and says: *When shall I come?* desiring to be clothed upon with *his house which is from heaven,* and calleth upon this lower deep, saying, *Be not conformed to this world, but be ye transformed by the renewing of your mind.* And, *be not children in understanding, but in malice be children that in understanding ye may be perfect,* and, *O foolish Galatians, who hath bewitched you?* But now he is not speaking in his own voice; he is speaking in yours who sent *the Spirit from above,* through Him *who ascended upon high* and *set open the floodgates of His gifts, that the force of His streams might make glad the city of God:* For that city the friend of the bridegroom sighs who has now the *first fruits of the Spirit laid up with Him, yet still groaning within himself, waiting for the adoption, to wit, the redemption of his body.* For that city he sighs, for he is a member of *the Bride;* he is jealous for it, because he is a friend of the Bridegroom; he is jealous for it, not for himself, because it *is in the voice of Thy waterspouts,* not in his own voice, that he calls to that other deep of which he is jealous and fears *lest as the serpent beguiled Eve through his subtlety, so their minds should be corrupted from the purity that is in* our Bridegroom, your only Son. And what a light of beauty is that, when we shall *see Him as He is,* and *those tears be passed away,* which have been *my meat day and night, whilst they daily say unto me, Where is now thy God?*

14 AND I TOO SAY "My God, where is He?" See where you are. In You I breathe a little when *I pour out my soul by myself in the voice of joy and praise,* the sound of *him that keeps holy-day.* And still my soul is sad, because it slips back again and becomes *a deep,* or rather it realizes that it is still *a deep.* And my faith speaks to it, my faith which you have kindled to be a light before my feet in the night, *and says: Why art thou*

sad, O my soul, and why dost thou trouble me? Hope in the Lord; His word is a lanthorn unto thy feet: hope and endure until the night, which is the mother of sinners, passes; until the wrath of the Lord passes, for we too were children of wrath, we *were sometimes darkness,* and we bear about with us relics of this darkness in our body, *dead because of sin, until the day break and the shadows fly away. Hope thou in the Lord; in the morning I shall stand in Thy presence, and contemplate Thee. I shall forever confess unto Thee. In the morning I shall stand in Thy presence, and shall see the health of my countenance, my God, Who also shall quicken our mortal bodies, by the Spirit that dwelleth in us,* because in mercy He has been *borne over* the flowing darkness of our inner deep. And as in our pilgrimage we have received *an earnest* that we should *now* be *light,* while we are still *saved by hope,* and *are* the *children of light and the children of the day, not the children of the night, nor of the darkness,* which yet *sometimes we were. Betwixt* whom and us, in what is still the uncertainty of human knowledge, *Thou* alone *dividest, Thou* who *provest* our *hearts* and *callest the light, day, and the darkness, night.* For who except you discerns us? *And what have we that we have not received of Thee? Out of the same lump vessels unto honor, from which others too* are made *unto dishonor.*

15 OR WHO EXCEPT YOU, our God, made for us a firmament of authority over us in your divine Scripture? For *heaven shall be folded up like a scroll,* and now it is stretched over us like a skin. For your divine Scripture is of all the more sublime authority because those mortals, through whom you gave it to us, have died their deaths. And you know, Lord, you know how you *clothed* men *with skins* when by their sin they became mortal. And so you have *like a skin stretched out the firmament* of your book; that is, your words which so well agree together and which, through the agency of mortal men, you have placed above us. By their death that solid firmament of authority in your words delivered by them was extended sublimely over all things that are below it; which, while they still lived here, was not so sublimely extended. For you had not yet *stretched out the heaven like a skin*, you had not yet spread abroad in every direction the glory of their deaths.

Lord, let us *look upon the heavens, the work of Thy fingers*. Clear away from our eyes the mist with which you have covered them. *There is Thy testimony, which giveth wisdom unto the little ones*. My God, *perfect Thy praise out of the mouth of babes and sucklings*. For we know no other books so destructive of pride, so destructive of *the enemy and the defender* who resists reconciliation with you by defending his own sins. I do not know, Lord, I do not know any writings so pure, so apt to persuade me to confess, to bow my neck to your yoke and take service with you for nothing. Good Father, let me understand them; grant this to me who am placed below them; for it was for us who are placed below that you established them so firmly.

There are, I believe, above this firmament other waters which are immortal and separated from all earthly corruption. Let them praise your name, let them praise you, those supercelestial peoples, your angels, who have no need to look up at this firmament, no need of reading to understand your word. For they always see your face, and there they read without syllables that are spoken in time what is willed by your eternal will. They read; they choose; they love; their reading is perpetual and what they read never passes away; for by choosing and by loving they read the very unchangeableness of your counsel. Their book is never closed, *nor is their scroll folded up*, for you yourself are their book and you are forever; because you have set them above this firmament which you established over the infirmity of the lower peoples so that they might look up at it and learn your mercy as it tells of you in times, you who made time. For *Thy mercy, O Lord, is in the heavens, and Thy truth reacheth unto the clouds*. The clouds pass away, but the heaven remains; the preachers of your word pass from this life into another life, but your Scripture is stretched out over the peoples until the end of time. *Heaven and earth shall pass away, but Thy words shall not pass away.* Because *the scroll shall be folded up,* and *the grass* over which it was spread *shall with the goodliness of it pass away,* but *Thy word remaineth forever,* which now appears to us not *as it is* but *under the dark image* of the clouds and *through the glass* of the heaven; because although we too are the well-beloved of your Son, it has *not yet appeared what we shall be. He looketh through the lattice of our flesh,* and He caressed us and set us on fire, and *we run after His odors. But when He shall appear, then shall we be like Him, for we shall see Him as He is.* It will be ours, Lord, to see Him *as He is,* though it is not for us yet.

16 FOR ALTOGETHER "as you are" is known to you alone, who are unchangeably, and know unchangeably, and will unchangeably, and your essence knows and wills unchangeably, and your knowledge is and wills unchangeably, and your will is and knows unchangeably. Nor does it seem right in your eyes that just as the unchangeable light knows itself, so it should be known by the changeable being that receives that light. And so *my soul is like a land where no water is,* since, just as it cannot by itself give light to itself, so it cannot by itself satisfy itself. For so *is the fountain of life with Thee* as *in Thy light we shall see light.*

17 WHO *gathered* the embittered *together into one* society? For they all have the same end, a temporal and earthly felicity, and for this they do everything that they do, however much they may waver here and there in the innumerable variety of their anxieties. Who except you, Lord, said: *Let the waters be gathered together into one place, and let the dry land appear,* which *thirsteth after thee?* For *the sea also is Thine, and Thou hast made it, and Thy hands prepared the dry land.* And what is meant by "sea" here is the *gathering together of the waters,* not the bitterness of men's wills. For you also restrain the wicked desires of the soul, and you set up bounds, how far the waters shall be allowed to go, so that their waves may break upon themselves, and so you make it a sea by the order of your power which is above all things.

But as to the souls which *thirst after Thee* and which *appear* before Thee (souls which are separated from the society of the sea by other bounds) you water them from a secret and sweet spring, so that *the earth may bring forth her fruit.* And she brings forth her fruit, and at your command, the command of her Lord God, our soul blossoms with works of mercy *according to their kind, loving our neighbor* in the relief of his bodily necessities, *having seed in itself according to its likeness,* since from our own weakness we feel compassion for others and are ready to help those in want, helping them as we ourselves would wish to be helped if we were in the same need, and not only in easy matters (like *the herb bearing seed),* but with help and protection given with all our strength (like *the tree yielding* fruit)—the sort of kindness as is shown, for example, in rescuing a man who suffers injustice from the grip of a powerful oppressor, or in giving him the shelter of our protection by the strong force of a just judgment.

18 So, LORD, let it spring up, as you already make it spring up, as you give cheerfulness and ability, so *let truth spring out of the earth, and righteousness look down from heaven* and *let there be lights in the firmament.* Let *us break our bread to the hungry* and *bring the* homeless *poor to our house:* Let us *clothe the naked, and despise not those of our own flesh.* And when these fruits have sprung from the earth, see that it is good, and let our temporary *light break forth,* and let us proceed from this lower harvest of action toward the delights of contemplation and, obtaining the word of life above, let us appear *like lights in the world,* clinging to the firmament of your Scripture. For there you instruct us so that we may distinguish between the intelligible and the sensible or between souls given either to the intelligible or to the sensible, as *betwixt day and night.* So that now it is not you alone in the secrecy of your judgment, as before the firmament was made, who *divide between the light and the darkness;* but, now that your grace is made manifest throughout the world, your spiritual children also, set and ranked in the same firmament, may *give light upon the earth, and divide betwixt the day and the night, and be for signs of times,* that *old things are passed away, and, behold, all things are become new,* and that *our salvation is nearer than when we believed,* and that *the night is far spent, and the day is at hand,* and that *Thou wilt crown Thy year with blessing, sending* the *laborers* of Thy *goodness* into Thy *harvest,* in the sowing of which *others have labored, sending* also into another field, whose *harvest* shall be *in the end.* So you grant the prayers to him who asks and *Thou blessest the years of the just; but Thou art the same* and in *Thy years* which *fail not* you prepare a granary for our passing years. For in your eternal place you bestow upon the earth heavenly blessings in their proper seasons. *For to one is given by the Spirit the word of wisdom,* as it were *the greater light* (for those who are delighted with the light of perspicuous truth) as *for the rule of the day. To another the word of knowledge by the same Spirit,* as it were *the lesser light; to another faith; to another the gift of healing; to another the working of miracles; to another prophecy; to another discerning of spirits; to another divers kinds of tongues.* And all these like stars—for *all these worketh the one and selfsame spirit, dividing to every man his own as He will,* and causing stars to appear *manifestly, to profit withal.*

But *the word of knowledge,* in which are contained *all Sacraments,* which vary in their *seasons* as it were *the*

moon, and the other *gifts* which are mentioned and reckoned up in their order as it were *stars* so far differ from
that bright light of wisdom in which the above-mentioned
day rejoices that they are only *for the rule* of the night.
For they are necessary to those to whom that most prudent servant of yours *could not speak unto as unto spiritual, but as unto carnal,* he who speaketh wisdom among
those that are perfect.

But the natural man who is as it were *a babe in Christ*
and must be *fed on milk* until he gains strength for *solid
meat* and has an eye strong enough to look steadily at the
sun must not have a night that is without light but must
be content with the light of *the moon* and of *the stars.*

So you instruct us, our God all-wise, in your Book, that
Firmament; so that in wonderful contemplation we may
discern all things, though still *in signs, and in times, and
in days and in years.*

19 BUT FIRST, *wash you, be clean; put away evil* from
your souls, and *from before mine eyes,* that the
*dry land may appear. Learn to do good, judge the father-
less, plead for the widow,* that *the earth may bring forth
the green herb for meat, and the tree bearing fruit,* and
come, let us reason together, saith the Lord, that there
may be *lights in the firmament of the heaven, and they
may shine upon the earth.* That *rich man* asked the *good
master what he should do to attain eternal life.* Let the
good master tell him (that good master whom he thought
to be no more than man; but He is good because He is
God); let Him tell him, *if he would enter into life,* he must
keep the commandments; he must put away from him the
bitterness of *malice and wickedness; not kill, not commit
adultery, not steal, not bear false witness;* that *the dry land
may appear, and bring forth the honoring of father and
mother, and the love of our neighbor. All these,* he says,
have I kept. Why then are there so many thorns, if the
earth is fruitful? Go, root out those rough thickets of
avarice; *sell that thou hast,* and be filled with fruit, by

giving to the poor, and thou shalt have treasure in heaven, and *follow* the Lord *if thou wilt be perfect,* in the company of those among whom *He speaketh wisdom*—He who knows what to distribute *to the day* and what *to the night,* so that you too may know it, and for you too there may be *lights in the firmament of heaven.* But they cannot be unless your *heart* is there; and your *heart* will not be there unless your *treasure* is there also, as you have heard from the *good master.* But that barren earth *was grieved,* and *the thorns choked the word.*

But you, *chosen generation,* you *weak things of the* world, who have *forsaken all* to follow the Lord, go after Him, beautiful feet, *shine in the firmament,* that *the heavens* may *declare His glory,* as you *divide between the light* of the perfect (though not yet as perfect as the angels) and *the darkness* of the little ones (who are still not without hope). Shine over all the earth; and let *the day,* all bright with *the sun, utter unto day* speech of *wisdom,* and *night,* shining with the moon, *show unto night the word of knowledge.* The moon and the stars shine by night, but the night does not obscure them; instead they themselves lighten it so far as it may be. For see, it is as if when God said: *Let there be lights in the firmament of heaven;* there *came suddenly a sound from heaven, as it had been the rushing of a mighty wind, and there appeared cloven tongues like as of fire, and it sat upon each of them.* And there were *made lights in the firmament of heaven,* having the *word of life.* Run, run everywhere, holy fires, fires of beauty. For you are *the light of the world* and you are not *put under a bushel.* He to whom you have clung has been raised up and he has raised you up. Run to and fro and be known to all nations.

20 LET THE SEA also conceive and bring forth your works, *let the waters bring forth the creeping creatures having life.* For you, *separating the precious from the vile,* are made the mouth of God, by which He said: *Let the waters bring forth,* not *the living creature* which the

*earth brings forth, but the creeping creatures having life
and the fowls that fly above the earth.* For your sacraments, God, by the ministry of your holy ones have crept
through the midst of the waves of the temptations of this
world to hallow the gentiles in your name by your
baptism.

Meanwhile great miracles were done, as it were *great
whales,* and there were the voices of your messengers
flying above the earth, in the open firmament of your
Book, which was placed above them in authority as
something under which they must fly wherever they
went. For *there is no speech nor language where their
voice is not heard:* since *their sound is gone through all
the earth, and their words to the end of the world,* because
you, Lord, by blessing them have multiplied them.

Can I be speaking untruly or mixing things up or fail-
ing to distinguish between the clear knowledge of these
things *in the firmament of heaven* and the corporeal
works in the wavy sea and *under the firmament of
heaven?* Certainly there are things of which our knowledge is solid and definite with no increase by generation,
as it were lights of wisdom and knowledge; but these
same things have many different corporeal operations;
one thing grows from another and they are multiplied
by your blessing, God; for you have made allowances for
our mortal senses which soon cloy, and have so arranged
matters that in the understanding of our mind one thing
may be represented and expressed in many different
ways through bodily motions. These things the waters
have brought forth, but still in your word; they have
been brought forth by the needs of people estranged
from the eternity of your truth, but still brought forth in
your Gospel; for they were cast out by those very waters
whose diseased bitterness was the cause why they were
sent forth in your word.

All things of your making are beautiful; and, see, you
who made all things are yourself inexpressibly more
beautiful. If Adam had not fallen away from you, there
would never have flowed from his loins the brackishness

of that sea which is the human race, so deeply curious, so stormily tossing, so restlessly flowing here and there, and then there would have been no need for the dispensers of your word to work *in many waters,* declaring in corporeal and sensible forms mysterious doings and sayings. For this is the sense in which I now take those *creeping and flying creatures;* people are trained and initiated to accept the authority of corporeal sacraments, but they would not get beyond this point unless their souls became spiritually alive on another level and after the word of admission looked forward to perfection.

21 SO IN YOUR WORD it is not the depth of the sea, but the earth separated from the bitterness of the waters which brings forth, not *the creeping creatures having life,* but *the living soul.* And this soul no longer has need of baptism, as the heathen do and as it did itself when it was covered with the waters (for there is no other *entrance into the kingdom of heaven,* since you appointed this as the entrance); nor does it seek after wonders and miracles to create faith; it is not of the kind which *unless it sees signs and wonders, it will not believe;* for now the faithful earth is separated from the waters that were bitter with infidelity and *tongues are for a sign, not to them that believe, but to them that believe not.* Nor does the earth which *Thou hast founded upon the waters* have any need of that *flying kind* which *the waters brought forth* at your word. Send your word into the earth by your messengers. For we speak of their labors, but it is you who are working in them so that they may work out a *living soul* in it. The earth brings it forth, because the earth is the cause that they work this in the soul, just as the sea was the cause that they worked upon the *creeping things having life* and the *fowls that fly under the firmament of heaven.* These the earth does not need, though it feeds upon that Fish which was taken out of the deep, upon that *table* which *Thou hast prepared in the presence* of those who believe. For He was taken from the deep so that He might feed the dry land, and the *fowl*, though bred in the sea, is nevertheless *multiplied upon the earth*. For it was man's infidelity which was the cause of the first preaching of the Evangelists, but the faithful too are exhorted and blessed by them every day in all sorts of ways. But *the living soul* takes its beginning from the earth, because only the faithful find profit in restraining themselves from the love of this world, so that their soul may live for you, a soul which was *dead while it lived in pleasures,* death-dealing pleasures, Lord; for you are the life-giving pleasure of the pure heart.

Now then let your ministers do their work on *the earth,* not as they did in the waters of infidelity by means of preaching and speaking with miracles and sacraments and mystic words—things which, through fear of such mysterious signs, attract the attention of ignorance, which is the mother of wonder. All this is a means of entrance to the faith for those sons of Adam who have forgotten you and, while *they hide themselves from Thy face*, have become a *dark deep*. But let your ministers now do their work as on the *dry land* which is separated from the whirlpools of the deep; let them be a pattern to the faithful by living among them and stirring them up to imitation. For in this way men hear not so as just to hear, but so as to do. *Seek the Lord, and your soul shall live*, so that the *earth* may *bring forth the living soul. Be not conformed to the world.* Restrain yourselves from it. The soul's life is in avoiding those things which are death to seek. Restrain yourselves from the monstrous savagery of pride, the sluggish voluptuousness of luxury, and the *false name of knowledge*, so that the wild beasts may be tamed, the cattle brought under the yoke, and the snakes made harmless. For these are an allegory for the movements of the mind. The arrogance of pride, the pleasure of lust, and the poison of curiosity are movements of a soul that is dead—not dead in the sense that it is motionless, but dead by *forsaking the fountain of life* and so engrossed in this transitory world and *conformed to it.*

But the Word, O God, is the fountain of life eternal and it does not pass away. Therefore, in your word that departure of the soul is checked, when it is said to us *Be not conformed unto this world;* so that *the earth* may in *the fountain of life bring forth a living soul*—in your word (delivered by the Evangelists) a soul that has become continent by imitating those who imitate your Christ. For this is what is meant by *after his kind,* since a man imitates the one who is his friend. *Be ye,* he says, *as I am, for I also am as ye are.*

So in the living soul there shall be *good beasts,* tamed in their behavior. For you have commanded, *Go on with thy business in meekness, so thou shalt be beloved by all men.* The cattle shall be good, for *neither if they eat, shall they overabound, nor, if they eat not, have any lack.* And the snakes shall be good, not dangerous and harmful but wise and full of caution, only searching into this temporal nature so far as is enough that *eternity may be clearly seen, being understood by the things that are made.* For these animals obey reason when they are checked from their death-bringing courses and live and become good.

22 FOR, SEE, LORD, our God, our Creator, when our affections, in which we were dying by evil living, have been restrained from the *love of the world* and we have begun to be by good living a *living soul,* and the word has been fulfilled which you spoke by your apostle, *Be not conformed to this world,* then there will follow next what you added directly afterward. *But be ye transformed by the renewing of your mind.* And now this does not mean *after your kind,* as in the cases of imitating one's neighbor who went before one or of following the example in life of some better man. For you did not say: "Let man be made *after his kind.*" What you said was: *Let us make man after our own image and* *similitude,* that we *might prove what Thy will is.* And, therefore, that great dispenser of your word who *begat* children by *the gospel,* not waiting to have them always as *babes* whom he must *feed with milk* and *cherish as a nurse* said: *Be ye transformed by the renewing of your mind, that ye may prove what is that good and acceptable and perfect will of God.* And so instead of saying: "Let man be made" you say: *Let us make man.* And instead of saying: "according to his kind" you say: *after our image and likeness.* For where man is *renewed in his mind* and sees and understands your truth he is in no need of another man to direct him in the sense of following *after his kind;* instead, with you to direct him, *he proveth what is that good, that acceptable and perfect will of Thine,* and, now that he has the capacity for it, you teach him to see the Trinity of the Unity and the Unity of the Trinity. So to the phrase in the plural, *Let us make man,* there is added in the singular *And God made man,* and after the phrase in the plural *After our likeness* there is added in the singular *After the image of God.* So man is *renewed in the knowledge of God, after the image of Him that created him,* and, having become spiritual, *he judgeth all things* (all things that are to be judged) yet *himself is judged of no man.*

23 By *"he judgeth all things"* is meant that he has *dominion over the fish of the sea, and over the fowls of the air,* and *over* all *cattle* and wild *beasts, and over all the earth, and over every creeping thing that creepeth upon the earth.* This he does by the understanding of his mind by which he *perceiveth the things of the Spirit of God,* whereas otherwise *man, being placed in honor, had no understanding, and is compared unto the brute beasts, and is become like unto them.* Therefore, our God, in your Church, according to your grace which you have given it *(for we are Thy workmanship created unto good works),* not only those who are in spiritual authority but also those who are spiritually subordinate judge spiritually; for in this way *you made male and female* in your spiritual grace, where according to bodily sex *there is neither male nor female* just as there is *neither Jew nor Greek, neither bond nor free.* So spiritual people, whether those in authority or those who are subjected to that authority, judge spiritually. They do not indeed judge of that spiritual knowledge *which shines in the firmament* (for they ought not to make judgment on such sublime authority at that); nor do they judge of your Book, even if certain passages are obscure, because we submit our intellects to that book and we regard it as certain that even what is closed to our gaze is still rightly and truly said. For so man, though he is now *spiritual and renewed in the knowledge of God after His image that created him* ought to be a *doer of the law,* not a *judge.* Nor does he take it upon himself to judge which men are spiritual and which carnal; these, our God, are known to your eyes and have not yet shown themselves to us by their works, so that by *their fruits we might know them;* but you, Lord, know them already, and you have *divided* and *called* them in secret even before the firmament was made. Nor, even though spiritual, does he judge of the unquiet and restless people of this world, *for what hath he to do, to judge them that are without,* when he does not know which of them will come into the sweetness of your grace and which will remain in the perpetual bitterness of ungodliness?

So man, whom you have made after your own image, did not receive *dominion* over *the lights of heaven,* nor over the secret heaven itself, nor over *the day and the night* which you called into being before the foundation of the heaven, nor over *the gathering together of the waters,* which is *the sea.* He received *dominion over the fishes of the sea, and the fowls of the air, and over all cattle, and over all the earth, and over all creeping things which creep upon the earth.* For he judges, approving what he finds good and condemning what he finds evil, and he exercises this judgment whether in the celebration of those Sacraments by which are initiated those whom your mercy searches out *in many waters;* or in that ceremony symbolized by the "Fish" which is taken out of the deep and which the good "earth" feeds upon; or in dealing with the significations and expression of words (which are under the authority of your book, as it were flying beneath the firmament) in interpreting, exposition, teaching, discussion, in praising you and in praying to you—signs proceeding from the mouth and sounding out aloud so that the people may answer: Amen. And the reason why these words have to be pronounced physically with the voice is *the deep* of this world and the blindness of the flesh because of which it is not possible to see thoughts, so that they have to be uttered audibly in our ears. So, although the *flying fowls are multiplied upon the earth,* their origin is nevertheless in the waters.

The spiritual man also judges by approving what he finds good and condemning what he finds bad in the actions and way of life of the faithful, in their almsgiving (which is like *the earth bringing forth fruit*), and he judges of the *living soul, living* by the taming of the affections, in chastity, in fastings, in holy meditations; also of those things which are perceived by the bodily senses. On all these things he is now said *to judge,* and in these things too he has the power to correct.

24 BUT HERE IS another mystery. What can it mean? See, Lord, you bless men so that they may *increase and multiply and replenish the earth.* Surely you are hinting here that there is something for us to understand, that we must ask ourselves why it was that you did not in the same way bless the light, which *thou calledst day,* nor *the firmament of heaven,* nor *the lights,* nor *the stars,* nor *the earth,* nor *the sea.* I would say, O God who created us after your image, I would say that you had wished to bestow this blessing peculiarly on men, if it were not for the fact that you had not in the same way blessed the fishes, and the whales, that they *should increase and multiply and replenish the waters of the sea,* and also that *the fowls should be multiplied upon the earth*. Again I would say that this blessing belonged properly to those creatures who are bred of their own kind, if it were not for the fact that I find the same blessing given to trees and plants and beasts of the earth. But now neither to the plants, nor the trees, nor the beasts, nor the snakes is it said *Increase and multiply;* although all these, as well as fish, birds, and men, increase and continue their kind by generation.

What am I to say then, truth, my light? That there is nothing here of importance? That the words are meaningless? Certainly not, Father of piety. Certainly a servant of your word must not say this. And if I do not understand what you mean by that phrase, then I hope that better people, that is, more intelligent people than I, will make a better use of it, according as you have given to each man his measure of understanding. And I hope that my confession will be pleasing in your sight when, Lord, I confess that I believe you did not speak thus for no good reason, and I shall say what is suggested to me by the reading of this phrase. For what I think it means is true, nor do I see what should stop me from understanding in this way the figurative expressions in your books. For I know that what is understood by the mind in a single way can be represented corporeally in a number of ways, and also that what is understood by the mind in a number of ways may have only one corporeal expression. Consider, for instance, the single idea of the love of God and of our neighbor. This is corporeally expressed in numbers of sacraments, in innumerable languages and, in each language, by countless varieties of speech. So do the offspring of *the waters increase and multiply.* And now I invite my readers to consider something which Scripture expresses and which the voice utters in only one way: *In the beginning God made heaven and earth.* Cannot this be understood in a number of ways, and not erroneously, but in different senses, each of which is true? So do the offspring of man *increase and multiply.*

So, if we think of the natures of things in their proper

sense and not allegorically, the phrase *Increase and multiply* applies correctly to all things born of seed. But if we regard the words as having been set down figuratively (which is what I think Scripture meant here, since it would not without some good reason ascribe this benediction only to the offspring of aquatic creatures and of men), then we shall find "multitudes" in creatures both spiritual and corporeal (as in *heaven* and *earth*); in souls both righteous and unrighteous (as in *light* and *darkness*); in the sacred writers who have been ministers of the law to us (as in *the firmament* which is established *between the waters and the waters*); in the society of peoples still in the bitterness of infidelity (as in *the sea*); in the zeal of holy souls (as in *the dry land*); in the works of mercy done in this life (as in *the herbs bearing seed and the trees bearing fruit*); in the *spiritual gifts set forth for edification* (as in the *lights of heaven*), and in the affections which have been reformed to temperance (as in the *living soul*). In all these cases we find "multitudes," "abundances," "increases." But only in signs corporeally pronounced and in things intellectually conceived do we find that kind of growth and increase where one idea can be expressed in a number of different ways and where one mode of expression can be understood in a number of different ways.

I take it that what is represented by the generation of aquatic creatures is the corporeally pronounced signs, which are necessary because of our deep immersion in the flesh, and what is represented by the generation of man is the things intellectually conceived, because of the fertility of reason.

And for this reason we believe, Lord, that you said to these two kinds *Increase and multiply*. For I take it that in this blessing you have granted us the faculty and the power both to express in many ways what we have grasped intellectually in only one way, and to understand in many ways what we find obscurely expressed in only one way. So *the waters of the sea* are *replenished,* waters whose movement indicates the variety of different significations, and so too *the earth is replenished* with human increase, and its *dryness* appears in its eagerness, and it is ruled by reason.

25 LORD, MY GOD, I wish also to say what the next phrase of your Scripture puts into my mind. I speak without fear; for, with you inspiring me, I shall speak the truth which from these words you have willed me to say. For by no other inspiration except yours do I believe that I speak truth, since you are *the Truth, and every man a liar.* Therefore *he that speaketh a lie, speaketh of his own.* So in order that I may speak truth, I must speak not "of my own" but "of yours."

See now, you have given us *for food every herb bearing seed that is upon all the earth, and every tree, in which is the fruit of a tree yielding seed.* And this not only to us, but also *to all the fowls of the air, and to the beasts of the earth, and to all creeping things.* But you did not give these things to *the fishes* and to *the great whales.*

Now we have said that these *fruits of the earth mean,* in an allegorical way, the works of mercy which are produced for the necessities of this life by the *fruitful earth.* Such an "earth" was the devout *Onesiphorus,* unto whose *house Thou gavest mercy,* because he often refreshed your servant Paul, and *was not ashamed of his chain.* The same was done by *the brethren,* and the same sort of fruit was borne by those who *out of Macedonia supplied what was lacking* to him. But how Paul grieves for some "trees" which failed to give him the fruit that was due! He says: *At my first answer no man stood by me, but all men forsook me. May it not be laid to their charge.* For these fruits are due from us to those who, from their understanding of the divine mysteries, minister the spiritual doctrine to us. They are due to them as men; yes, and they are also due to them as to *the living soul,* since they offer themselves to us as patterns for imitation in all kinds of continence. And they are due to them as to *flying creatures,* because of their blessings which are *multiplied upon the earth,* because *their sound went out into all lands.*

26 THOSE WHO FIND JOY in this food are fed by it,
and those *whose God is their belly* find no joy in
it. And also in those who give these fruits; the fruit is not
in what they give, but in the spirit in which it is given.
And so in the case of Paul who *served God and not his
own belly*, I see clearly whence comes his joy; I see it and
I greatly rejoice with him. For he *had received from the
Philippians* what they sent to him *by Epaphroditus*. But
still I see the reason for his joy. He feeds upon what he
finds his joy in, for, speaking in truth, he says: *I rejoiced
greatly in the Lord, that now at the last your care of me
hath flourished again, wherein ye were also careful but ye
had grown weary.* These Philippians, as we see, after a long
period of weariness had become as it were parched and
dried up for the bearing of *the fruit* of a good work, and
Paul rejoices for them because *they flourished again,* not
for himself because they supplied his needs. For he proceeds as follows: *I speak not in respect of want, for I have
learned in whatsoever state I am, therewith to be content. I
know both how to be abased, and I know how to abound;
everywhere and in all things I am instructed both to be full,
and to be hungry; both to abound and to suffer need—I
can do all things through Him which strengtheneth me.*

In what then do you rejoice, great Paul? In what do you
rejoice? On what do you feed, you *man renewed in the
knowledge* of God; *after the image of Him that created
Thee,* you *living soul* of such continence, tongue like *the
flying fowls,* speaking mysteries? (For to such creatures is
this food due.) On what do you feed? Joy. Hear what
follows: *notwithstanding, ye have well done, that ye did
communicate with my affliction.* It is in this that he rejoices
and it is upon this that he feeds—that they had acted well,
not that his own wants had been relieved. He says to you:
Thou hast enlarged me when I was in distress; for he knows
how *to abound and to suffer want in Thee Who strengthen-
est him.* He goes on to say: *For ye Philippians also know
that in the beginning of the Gospel, when I departed from
Macedonia, no Church communicated with me as concerning giving and receiving, but ye only. For even in Thessalon-*

ica ye sent once and again unto my necessity. He now rejoices because they have returned to these good works, and he is glad that they have flourished again, as when a field becomes fertile once more.

Was he thinking of his own necessities when he said: *Ye sent unto my necessities?* Was that the reason for his joy? Certainly not. But how do we know? Because he says immediately afterward: *not because I desire a gift, but I desire fruit.* I have learned from you, my God, to distinguish between a *gift* and *fruit.* A *gift* is the actual thing that is given to meet these necessities of ours, such as money, food, drink, clothes, shelter, help; but the *fruit* is the good and right will of the giver. For the good Master did not say only: *He that receiveth a prophet;* he added: *in the name of a prophet.* He did not say only: *He that receiveth a righteous man;* he added: *in the name of a righteous man.* And indeed the one shall *receive the reward of a prophet* and the other *the reward of a righteous man.* Nor did he say only: *He that shall give to drink a cup of cold water to one of my little ones;* he added: *in the name of a disciple,* and went on to add: *Verily I say unto you, he shall not lose his reward.*

The *gift* is to receive a prophet, to receive a righteous man, to give a cup of cold water to a disciple; but the *fruit* is to do this in the name of a prophet, in the name of a righteous man, in the name of a disciple. It was with *fruit* that Elijah was fed by the widow who knew that she was giving food to one who was a man of God and gave him food just for that reason; but he was fed by the raven with a *gift,* and it was not the inner man of Elijah that was fed by the raven, but the outer man, which might have died for lack of that food.

27 So, LORD, I will say what is true in your sight. We suppose that what is meant by the *fishes* and *whales* are the ignorant and the infidels who have to be won over and initiated by sacraments of initiation and the wonders of miracles. And when these men give bodily refreshment to your children or help them in any way that is useful to this present life, they do not know why they ought to do as they are doing nor what is the real direction of their actions. Thus neither do they really feed these children of yours, nor are your children really fed by them, because they are not acting out of a holy and right will and your children do not rejoice in their *gifts*, since they do not yet see the *fruit*. For it is certain that the soul feeds on that in which it finds joy. And that is why the *fishes* and *whales* are not fed on that food which is only brought forth by the earth after it was separated and divided from the bitterness of the waves of the sea.

28 AND *Thou, O God, sawest everything that Thou hadst made, and, behold it was very good.* We also see these things and indeed they are very good. With regard to each particular order of things, after you had said "Let them be made," you saw each of them in turn *that it was good.* I have counted that there are seven times when it is written: *Thou sawest that that which Thou madest was good,* and then, the eighth time, we find: *Thou sawest everything that Thou hadst made* and, behold, it was not only *good,* but *very good,* being now considered altogether. For taken individually they were only good, but taken all together as a whole, they are both good and very good. The same truth is expressed by all beautiful bodies. A body made up itself of members which are all beautiful is very much more beautiful than the individual members out of whose well-ordered harmony the whole is made up, even though all those members taken separately are beautiful.

29 AND I LOOKED closely to see whether it was seven or eight times that you saw that your works were good when they pleased you. And in your seeing I found no time by means of which I could understand what was meant by "how often" you saw what you had made. And

I said: "Lord, is not this Scripture of yours true, for you are true and you who are Truth have spoken it? Why then do you tell me that in your seeing there is no time, yet your Scripture tells me that with regard to what you made each day, *Thou sawest that it was good,* and when I counted I found how often?" In answer to this you say to me, for you are my God and you speak out loud into the inner ear of your servant, breaking through my deafness and crying out: "O man, what my Scripture says, I say. But my Scripture speaks in terms of time, and time does not affect my Word, because my Word stands together with me in an equal eternity. So the things which you see by my spirit, I see; just as the things which you say by my spirit, I say. And thus, although you see these things in time, I do not see them in time; just as, although you speak in terms of time, I do not speak in terms of time."

30 AND I HEARD YOU, Lord my God, and I sucked a drop of sweetness from your truth and I understood. Because there are some people who find your works displeasing and who say that you made many of them under the compulsion of necessity—the fabric of the heavens, for instance, and the harmonious order of the stars. They say that you did not make them out of what was yours, but that they were created elsewhere and from some other source, and that you merely brought them together and fixed them and set them in place, and that you did this at the time when you had conquered your enemies and built up the ramparts of the world so that these enemies might be held down by that fortification and never rebel against you again. And they say that other things were neither made by you nor even put together by you—for example, all flesh, and very small living creatures and all things which are rooted in the earth—and that these things were brought into existence and given form in the lowest levels of the world by a mind hostile to you, a nature different from you, not created by you and contrary to you. Those who hold these views are mad; they do not see your works by your spirit, nor do they recognize you in them.

31 BUT WHEN WE SEE these things by your spirit, it is you who see in us. Therefore, when we see that they are good, you see that they are good, and when things please us for your sake, it is you in them who please us, and when things please us by your spirit, they please you in us. *For what man knoweth the things of a man, save the spirit of a man, which is in him? Even so the things of God knoweth no one but the Spirit of God. Now we (he says) have received not the spirit of this world, but the Spirit which is of God, that we might know the things that are freely given to us of God.*

And here I am moved to say: "Certainly *the things of God knoweth no one but the Spirit of God*: how then do we also *know the things that are given us of God?*" And the answer is given to me: "Because in the case of those things which we know by His Spirit, even so *no one knoweth them but the Spirit of God.* For just as it was rightly said to those who were to speak by the Spirit of God *it is not ye that speak*, so it is rightly said to those that know through the Spirit of God: "It is not you who know." And it is just as right to say to those who see in the Spirit of God: "It is not you who see." Therefore, whatever a man sees in the Spirit of God as good, it is not he but God who *sees that it is good.*

It is one thing to think that what is good is bad, like the men mentioned above, and it is another thing for a man to see that what is good is good in the way of those who are pleased by your creation because it is good, but who still do not find their pleasure in your presence in your creation, so that they prefer to enjoy the creation itself rather than you. And it is another thing again when a man sees that something is good, but it is God in him who sees this, so that God should be loved in the thing made by Him. And God could not be loved in this way except through the Spirit which He has given. *Because the love of*

*God is shed abroad in our hearts by the Holy Ghost, which
is given unto us;* by whom we see that whatever in any
degree is, is good; for it is from Him who is not in degree,
but Is what He Is.

32 I THANK YOU, LORD! We see *heaven and earth*—
whether it be the upper and lower parts of the
corporeal world or the spiritual and corporeal creation—
and for the adorning of these two—whether they constitute
the whole mass of the world or the whole total of creation—we see *light* made and *divided from the darkness.*
We see *the firmament of heaven,* by which may be meant
either that primary body of the world between the upper,
or spiritual, waters and the lower, or corporeal waters, or
else (since this is also called heaven) the space of air
through which the birds of heaven go wandering, *betwixt
those waters* which rise above them in vapors to fall again
in clear nights as dew, and those heavier *waters* which flow
upon the earth. We see the face of the *waters gathered
together in* the fields of *the sea;* and *the dry* land, both void,
and formed so as to be visible and set in shape, the mother
of plants and trees. We see the lights shining from above,
the sun sufficient for *the day, the moon and the stars* to
cheer *the night,* and time marked and signified by all of
these. We see on all sides of us a moist element teeming
with fishes, animals, and birds; because by the evaporation
of the water the air acquires the density which supports
birds in flight. We see the face of the earth decked out
with land animals, and *man, created after Thy image and
likeness* with dominion over all irrational creatures simply
because of that *image and likeness,* that is, because of the
power of reason and understanding. And just as in man's
soul there is one part which rules by taking thought and
another part which is subject to obedience, so for man,
also corporeally, a woman was created to have a nature
equal indeed to his in mind and rational intelligence, but
to be in sex subjected to the masculine sex, in the same
way as the appetite which leads to action is subjected to

the skill, mentally derived, of acting rightly. We see these things, and they are individually *good* and all together *very good*.

33 LET YOUR WORKS praise you that we may love you, and let us love you that your works may praise you. For they have a beginning and an end in time, a rising and a setting, growth and decay, form and privation. So they have their succession of morning and evening, in part secretly, in part evident. For they were made of nothing, by you, not of you; not of some matter not made by you or previously in existence, but from matter which was concreated, that is created by you simultaneously with the things made of it, because without any interval of time you gave form to its state that was *without form*. For the matter of heaven and earth is a different thing from the form of heaven and earth, and while you made the matter out of absolutely nothing, you made the form of the world out of the formless matter; but, nevertheless, you made them both simultaneously so that form should follow matter with no intervening space of time.

34 WE HAVE ALSO CONSIDERED what you wished to be allegorically intimated by the particular order in which you made these things or had their creation described. And we have seen that things are individually *good* and all together *very good,* in your Word, in your Only-begotten, both *heaven and earth,* the head and body of the Church, in predestination before all times, without *morning and evening.* Then you began to work out in time what you had predestined, so that you might reveal what was hidden and bring order into our disorder; for our sins were over us and we had gone away from you, into the *dark deep,* and your good *Spirit was borne* above us to help us *in due season.* And you *justified the ungodly* and *divided* them from the wicked, and you established the authority of your Book between those *above* who were to be docile to you, and those *under*, who were to be subject to them. And you *gathered together* the society of the unbelievers *into one* membership, so that the zeal of the faithful might appear, and they might *bring forth* for you works of mercy, distributing even to the poor their earthly riches so that they might obtain heavenly riches.

And after this you kindled *lights in the firmament*, your saints holding the word of life and shining in sublime authority raised up by spiritual gifts. And then for the initiation of unbelievers, and as a blessing also to believers, you brought out of corporeal matter the sacraments and visible miracles and the sounds of words according to the firmament of your book. Next you formed the *living soul* of the faithful through affections set in order by the strong force of continence. And then you took the mind, subjected to you only and needing to imitate no human authority, and you renewed it after your *image and likeness*, and you subjected rational action to the excellency of the intellect, as the woman to the man, and to all offices of your ministry necessary for the perfection of the faithful in this life you willed that these same faithful should bestow gifts for the temporal uses of your ministers, gifts which would bear fruit in the future for the givers.

All these things we see and they are *very good*, because you see them in us—you who have given us the Spirit by which to see them and in them to love you.

35 LORD GOD, GIVE US PEACE—for you have granted us all things—the peace of quiet, the peace of the Sabbath which has no evening. For indeed this most beautiful order of things that are *very good* will finish its course and pass away, since in it there was *morning and evening*.

36 BUT THE SEVENTH DAY is without evening. The sun does not set on it, because you sanctified it to last forever. For after all your works which were *very good, you rested on the seventh day*, although you made all these works in an unbroken rest. So may the voice of your book tell us in advance that we too, after our works (which are *very good* only for the reason that you have given them to us), may rest in you in the Sabbath of eternal life.

37 THEN TOO YOU WILL rest in us just as now you work in us, and so that rest will be your rest in us just as now these works are your works in us. But you, Lord, are always at work and always at rest. You do not see in time nor move in time nor rest in time. Yet you make the things which we see in time, and time itself and the rest which comes from time.

38 WE SEE THE THINGS you have made, because they are, and they are, because you see them. Outwardly we see that they are; inwardly we see that they are good. But you saw them made when you saw that they were to be made. And we at a later time, after our heart had conceived by your Spirit, were moved to do well; but previously we were moved to do evil, forsaking you. But you, the one, the good God, have never ceased to do well. And we, too have some *good works,* of your gift, but not eternal; *after them* we hope for *rest* in your great *hallowing.* But you, the Good which is in need of no other good, are always at rest, because you are your own rest.

How can one man teach another man to understand this? What angel will teach an angel? What angel will teach a man? This must be *asked* of you, *sought* in you, *knocked* for at you. So, so shall it be *received*, so shall it be *found*, so shall it be *opened.* Amen.

After *The Confessions*

In religious traditions where people "go to confession" and "make their confessions," as Augustine would and did, they are expected to be different from what they were before. There is no way to predict whether any particular reader or readers will be different in any coherent set of ways, though I suppose we are all made different by all new knowledge or perspective, whether gathered from *The Divine Comedy*, a hardware or software catalog, or a walk in the woods. Without aspiring to read readers' minds, discern coherences where they may not have developed, or offer templates into which others may or must force their ways of being different, I do think it in place to put a few signposts up for those who, like Augustine—who presumes he speaks for all humans in this one respect—are restless, perhaps searching.

It is hard to get up from a reading of *The Confessions* without having a new appreciation for the role of memory in life: memory as an agent that haunts; memory that can include liberating incidents and words. I hope readers will revisit the pages beginning with Book X, 8. There we see Augustine speaking of it as a huge palace, a storehouse that is both capacious and deep; it has awesome power, and contents whose origin elude the author's ability to discover. He can be a bit crude when he describes it as a stomach of the mind, where good and bad things alike can lose their taste. He connects its stored contents to what his senses tell him, but he does not slight what he learned in academies: information, grammar. While he wishes pain were not memorable, it is, along with pleasure. One gets ideas of happiness from glimpses of it in memory.

Not all will follow him but all can follow his reasoning as he describes a peculiar dimension of his experience: Humans, he suggests, have a memory of God (X, 25–37). God was within him but he was "outside" himself. The notion is philosophically complex—we reach into his Platonism for this—and not something we need pursue into the "abyss" at this point. Instead, think of the notion as one more dimension of his celebration of memory. Book X provides a launch for anyone who wants to explore the concept of memory.

A second feature of *The Confessions* that readers of all sorts, restless and searching or complacent alike, will find worth revisiting, is Augustine's celebration of friendship. Philosophers and theologians like to take on the cosmic subjects like hate and love—Augustine is a master of the latter subject—but they tend to pass over what look like middle-size virtues and benefits. Not Augustine. He uses the death of his close friend to begin the musing in Book IV. (So touching is his description of loss that some contemporary commentators, on extremely limited evidence, think there must be a homosexual tinge to the friendship. No matter.)

How he connected the experience of grief with the external environment tends to ring true in the recall of many who lost someone close to them. But Augustine uses the event to throw friendship against what we might call a cosmic backdrop of grief and exaltation, as those who have risked bonds of friendship have to know and may freshly ponder.

The Confessions helps induce fresh reflection on the roles of chance and purpose; some call it Providence. The most famous scene of the book has to do with Augustine's conversion. Did he or did he not hear the actual voice of an actual child saying, "Take, read!"? What was the significance of the fact that the scroll he was to read was turned to Paul's Letter to the Romans that so spoke to his soul? Chance, one might or must call this.

Modern banner makers would have chosen something like the "John 3:16" that some Americans like to unfurl in stadiums when the camera roams the crowd at sporting events. Augustine knew all about what John 3:16 said. The Romans passage spoke to his conscience.

For that matter, Augustine's whole language about conversion speaks to believers and nonbelievers alike. He explores at great length what a new start in life means. His new start is located in God, a God not all readers will share. It finds its focus in Jesus Christ, commended by that Romans text in the garden where he heard the child's voice. Paul's readers, and now Augustine, were to put aside the revels of the sort this not-yet-saint had known and to "put on the Lord Jesus Christ and [consequently] do not make forethought for the flesh with inexhaustible desires." (VIII, 12, 29). Christian readers, no doubt the majority through the ages, resonate to that. But the idea of "putting on" a reality that alters other reality speaks to searchers on paths other than Christian.

I have perhaps disappointed and frustrated some readers and may look evasive to others by not having lifted up in either "Before 'Confessions'" or "After 'Confessions'" the large role that sex, lust, "the flesh" play in Augustine's lifelong wrestling with himself and God. This was not done to downplay it. One can simply take for granted that this will leap out at a reader in our culture, and does not need the pointing of fingers or the placement of "Nota Bene" signs. But now at the very end, it is valid to point out to what extent these contributed to his restlessness and the relative peace he achieved when he found, or as he would put it, was found by a stronger force, a greater lure, where he found his depth, his peace.

Whatever else a commentator might do, Augustine himself, on this subject and on so many others, will not have disappointed or frustrated readers, or been evasive. He reaches for the heights and depths of human experience with his confessions, his testimonies, his book-length prayer, his classic autobiography, his invitation to others to join in acts of seeking.

—Martin E. Marty
The University of Chicago
Fairfax M. Cone
Distinguished Service Professor
Emeritus

Selected Bibliography

Arendt, Hannah. *Love and Saint Augustine*. Ed. Joanna Vecchiarelli Scott. Chicago: University of Chicago Press, 1996.

Brown, Peter. *Augustine of Hippo*. Berkeley: University of California Press, 2000.

Cary, Philip. *Augustine's Invention of the Inner Self*. New York: Oxford University Press, 2000.

——. *Inner Grace: Augustine in the Traditions of Plato and Paul*. New York: Oxford University Press, 2008.

Chadwick, Henry. *Augustine*. Past Masters. New York: Oxford University Press, 1986.

Courcelle, Pierre. *Recherches sur les Confessions de Saint Augustin*. Paris: E. de Boccard, 1968.

Enno, S. S., and Robert B. Enno, ed. *Saint Augustine, Letters*. Washington, D.C.: Catholic University of America Press, 1989.

Gilson, Etienne H. The *Christian Philosophy of St. Augustine*. Trans. L. E. M. Lynch. New York: Random House, 1960.

Harrison, Carol. *Augustine: Christian Truth and Fractured Humanity*. New York: Oxford University Press, 2000.

O'Donnell, James J. *Augustine: A New Biography*. New York: Ecco, 2005.

——. *Augustine, Confessions*. 3 vols. Oxford: Oxford University Press, 1992.

O'Meara, John J. *The Young Augustine: An Introduction to the Confessions of Saint Augustine*. London: Longmans, 1980.

Stock, Brian. *Augustine the Reader: Meditation, Self-Knowledge, and the Ethics of Interpretation*. Cambridge, MA: Harvard University Press, 1996.

Wills, Garry. *Saint Augustine*. Penguin Lives. New York: Viking, 1999.

READ THE TOP 20
SIGNET CLASSICS